You started so you should finish.

With the complements of the author

Andy Lang —
05/10/2013

ANDY'S STORY

STORY

TOO MUCH FOR A LIFETIME

D1807691

R. A. LANG

Produced by:

FriesenPress

Suite 300 – 852 Fort Street
Victoria, BC, Canada V8W 1H8

www.friesenpress.com

Distributed to the trade by The Ingram Book Company

ACKNOWLEDGEMENTS

Ward G in Morriston Hospital (Swansea) for their Pancreatic Centre of Excellence that saved my life in May 2012 and allowed me to write *Andy's Story*.

★★★

Sonja, her mother and father, Myrthe, Pete, Fluer, Koos, Marianne & Robbie, Eugene and Renee (from the Café Koeport in Delft, Holland) for all their inspirational support and friendship while I worked in Holland. We'll be friends forever.

★★★

Jo and Richard, proprietors of the Pilot (Mumbles, Swansea) for their warm welcome and excellent selection of real ales – in addition to their own ales. They inspired me to start rewriting *Andy's Story* after so many years.

TABLE OF CONTENTS

AUTHOR'S NOTE

Dear reader,

Kindly forgive any spelling, punctuation or grammar mistakes you may find in my story. I am an Oil and Gas Professional and didn't go to grammar school. I just wanted to share my life experiences with the rest of the world to describe the *real* world. The *real* world isn't always what you see on the television, internet or read in newspapers.

For legal reasons, I have not mentioned any companies, projects, or people's names throughout my story. They, if they read my story will know whom they are. The good guys names are real by personal requests, the bad guys names have been changed.

I sincerely hope you enjoy what you are about to read and the journey I am about to take you on. You may feel shocked, horrified and also amused, but nevertheless what I have recorded is factual and exactly how it happened. Due to some events, I should not have survived to write my story but as you will read, I am not the type to give up without a fight. Enjoy.......and thank you!

CHAPTER 1

How It Began

It all started in 1978, when I moved back to Wales at the age of sixteen to complete my apprenticeship as a Plater in a heavy engineering fabrication shop. The fabrication shop was called Bercon Engineering, and it was located in a small, Welsh village called Penclawdd, which was better known for its cockle factories than its fabrication workshops.

There were still remnants of foundations where anti-aircraft guns had helped defend the steel works in Llanelli just across the estuary during the Second World War.

Penclawdd wasn't the easiest place to work for someone who had completely lost his Welsh accent after seven years living just outside London, in Hindhead, Surrey. My accent caused quite a bit of hostility, but that was eventually overcome.

My apprenticeship was to last for four years, and I had to spend every Wednesday in the West Glamorgan Institute for Higher Education for the theoretical part. Because my apprenticeship was long before the days of health and safety codes, the workshop left a lot to be desired. There weren't any machine guards, eye shields, or other safety measures installed.

The only thing we could do was complain to our union representative when we needed to pay our dues on Friday nights once a month. The union representative would eventually visit the office, but nothing was ever done to improve things.

As an apprentice, the usual jokes were played on me, and I was very gullible for the first couple of years. I needed to arrive earlier in the mornings than the tradesmen so I could go outside to the red diesel tank and fill a twenty-two litre can. I would use that can to refuel the old-fashioned, very unhealthy, diesel salamander heaters in the workshop. These were dangerous, and they often blew back in my face when I lit them.

We'd all huddle around the heaters, holding our damp coveralls near the heat to dry them as much as we could before wearing them. Our gloves would often be wet from the day before – and also frozen in the winter. Meanwhile, I got burnt regularly when I picked up hot steel without realising the gloves had holes in them.

They didn't like to issue new gloves until the old pair was in a really bad condition. The same went for respirators and facemasks. I often become ill when welding galvanised steel because I couldn't avoid breathing in the zinc fumes from inside my welding head shield. We called it chemical flue.

We didn't have any welding curtains or screens either, so we regularly experienced "arc eye" symptoms. Arc eye occurred when the powerful, ultraviolet light entered the corner of passing workers' eyes as another worker was striking an arc to start welding.

The light caused the membranes protecting the surface of the eyes to dissolve, exposing thousands of nerve endings. It felt like grains of sand in the eyes until the membrane had time to grow back which sometimes took a couple of days.

Sometimes, the arc eye symptoms were so bad that I couldn't open them (which meant going to work the next day was impossible, so I'd have to lose a day's pay). It helped to put slices of cold cucumber over my affected eyes and stay in a dark room, out of any sunlight.

I suffered many accidents, mostly caused by my own clumsiness and sometimes the clumsiness of others.

Our office secretary hated the sight of blood. Therefore, when I needed to report an accident and ask to go to hospital, I had to enter her office with my smashed fingertip or broken thumb behind my back so she wouldn't faint.

I visited Singleton Hospital, Swansea regularly to have sparks and fillings removed from my eyes. The other workers underwent the same procedures.

Creating patterns to cut out the necessary steel shapes was a natural skill I developed, and I was soon given more and more complicated fabrications to do, which I enjoyed.

I became fluent in parallel line development, triangulation, and the common central sphere, and sometimes I used all three methods to develop the more complex patterns. Soon, word got around so I had started getting job offers from other fabrication shops in West Glamorgan.

Nevertheless, I was comfortable continuing on in the sweat-shop until I had at least completed my apprenticeship.

For the first two years, everything seemed to progress in a normal way. I got filthy at the fabrication shop by day, and I played with cars by night (like most of my friends at that age).

I also enjoyed underage drinking at the bottom of the lane near our house in the Woodman Inn in Blackpill, and playing the motorbike touch game while riding through the streets of Mumbles at high speed – all the while trying to avoid getting caught by the police.

In March of 1981, things took a dramatic change for the worse. Something happened that changed the rest of my life.

I had been meddling with an old vacuum cleaner motor in our old, wooden garage, which had been left standing after my father had built a new garage. It was just for me, and I enjoyed pottering around in it. I had built up quite a comprehensive collection of tools by that time, and a friend of mine, Dale, spent a lot of time with me repairing cars for extra income. Each week, I'd collect my pay and go into John Hall tools on the Kingsway in Swansea to buy another tool.

I decided I needed something to sharpen tools with, so I got hold of a nine-inch grinding disk, which was made in Germany. We used them in the fabrication shop to grind steel. Not once did I take a moment to consider the motor speed of the old vacuum cleaner with regards to the safe working speed limit of the grinding disk I was mounting on it.

On March 30, 1981, my father returned home with our young Rottweiler after taking her to dog training class at nine o' clock in the evening. By a quarter past nine, my father lay dead on the living room carpet, surrounded by a huge pool of blood. He asked to see the machine working, so I went into the kitchen, plugged it into the wall socket, and switched the motor on.

With 240 volts running up my arms from my fingers touching the bare terminals, and the disk running at twenty thousand ramps per minute, the disk was uncontrollable. It was similar to a gyroscope keeping the motor too ridged to move or throw.

After what seemed like only a few seconds, there was a load bang, a sting in the corner of my left eye, and a torrent of blood shooting out from my father's chest. He stood there, clutching his heart with both hands for one or two seconds before collapsing into the entrance of the living room.

Though I was stunned, I went to see to my father, but there wasn't anything that could be done for him. He was lying face down on the living room carpet, and when my mother tried to turn him over, we could see that the carpet below his chest was totally saturated in a pool of blood. The blood seeped about two feet from his body.

I remember my mother keeping her cool. She dialled 999 and calmly asked for an ambulance before giving them our address and other relevant information. I picked up a torch and waited at the top of the drive so the ambulance could see where to stop without wasting time looking for the house name.

It only felt like three or four minutes before the sounds of sirens grew closer. I was surprised to see two of them – I hadn't heard my mother request a second for me. I hurried back to the house with the paramedics and showed them where my father lay motionless.

By the look on the first paramedic's face, it was clear what he was thinking. He slowly shook his head from side to side. The other paramedic moved me back into the kitchen where he had better light to attend to me.

The slight sting I had felt when the accident happened was from fragments of the broken grinding disk penetrating deep into the skin at the corner of my eye, just missing my tear duct.

After what had happened to my father, I wasn't aware of the blood running down the front of my face – nor did it matter. I watched as my father was strapped to a stretcher and taken to the first ambulance. Shortly after I had been temporarily dressed, I was taken to the second.

In those days, Swansea Hospital had a casualty area, and it was just a few minutes down the Mumbles Road.

My father and I were taken to separate rooms, so I couldn't see anything that was being done to him. I was waiting to be treated, and a nurse was near me, sitting quietly by the wall.

After what felt like hours (but was probably just minutes), my sister came in, looked at me, leaned in close to my face, and said, "Dad's dead." Just two words which I will keep hearing for the rest of my life.

I tried to jump up and see for myself, but the nurse prevented me from doing so. A couple of other nurses rushed in to hold me down, which added to my sense of frustration and helplessness.

After a while, I was taken to a treatment room where as many fragments as possible were removed from my eye before they stitched it up. My father's brother had arrived by that time, together with police officers who wanted a statement while I was being treated. A nurse asked the police to leave because it was not an appropriate time. I was a mess and on a lot of tranquillisers – medication that I ended up taking every night before bedtime for the following two years. It took several more years for the rest of the fragments to work their way out from my eye area.

The funeral was held in Bishopston Church, which was very close to my father's birthplace. It was one of the biggest funerals held at the church because my father knew many people through his job, and people came from all over the United Kingdom to pay their respects, including my workmates.

Just two weeks after the funeral, I was advised to return to work in order to occupy my mind with other things.

Eventually, I completed my four-year apprenticeship and settled into a life of work, but I was far from satisfied. I knew there had to be more to my life than a set routine, and I began thinking about ways to change things. My father had never been happy with my chosen career, so I decided to change my career to better suit his wishes.

I heard about a new course at my local college, welding inspection, so I immediately enrolled for the September start. While taking the course, I signed up for another course: radiograph interpretation of welded joints.

The two courses complemented each other and took up four evenings per week. I attended them after working in the fabrication shop during the day. I figured taking the two courses were the easiest way to change my career path – and the choice paid off.

Previously in the year of 1984 an Auntie had died and left a Thai Buddha made out of cast brass, which sat on a hand carved wooden stand. I was later to learn that it was an original antique Thai Buddha aged over three hundred years.

Many years later, I was to learn the true significance of why this Buddha had found its way to me. I was to return it back to the country it had originated in person.

CHAPTER 2

South Africa

I had a South African friend who had a double glazing business in Swansea. He met me regularly for a few beers after work. He always told me about his time in South Africa and how good life was when he was living in Cape Town. It sounded like such a wonderful place, and I became even more eager to restructure my future and get away from the United Kingdom for a while.

I was twenty-seven years old, and I was becoming increasingly frustrated with my day to day routine. In May of 1989, I read in a London newspaper that there was going to be a seminar regarding immigration to South Africa. It would be held in a London hotel.

I didn't need to waste time thinking about it: I decided to attend, compiled my first curriculum vitae, and headed to the seminar. At the seminar, I met a guy who had a business partner based in Johannesburg. I gave him my CV, and he faxed it over.

Just a week later, I was flying to Johannesburg to start my very first overseas contract as a welding inspector representing the client on the first offshore gas platform to be built in the country.

The long-haul flight began in London, Heathrow, and went to Amsterdam and Nairobi before landing in Johannesburg. The day I left Swansea was a terrible day filled with torrential rain. I got soaked walking to the coach station with my mother.

I was both excited and also nervous – not knowing what was in store for me. Emotions were running a little high. I felt a little choked up when it was time to bid my mother goodbye, but I managed to put on my bravest face and made the exchange brief. Soon, I was on the coach.

I waved her away so I could start thinking about the journey ahead. I figured that I wouldn't see of her for at least a year. The coach pulled out of Swansea Quadrant bus station a few minutes later and headed towards the junction with Oystermouth road.

There, waiting at the junction in the torrential rain without an umbrella, stood my mother. She gave me one last wave farewell before the coach pulled out onto the main road and headed towards London.

You could see by the look in her eyes that she was excited about her only son's first journey overseas, but she was also saddened to see him leaving with little idea when she would next hear from him or see him again.

My KLM flight finally reached African soil in Nairobi where some passengers got off and others joined the flight.

We were invited to get off the flight to stretch our legs, which I took full advantage of.

I walked into Nairobi's airport for a look around, and I was quite surprised to see how expensive it was. I figured that, because Kenya was a popular tourist destination, the prices were deliberately high to milk the tourists of their remaining holiday money.

Upon arriving in Johannesburg later the same day (around five o'clock in the afternoon), I was met by a representative from the company I would be working for. I was expecting to be handed my domestic flight tickets to Cape Town, but I was instead handed three maps, some car keys, four hotel booking references, and instructions that Cape Town was "in that direction, straight down the N1 highway."

Although Johannesburg is the commercial centre of the country, it is not one of the three capital cities in South Africa.

The company rep helped me with my luggage and drove the car to the hotel: the Travel Lodge. He helped me carry my luggage to my hotel room because it would not be very safe in the car. After that, he showed me the way to the bar.

Tired from not getting any sleep on the flight the night before, my first South African beer hit me hard. The second was easier ... so was the third ... and the fourth. Eventually the rep had to leave me to meet his wife.

I proceeded to drink a few more beers to ensure a good nights sleep before going to the restaurant and then head for bed. I slept very well that night, and I got up early the next morning to leave at six o'clock (while the roads were still quiet).

I had no idea at that time that the South Africans had placed bets on whether I'd make the trip without getting lost. I pulled out of the Travel Lodge and arrived at a cross-roads. *Right,* I thought, *no signs saying Cape Town, or N1, or "Andy this way?"* When the lights changed to green, I pulled away and suddenly thought I was going in the wrong direction.

I made a U-turn to retrace my steps, but then I made another U-turn and went back the way I went first. Ultimately, I pulled over to the side of the road to think about it. Luckily, there was a group of local road workers doing some repairs, so I shouted out, "Which way to Cape Town?!" They all burst out laughing and pointed me in the right direction, and I continued on my journey.

My fuel tank was full when I left, but I was warned not to pass a fuel station without filling up because they were spaced far apart along the N1 – if you missed a station, you would run out of fuel before getting to the next one. Sure enough, it was almost three hours later before I saw my first fuel station. I was running low, so I pulled over and filled my tank to the top.

After ten hours of driving down the N1 (through the Orange Free State) with hardly a bend in the road I arrived at my second hotel. The place was called Bloemfontein.

The Republic of South Africa has three capitals: Pretoria, Cape Town, and Bloemfontein.

Pretoria was the home of the executive branch of government, Cape Town held the assembly, and Bloemfontein housed the supreme court.

The N1 went straight through the middle of the city, and I found the hotel right alongside the road. It was dark by then, so I had no desire to explore the place. Instead, I checked in, ate, and went straight to bed. There weren't any bills to pay because my company had arranged to pick up the bills from all four hotel stays.

After seven hours of driving (after another early start), I could finally see the awe-inspiring sight of Table Mountain – albeit far in the distance. It was a hot day, and due to the shimmering effect on the road in front of me, I couldn't see too far ahead. Still, Table Mountain stood out. Throughout the entire trip, I don't think I drove around a single bend.

As I got nearer to Cape Town, the dual carriageway I was on began featuring some planted flowers. The flowers divided up the two sides of the road. I observed them for a few miles before I entered the city itself, which felt quite welcoming.

The only time I managed to get lost was after I pulled over in Cape Town to ask directions to the Plein Park Travel Lodge Hotel. A friendly local police officer explained that I was just a couple of "robots" away, so off I drove looking for robots.

I drove around for almost an hour looking for robots before I pulled over again and asked another police officer where the robots were. He realised I was from out of town, and he explained that *robots* were traffic lights. When I thanked him, he told me to buy a donkey. In fact, everyone

I met in South Africa told me to buy a donkey until I learnt that *bia dankie* meant *thank you* in Afrikaans.

The next day, I made it to the site office in Saldanha Bay, which was only an hour from Cape Town (driving north along the coast on the R27). After being introduced to the project team and checking out the job site, it was time to settle in to my new role.

After work, I followed a new colleague to the Saldanha Bay Hotel, which had also been reserved for me. After meeting him, we went to their usual bar. The place, which they frequented after work, was in a place called The North Western Hotel in a nearby village called Vredenburg.

It was by chance that I met a local South African motor-bike police officer called Guy Stokes. He introduced me to a new, South African way of life.

Guy helped me find a bungalow to rent in Vredenburg, not far from where he lived. After I was in the country for just a month, Guy came around to my bungalow on a Saturday morning and invited me to join him in target practise. I thought it sounded like fun, so off I went. I was thinking of black and white paper targets with sandbags behind them – how wrong I was!

Guy handed me his standard, police-issue, 9 mm CZ semi-automatic and explained that he'd use his unlicensed, Russian, 9 mm semi-automatic Tokarev. I innocently asked Guy what targets we would be shooting at, and he replied, "Anyone holding a stone, pitchfork, machete, or anything else in their hands!"

I thought: *hang on*, I was in Swansea just a month ago, and now I am getting involved in an African tribal riot on a Saturday morning. Guy said I shouldn't wait for someone to throw anything. Rather, he encouraged me to fire as many rounds into them as I could before they hit the ground.

I thought he was a madman until he explained that the South African police often made an example of a few aggressive rioters so the rest would run away and live to fight another day.

He explained that they saved a lot of lives by doing it this way, that they were preventing a bloody massacre. I've often wondered why they didn't just throw some gas canisters and be done with it instead of resorting to a more permanent solution. Fortunately no shoot needed to be fired.

The following weekend, Guy pulled up again and told me that he wanted me to see Saldanha Naval Base (where he was a member). The place was simply amazing. We got through the security gate using Guy's pass, and then we went straight to the officers' mess. I was well received by the officers and made to feel at home – including a guided tour.

It was clear how proud they were of their set up. The design of their barbecue was unique: it was made from a big sea buoy that had been mounted on a huge propeller bearing. It had a chimney and handles to rotate it according to the wind direction.

Every Saturday morning, they used one of the naval boats to troll Saldanha Bay for barracuda, which some like to call *snook*. Later, they cooked them on the barbecue with copious amounts of Castle or Amstel beer.

The beer was subsidised. At 10p per beer, we drank loads of the stuff whilst eating barracuda and watching the Northern Transvaal playing the Western Province at rugby.

I got on so well with the officers that, after a few months, they made me an honorary member of the naval base. They explained that I was the first in the history of the South African Navy to be made an honorary member without having any naval history in my family.

I've still got my black beret, which they presented to me, and I assume my name is still on their board in gold lettering.

It wasn't long before senior management learnt of my naval base hideaway, they asked me if I could get them in. I spoke to the officers, and they thought it would be a great social event to pit themselves against the project staff in a games night.

It took a few weeks to arrange because everyone's car license plate number had to be given to the naval base security office and visitor passes had to be printed. Sadly, I couldn't enjoy the event I had organised because they put me on nightshift the night of the party.

This infuriated my friends at the naval base – they couldn't believe how selfish and idiotic my co-workers were to do that to me. As a result, the naval base banned everyone from visiting the officers' mess again. They seemed to give me an even bigger welcome after that night, and I miss them all to this day.

I was still renting the small, two-bedroom bungalow in Vredenburg, but because I had rented the house unfurnished, it was hard going sleeping on the floor. Because Guy took up so much of my free time, I couldn't furnish it as quickly as I needed to.

I eventually met a local lady in the nearby supermarket who offered to help me partially furnish the place, starting with all the usual essentials. She also dropped her maid off at the bungalow once a week to clean until I was able to find my own maid.

Eventually, I bought some furniture, kitchen utensils, and rented a cable TV. This made all the difference. Also, because the little bungalow had a barbecue built outside the kitchen, I was able to invite friends around on the weekends.

All was going well. I continued to work shifts: one week working days, the next week working nights. I still hadn't got around to fitting any curtains in the living room of the bungalow, however, so it wasn't long before it was noticed.

I'd only had my TV and cable decoder a week when I returned home from work one morning to find that my little place had been trashed. Local thieves had entered through the kitchen window (completely invisible to anyone passing by).

They stole just about everything I had, but they couldn't get my rented TV through the kitchen window. What they couldn't take, they smashed. The most annoying thing they did was urinate over all my vegetables in the drawer at the bottom of the small, second-hand fridge I'd bought.

I called Guy as soon as I saw the devastation, and he wasted no time calling his police colleagues who came over a short time later. Several police officers arrived, and as they looked around, the guy in charge told me it had been the work of locals who lived close by in a Township. After all, they had only taken what they could carry on them.

He also pointed out that they were too stupid to open my back door, which had its key in the lock. If everything had a funny side, this had to be it.

The police recommended that I get window grills fitted all around the house. Guy notified the owner, and he was more than happy to oblige. The very next day, a pickup truck arrived, and a local wrought ironworker took all the measurements around the house. He was ashamed that a foreigner had had such a bad experience in his country, and he made very nice wrought iron window grills for the bungalow.

I could appreciate his workmanship because I had made people gates, railings, balustrading, and other iron works when I was in Swansea for extra income. I was always interested to see how others did the same kind of work.

His name was Peter. Once he'd finished fitting his handiwork onto the house, we sat outside with a couple of cold beers and chatted. He asked if I had a maid. I told him I hadn't been lucky because everyone I tried stole miniscule things from me, which was annoying.

He recommended that his sister, Elizabeth, be my maid. She wasn't working, so it seemed logical. Later the same day, he brought her over to me. She arrived dressed in a newly purchased maid's outfit, which certainly impressed me. I heartily welcomed little Elizabeth.

Elizabeth was as honest as the day was long, and she kept the little bungalow immaculately clean. Because it was so sparsely furnished, there wasn't actually much to keep clean. I didn't have a vacuum cleaner or a washing machine, but that didn't matter to Elizabeth.

She had all day, and she paced herself as she swept the carpet and hand washed my clothes. She seemed happy.

The grass in the front of my garden badly needed cutting, so she asked whether her grandfather could take care of my garden for me. *Great,* I thought. The next day, I arrived home to see an old man sitting down on the grass using my front door mat, cutting my grass by hand with what looked like a sheep sheers. The grass didn't seem to grow very fast, so he'd spend all day, every day snipping away at it.

He liked to smoke marijuana, which made him sleepy. When Elizabeth couldn't see him working, she'd go out and find him sleeping under a big rubber tree in the corner of the back garden. She'd angrily kick him to wake him up and get him back to work. I felt quite sorry for the old man, but Elizabeth made a better boss than I did, and she wouldn't allow him to snooze while I was paying for his services.

Elizabeth was always preparing meals for me with whatever she could find available. Meatballs were a regular preparation – even though that meant chopping up my prized fillet steak sometimes.

We developed a nice routine. Elizabeth would light the barbecue an hour before I was due home, and it was ready to use as I arrived. She'd hear my car pull into the short drive, which was her cue to throw a rib-eye steak on the grill.

By the time I had entered and taken my shoes off, she knew it was time to turn my steak. And then, after I'd had a wash and freshened up, the steak was ready to be placed on a plate (together with the maize meal she'd prepared). In South Africa, they called it *mealy pup,* and it was often served with homemade onion and tomato sauce.

I insisted that she eat with me because she looked a little on the skinny side. Therefore, her steak would go on the grill well before mine as she liked hers well done.

Our meals together weren't without their surprises. I didn't have a table, so we had to sit on the little, scruffy sofa I'd bought. We ate off our laps. The first time we ate together, I sat on the sofa and little Elizabeth sat on the carpet beside me.

I asked her what she was doing down there and told her to sit on the sofa, but she answered, "Master, if any of your South African friends call around and see me eating with you, it wouldn't look good for you!"

I thought, *First, I'm not involved − and have no intention of getting involved − with the apartheid, which was still in full force in South Africa; and second,* Master *is not my name.*

I explained to her that apartheid didn't exist where I came from, and it would never exist inside my house either. She began to call me Andy, and the atmosphere changed dramatically. It was so nice having a little angel in the house − and that was how it remained.

At that time, I was engaged to get married to a girl back in Swansea called Rita. Rita was becoming increasingly interested in staying with me in South Africa due to the lifestyle I told her about in my letters. I explained to Guy that she was interested in joining me, and he asked whether I would still be required to work nights. "Yes," I said to him. Guy recommended I buy a sidearm, just in case I was broken into a second time – it wouldn't be good for the robbers to find a white girl alone in the house.

With that in mind, Guy took me to a local gun dealer, and after a short time, I settled for a small, 7.62 mm semi-automatic. It fitted into my small hands better than the 9mm guns I also picked up, and it held fourteen rounds in its clip.

The sequence required for the purchase of a gun by a foreigner was to first buy a gun and then take the receipt to the local police station along with a passport.

The police took my fingerprints and a number of other pieces of information before sending the passport to Pretoria, where a gun license could be stapled in the back of it.

A week later, my passport was returned to me with my license, and I went back to the gun dealer to collect my gun. As part of the requirements, I had to buy a gun safe and have it securely bolted to a wall in a discrete place in the bungalow. Guy advised me to use the fitted wall cupboard in my bedroom, so that's where we installed it.

Three weeks later, my fiancée arrived, but this was not such a good move. She became increasingly homesick, and it was a long way from home for her first overseas visit.

There were many time when she did enjoy herself, however. Guy's wife picked her up in the daytime, and she introduced her to all the other local ladies. Due to the reduced intensity of the project, we began getting long weekends every two weeks. We'd leave work on Friday at lunchtime, and we'd start again on Monday at lunchtime. This was great because there was a mass exodus to Cape Town every long weekend for a change of scenery. We stayed in the Ritz Hotel in Seapoint, which was just behind a mountain they called the Lion's Head due to its appearance.

The hotel offered an amazing buffet breakfast and had a revolving restaurant on its roof. In the restaurant, someone was always playing a white grand piano. I always walked the wrong way when returning from the restroom because the table had moved, which was very disorienting.

The stay at the hotel didn't improve her homesickness, though. One night back at my house, Rita felt terribly homesick and decided to walk home to Swansea. I knew she wouldn't get far before getting into trouble, so I stopped her.

Just two days before Christmas, I caught her trying to walk out the front door – not once, but three times! Eventually, she punched me in the mouth, snapping the root of my front tooth. All the dentists were on holiday for the week, so I couldn't eat anything. I just had to wait while my front tooth dangled painfully in my mouth.

In February of 1990, my mother came to visit me. She'd never flown further than Greece before, so it took a lot of persuasion to get her to come. The weekend she arrived, we stayed in Cape Town before driving along the N2 through the Garden Route and the Wilderness to Port Elizabeth.

The first place I wanted to show her was the massive Sunday market held in Seapoint. It was located in the national stadium's car park near the Lion's Head. As I drove out of the hotel, I couldn't understand why all the roads were so deserted in Cape Town.

On the way back, we found out why. It was February 22nd, the day Nelson Mandela was freed after twenty-two years in captivity. We were foolishly waiting at a red light when is all started.

Thousands of Africans rushed through the streets and totally surrounded my car. I put my semi-automatic in the car door in case of trouble – not that it would have helped. Instead, as I beeped the car horn and waved at the guys, they moved out of our way and let us drive on through the middle of them all. They didn't give us any trouble.

The following day, we drove east towards a place called George to spend a few days at the popular Victoria Bay. Every day, we'd see the narrow-gauge Apple Express steam train from Port Elizabeth to Loerie going past on the cliff above us. A number of its original coaches were manufactured in 1905 by Bristol Carriage & Wagon in the United Kingdom. By 1924, however, those coaches were taken out of service.

George was a very nice place, and it was home to the crocodile and ostrich farms – not to mention the huge Kango Caves, which we also visited. It was at one of the ostrich farms that I had the opportunity to ride one around the enclosure. Some Japanese tourists watched on with great interest taking many photos.

We left George and headed to Port Elizabeth (also known as the friendly city), where we spent a couple of nights. Whilst there, we drove northeast one day to the Addo elephant park.

After four hours of driving around without seeing an elephant anywhere, we found all forty-seven of them at a watering hole. I managed to take some really nice photos of a mother with its baby, which I eventually had blown up to three feet by two feet and framed.

We worked our way back the same we came, and we spent a couple more nights in George until we arrived back in Cape Town. From there we went directly to my bungalow in Vredenburg. Just a couple of days later, my mother's three week visit was over. It was time for her to travel back to Swansea.

By March, my fiancée couldn't shake off her homesickness any longer. The only solution was to get her a flight back to Wales. She flew back, and I've never seen her to this day. Nevertheless, I've heard stories that she's doing well for herself so that's nice to know, as she was terrific company.

Just a couple of weeks later, on a warm evening, I was rushing to start my nightshift with my driver's side window fully open. Someone walking at the side of the road – maybe drunk, but definitely angry – threw a broken beer bottle at my car. It all happened so fast: all I could do was put my hand up just in time to stop the bottle from hitting me in the face.

With the combined speed I was driving and the force of the throw, the bottle nearly severed my entire thumb. I wasn't sure where the local hospital was, so I got myself to the office where the contractor's nightshift inspector would be waiting.

His name was Ben. He was a Scottish man who was very much the *old school* type. He immediately stopped what he was doing and drove me straight to hospital. By the time we arrived, the blood had saturated my shirt and jeans. Thus, as we entered the hospital, the nurse rushed me into a treatment room.

In an instant, a doctor joined us. I was still holding my thumb together against my right hand. Infection had already set in, and the pain was rising fast. It was difficult for me to let go of my thumb because areas of the blood had set like glue.

I put my confidence in the doctor while he lowered my arm down and slowly separated my left hand from my thumb to begin his assessment. Without needing time to think, he said, "It's lost. We just need to cut this small piece of skin remaining and stitch you up the best we can."

I couldn't accept this. I asked him to do whatever he could to save my thumb. He said, "There's nothing left to save. All nerves, tendons, everything has been cut through." And then he repeated his words: "There isn't anything left to save."

Again, I asked him to at least try. I told him my right hand would be useless without a thumb, so he agreed. He stated, "I'll do my best, but it'll probably be a waste of time."

The doctor was a general practitioner, not a surgeon, and he spent five and a half long hours doing all he could before stitching my skin back together. He had to keep injecting more and more painkillers into me, but they did nothing to stop the burning sensation I was feeling in my thumb.

He wrote a prescription for a course of antibiotics and a few other drugs, and he told me to clean the area and change the dressing daily until I returned to have the stitches removed.

I couldn't clean my wound myself because doing so required two hands to slowly unwrap the blood soaked bandage. Luckily, two local barmaids from the North Western Hotel took turns helping me.

The two girls, Julie and Dalmaine, decided who would visit me each day. And for the following two weeks, they were always on time, never missing a day. The wound was badly infected, and the pain prevented me from sleeping.

Sometimes, I had to stop the girls from pulling on the bandage when trying to separate it from the dried blood because the pain was too great. Plus, there was the risk of opening the wound. Instead, they gently dampened the blood with warm water until it was soft enough to pull the bandage free.

I kept off any kind of alcohol with the hope that the antibiotics would succeed against the infection. Ultimately, my choice paid off. Eventually, back at the hospital, the stitches were removed. Still, they didn't have any confidence that I would ever be able to use, feel, or move my thumb again.

Eighteen months later – after spending every opportunity trying to bend the frozen joint using my left hand – it begin to move slightly. A few months later, I could feel the tip of it tingling, but only slightly. I continued bending and stretching my thumb for another two years until full feeling had returned. In the end, I could move it without any help from my other hand!

CHAPTER 3

Back to Wales

I returned back to Swansea in June of 1990, after recovering from a very hospitable twelve months in South Africa. It wasn't too long before I secured a short contract for a three-month shutdown on a nuclear power station in Dungerness, New Romney, Kent.

New Romney was a really nice place to be, and so was the pub I stayed in while there. The shutdown crew was from North Yorkshire, and were a real mix of characters. They were great to work with, and they all knew their roles. I was still a little new to the business, but I had learnt enough from South Africa to hold my own. Plus, I knew what was required of me.

Because I was the quality assurance engineer, I was the only person taking care of the quality for the shutdown. I also needed to work late every night to keep up with the progress and large amount of paperwork. I had contractors for site coverage, inspection, heat treatment services, etc., but in the end, the responsibility fell on my shoulders.

We had one particular labourer who was so efficient that the company always kept him employed. It was great for him because it was the only way he could avoid going to an asylum, where the rest of his family lived.

One night, I left the site office long after everyone else had gone. I quickly noticed that the entrance of the pub had traces of fresh blood on the walls. As I entered, I found more blood on the walls and the floor ... and then a lot more as I entered the main bar. A few crew members were sitting at the bar finishing their beers, but the whole place was badly messed up.

The site engineer was one of them, so I asked what the hell had happened. He explained that a local man had entered earlier and demanded a beer, but he was refused and asked to leave. Apparently, this man was no ordinary man: he had a military background − and not a normal military background.

The police were called the moment he entered, but when they arrived, they stayed outside. They knew who was inside. The man demanded to be served again, but again, he was denied. He quickly became aggressive and started breaking up the place.

The landlord's son hit the man over the head with a baseball bat, which started the blood flow. And then the son's mother hit the man with a large beer bottle, which added to his injuries. Still, nothing seemed to affect him.

During all the commotion, our industrious site labourer finished his beer and went to the bar for a refill. The land-lady explained to Keith that they couldn't serve any beer until they got the man out of the pub, which seemed to register something in the labourer's head.

He calmly went over to the crazed man and said, "Get out." The man didn't react at all, so the labourer asked him a second time: "Get out." Again, he didn't get a reaction.

After that, the crazed man tried to return to the bar. The labourer responded by punching him in the jaw, which knocked the man out cold. He barely move his arm a few inches, apparently.

The landlord opened the front door and shouted to the police that they could come in. One police officer asked who had apprehended the man, and they pointed to Keith. The officer went over to him and thanked him for helping the community. The labourer completely ignored him; he just sat at the table like nothing had ever happened.

The shutdown was completed with time to spare. Luckily for me, I was approached by a new agency before that job was finished. They offered me a two-year contract in the Islamic Republic of Iran.

I signed the contract in London in September of 1990, but before I could mobilise, Saddam Hussein had popped across the Kuwaiti border, which delayed my departure.

I needed to wait at home until the Japanese firm I was going to work for considered it stable enough in Iran for me to fly. After a month, I called the London office to say that I couldn't wait indefinitely – I needed to make money.

The administration manager, a lady from Yorkshire, asked me to check my bank account. Evidently, the Japanese had started paying me from the day I'd signed contracts. This was wonderful news. I enjoyed watching the news about the Iraqi war in my local pub knowing I was on full salary.

It wasn't to last, however. Early one morning, in January of 1991, I received a phone call from London. I was advised that my flight from London, Heathrow was scheduled for later that day.

I had very little time to get my inoculations, but I managed. After that, I headed straight for the Quadrant bus station to catch the coach to Heathrow.

In the meantime, it had begun to snow very heavily. By the time I arrived at Heathrow, the snow was quite deep. By this time, both my arms had seized up due to the injections I'd had earlier that day; I could hardly move them to manage my suitcase. As luck would have it, the snow caused my flight to be postponed until the next day. I called the London office, and they told me that I'd already been booked into the Edwardian International Hotel near the airport.

Once in the hotel – and after looking at some of the prices on the bar and restaurant menus – I rang the administration manager again to explain that I didn't have money put aside for such expenses. To my surprise, I was told to enjoy the lobster and sign everything to my room because it was probably the last good meal I'd have for months!

I spent three nights in the hotel waiting for a flight to Tehran. Each day, I would check out and return to the airport to see whether I had a flight. I spent twelve to fourteen hours every day waiting near the check-in counter but finally on the fourth day, I finally managed to get a flight by way of Frankfurt to avoid flying anywhere near the Middle East.

By the time I got to Frankfurt, I was just in time to miss my connection to Tehran. I had to stay in yet another hotel – compliments of the airline.

That night wasn't unlike any other night for an expat in transit. I sat at the hotel bar the whole evening and chatted with a German journalist on his way to Baghdad to provide war coverage.

The next day, I was on the flight to Tehran. I asked the airline to forward my details to my Tehran office, which they said they would – not.

There were only twenty-four passengers on the entire flight, so the flight attendant understandably left the drink trolley next to me and an Irish guy – how civilised I thought as I was going to spend the next four months in a *dry* country.

CHAPTER 4

Islamic Republic of Iran

I finally arrived in Tehran at eleven o'clock at night – a little worse for wear due to the damn drink trolley. But I soon found out that nobody was there to meet me. I saw on CNN that numerous Iraqi air-force jets were believed to have defected to Iran. Those jets, supposedly, were located at the airport where I was about to arrive.

In fact, as we came in to land, I could see hundreds of MiG-29s along the length of the runway. In actual fact, the Iraqi fighter's had lined the length of the runway two and a half times!

Luckily, I had a number to call. After an hour of trying to wake somebody up, I was finally able to announce my arrival. It took over an hour for a Japanese guy to get to the airport because the traffic in Tehran was like permanent rush hour. As I stood there, guarding my suitcase in the freezing cold, Iranian black marketers tried to buy my dollars off me.

The best was yet to come. The next day was a national holiday in Iran, so there were no domestic flights. After catching just four hours of sleep, they woke me up and explained that my taxi was waiting to take me south on a nine-hour drive from Tehran to Mobarakeh, near Esfahan.

After a short time in the battered Hillman Hunter taxi (which didn't even have headlights), I heard gunfire all around us. I asked the driver what the hell was happening, and he calmly smiled and said, "It's Revolution Day in Iran. We celebrate this every year." It was quite dangerous outside because everything they were shooting up into the air was coming back down all around us!

It was pitch dark for the last couple of hours, and we were relying on the moonlight to avoid all the potholes in the road. I remember telling the driver to slow down because we were going far too fast. I didn't want an accident in the middle of nowhere. The driver told me it was okay because Allah was watching over him. I reminded him that Allah certainly wasn't watching over me, and I told him to slow down again.

Working in Iran was a good experience, and the Iranians were wonderful people. I was always getting invited to somebody's home on my Fridays off. I'd buy a bottle of black market whisky to take along, which was always appreciated. Sadly, I did see a sick sight on one of my trips into Esfahan. As we drove through a small village, the driver stopped the taxi to show me a public execution.

I saw a young man's head placed in a noose, which was tied to the hook of a very small crane (called a cherry picker). There was a young girl standing against a wall with her hands tied behind her back. Her head was covered with a black, cotton sack. Near the girl were piles of rocks, and fat old women stood next to them.

The execution was just about to begin, so I ordered my driver to go. He was hesitant because he wanted to watch, but I strongly insisted. Fortunately, he drove away just before they murdered the young couple.

My heart wasn't into visiting anyone after seeing such a terrible sight, but I went to visit the family anyway. They understood my feelings on the matter, and they didn't agree with how Iran handled young couples holding hands or caught having a little cuddle.

Alcohol was legal in Iran if you weren't a Muslim, but there was no tolerance if you were caught carrying it into your home. The easiest answer was to make your own, so that was exactly what I did. First, I bought a pressure cooker and a few feet of 8 mm copper piping. And then I managed to find a short plastic tube to connect the copper pipe to the safety valve connection on the pressure cooker's lid.

The copper pipe was pulled around an empty bottle to form it into a coil, and that ran from the pressure cooker into the kitchen sink (which was full of cold water). During the distilling process, I left the cold water tap running, allowing the water to run out through the overflow. This helped condense the vapour going through the pipe. I had to be careful not to let the liquid inside the pressure cooker reach over 89 degrees because alcohol evaporates at 89 degrees and methanol evaporates over 90 degrees.

I regularly lit the clear liquid dripping from the end of the copper pipe to ensure that the liquid was producing a very clear blue colour. Any hint of orange, purple, or red would mean that I had to stop the process and pour the remains down the toilet. I had the shiniest, cleanest toilet on the camp.

It took several hours to fill a water bottle full of the uncut alcohol, but that was just the first part of the process. Once I had filled a bottle two-thirds full, I filled the rest of the bottle with raisins.

After that, I turned the bottle once per day for a month before using it as a rough brandy. It tasted okay mixed with Coke. I never bothered to cut it back with 50% water; instead, I used more Coke and ice.

Apart from my still, I brewed beer from cases of alcohol-free cans. I'd just add dark brown sugar and yeast. This process was much simpler and quicker. For each case of alcohol-free beer, I would dissolve a kilo of dark brown sugar. I'd pour a sachet of dried yeast into a cup of warm water with a little sugar to start the fermentation process, and then I'd add it to my plastic bin with four cases of beer and four kilos of dissolved brown sugar.

After ten days, I'd siphon the beer into empty Coke and lemonade bottles, which were capable of taking the pressure. And then I'd add a tablespoon of white sugar to each bottle and replace the tops as quickly as possible (before the yeast reacted to the additional sugar).

I'd keep the filled bottles in a dark place for another seven days before moving them into my refrigerator. And then I'd wait until they were so cold that the internal pressure was low enough to open them without having them spray all over the place. I continuously poured the liquid into a large jug until the sediment arrived at the bottles neck, which meant it was time to stop.

And then there was the wine. Originally discovered in that region well over four thousand years before Christ (and even earlier in some places), it seemed like a natural choice. Plus, it was easy to do. I just bought twelve bottles of grape juice, two-and-a-quarter kilos of white sugar, and a sachet of dried yeast. From there, I simply mixed everything together and let it sit for twenty-one days before bottling.

I made an air lock in the shape of an *s* with a little water and some cotton wool. That way, the carbon dioxide could escape, which stopped the explosions from happening. The original airlock was just a prototype, but later, I was able to smuggle in purpose-made airlocks bought from winemaking shops. They were perfect for the job.

During the construction phase of the project, we heard that the Iranian president was planning to visit the site. Nobody was told which day he would arrive for security reasons, but I saw numerous people planting evergreen trees all along the entrance roads to the steelworks to prepare for his arrival.

One day, I was walking around one of the five direct reduction iron ore modules where nobody was working. I was checking the status of piping that had been installed, and I lost track of time. A couple of hours must have passed before I realised how quiet the site had got, so I became suspicious and decided to return to the office to find out what was happening.

As I walked out from under the module, a large group of Iranians ran towards me and pointed their Kalashnikov

AK-47s at me. And there he was: Rafsanjani. He briefly saw me before I was totally surrounded and hastily escorted off the site.

My work rotation was sixteen weeks of work and just ten days break, back in the United Kingdom. Fortunately, due to the flight timetable, I was able to have twelve days back at home. I always tried to time my home breaks so I would be home at the same time as a friend of mine who was working in the merchant navy as a marine engineer. In March of 1992 I was presented with my usual home leave flight tickets.

My flight home consisted of a domestic flight from Esfahan to Tehran, where I would stay overnight and then two international flights; one from Tehran to Amsterdam, and a final flight from Amsterdam to Cardiff airport in Wales. On this particular home trip, my scheduled arrival date was a week before my friend would arrive back from the ship he was on, leaving me with just a few days to have his company.

We were quite busy on site at that time with all the piping which I was responsible for, so the Japanese project manager allowed me to postpone my home leave by a week. This was great news as I'd earn an extra weeks salary, plus have my friends company the whole time I was home.

Unbeknown to me at the time, my original flight wasn't going to make it to Tehran — at least, not in one piece. The day I was originally booked to fly to Tehran was a busy one for me. I was on site most of the day supervising the pressure testing of a large piping system and also air flushing any remaining debris from inside the piping loops by opening valves wherever there was a pipe branch etc. It was late in the afternoon when I returned back to my office to update the records I kept of all piping activities and progress records, when a young Iranian documentation engineer came running over to me.

He was very hard working and had managed to learn very good English in just six months! He asked me if I had heard the news, to which I replied, "how? I've been on site almost the whole day." We entered into my office and sat down at my desk where my original flight schedule was still visible amongst the piles of other papers.

The young Iranian immediately put his index finger on my flight schedule and told me that I was one very lucky man. Puzzled I asked why? He told me that my flight had had a bomb planted onboard and the fully laden flight blew up just as it neared Tehran. It was later printed in the Tehran Times that the flight was carrying some high-ranking VIPs from the National Iranian Steel Company (NISCO), which may have been the reason for the bomb on board? There were no survivors. I kept that flight schedule for quite a long time until it eventually was lost.

The Iranian's also made new postage stamps to commemorate the project we were working on and each of us in the office were given a full sheet of the stamps from their first printing. The stamps were of an artist's impression of an aerial view of the steelworks we had built. At that time it was the second biggest in the world; the biggest being in Russia. It didn't feel right that we, as foreigners were given such a unique gift, whilst our Iranian contractor received nothing, so I gave mine to the young documentation engineer as they would surely be worth something in years to come.

In December of 1992 I was responsible for pressure testing a natural gas 'header' (pipe manifold) which was one hundred meters long. Due to budget restrictions and lack of chemical consumables, I had to pressure test with water (hydro-test), without any anti-freeze chemicals added to the test water.

The daytime temperature was minus twenty two degrees centigrade so if I raised the internal test water pressure, the entire pipe line would have frozen in seconds, causing it to burst along its entire length, including some very expensive globe, ball, check and gate valves at the same time with a serious dollar and schedule value. It was a genuine mission impossible for the time of year. At that time, there was something playing on my mind that nothing was impossible. I checked the sites general arrangement drawings, the process and instrumentation diagrams (P&IDs), isometric drawings and any other drawing I could find relating to the area I needed to pressure test.

Eventually, and so conveniently, I discovered that there was a super heated water supply right at the beginning of the piping I needed to test. The super heated water supply came from the Italian part of the site, as they were building the steel rolling mill, and their site was segregated from my side of the complex by a chain-linked fence. Unfortunately for the Italians the fence didn't cover access to the drain valve of their super heated water supply piping. I had my brilliant Iranian piping gang to connect a high pressure hose to the Italians super heated water drain valve, so we could run the hot water down the pipe manifold I needed to pressure test.

The super heated water was able to keep the internal water temperature to just above freezing and we were able to apply pressure from time to time to search and seal any leaks along the one hundred meter manifold. We had the vent valve at the far end of our manifold open with a flexible pipe fitted to it to take away the continuous water flow into our industrial drainage system. We had to maintain a flow of super heated water continually for twentyfour hours a day to stop ice crystals forming. At pressure, the ice crystals would have taken just seconds to form, and in minutes explode the entire manifold.

Eventually, after my piping team had succeeded in closing all leaks on the manifold, they called me to witness the final pressure test and endorse its success. It was a freezing cold morning with snow and ice everywhere, and my piping team had worked continuously all through the night. I later discovered, they'd worked for seventy two hours with very little sleep out of respect for me, making final preparations for the pressure test. The test had to be completed so that my commissioning group could start earning their salaries.

Failure would have meant dozens of expats hanging around without anything to do until I had successfully completed the pressure and leak test of the manifold.

It was Christmas day when we finally applied the full test pressure. I nervously walked along the pipe manifold which ran along a four meter high pipe rack, expecting the worst but it never came. My Iranian piping team had done an impossible job due to the ambient temperatures at that time of year and had successfully achieved the impossible without antifreeze chemicals!

I gave the instruction to totally drain the manifold of all test water, including the opening of valve drain plugs and any other drain location where I could foresee water traps to avoid freezing ruptures. This took the rest of the morning to complete, before using nitrogen to dry the inside of the manifold.

Test completed, I stood at the beginning of the hydro-test, and heard the voice of an Italian process operator as he ran towards the chain link fence.

He spoke perfect English, but didn't have too much hair left since I'd last met him at a party on our compound a few days before. He was distraught and totally beside himself. He explained that all the gauges in his control room had been fluttering around for days and he couldn't find out where all their super heated water was going?

I was standing on the hose that was still connected to his super heated water supply and positioned my body so he couldn't follow its connection to my test manifold. I assured him to have faith, and that I was sure, that by the time he had returned back to his control room his gauges would start reading correctly!

My Japanese senior management were beside them-selves once I had returned and announced the gas manifold had been finally and successfully pressure tested, and they immediately arranged a celebratory party in true Japanese style. Needless to say I supplied the illegal alcohol.

During one of my home leaves I had bought several welsh flag 'sew on' badges to give to my Iranian piping gang. My original intention was for them to sew them onto the breast pocket of their coveralls. Instead, they put them on their jeans and proudly walked around the streets of Esfahan and Mobarakeh displaying my countries flag for all to see.

I didn't know at that time that *apparently*, the dragon on the welsh flag originated from Persia. The Romans had copied it for one of their flags and the welsh had taken a liking to it while the Romans were in Wales!

One of my Iranian piping guys lived on a farm. His father grew vegetables and fruit but was also a beekeeper and had over forty beehives. He came to the entrance of my office one morning and asked the security guards if they could call me to the door. Our guards didn't speak any English but I had got very good at sign language and understood I needed to go to the office entrance.

The young Iranian presented me with a full comb of honey extracted from one of his father hives as a gift in return for the little welsh flag sew on!

I was quite overwhelmed by his generosity and accepted his gift, not knowing quite what to do with it? It was in a cardboard box and quite heavy. It felt like it was about five kilos in weight and it was held together with a wooden frame. I showed a French Canadian electronics engineer who was working with me and he explained what I needed to do with it. As the daytime temperature got to fifty degrees centigrade in the shade, I was told to hang it outside the back of my bungalow in direct sunlight with a bucket strategically placed underneath it.

This I did as soon as I got home, as there was a cloths line stretching across my back yard. The following afternoon, when I arrived home I went straight out to my back yard to see what condition my honeycomb was in. All the honey had been melted by the intense sunshine and had dripped into the bucket. It had also made an excellent flytrap as the entire surface was covered with sticky flies, which I'm sure, were busy doing what flies do!

As the heart warming gentleman which I tried so hard to be, I held back the flies as I poured the full contents into plastic containers and gave it all to my Japanese colleagues. The French Canadian had already reserved the comb itself for his family. The honey was very nice, the one time I dipped my index finger into the clean part of it just to try it.

One Iranian working on the site brought me in a large family-sized coffee jar full of marijuana seeds. Just for fun, I dug the three flower borders in the back yard of my camp bungalow and scattered the entire jar over the soil. I watered them, but I didn't think anything would become of them. In just a couple of days, however, I had a green back yard. After a couple of months, I had a jungle.

A few months later, a Canadian commissioning engineer joined us. We got on very well from the day he arrived. In no time, he said he could do with something to smoke. He mentioned that he'd heard there was good quality hashish in Iran. I told him what I had in my backyard, which he found hard to believe. That evening, he came to my place to see for himself.

Apart from being totally amazed by the size of my jungle, he noticed that my male and female plants were all together.

He immediately removed all the male plants and piled them up separately. He explained that removing them would make the female plants produce more resin.

Despite my success, I decided to get rid of the whole lot. After all, it was only meant to be a bit of fun. The Canadian took several bags back to his place because he kept rabbits and rabbits love the leaves (as did his mad, local, feral cat). Later, we pulled the rest up and dumped them into a big pile for drying and eventual burning.

The following weekend, after a few smuggled whisky's, we thought it was a good time to burn the lot. It was so dry that it burnt immediately, and because we couldn't avoid the smoke … *wow*. Enough said.

In addition to my brewing, distilling, and fermenting activities, I made several black market friends who could supply whisky at fairly reasonable prices. The Japanese expats also bought whisky, but they made the mistake by using the local currency – therefore paying ridiculous prices for the very same stuff.

I knew the black market needed good, old American greenbacks because that was what they used to buy foreign goods. In other words, Iranian Riyals were useless outside the country.

I could buy a bottle of black market whisky for just thirty dollars in those days. That was quite cheap compared to what the Japanese paid which was the equivalent of ninety dollars in local currency.

One night, the Japanese expats were having a party and didn't have enough whisky to go around. One of them suggested that they knock on my door to see whether "Lang-san" could save their party with a few bottles.

When I let them in, they looked a little shy as they explained that they were looking for some more whisky for their party – which I hadn't been invited to!

I asked them how many bottles they needed, and they answered, "As many as possible." They were probably thinking that I had one or two bottles available.

I took them to the spare bedroom which I used for storage so they could choose which make of whisky they preferred. They nearly collapsed when they saw 366 bottles neatly placed on the floor according to its manufacturer.

It wasn't possible to order or request a particular brand in Iran – you just had to accept whatever was available at the time.

The Japanese wanted five bottles to start with. I quoted them fifty dollars per bottle, which they found very reasonable. They tried to pay in local currency, but I insisted on dollars. So off they went and returned minutes later with two hundred and fifty bucks.

The twenty-dollar-per-bottle profit helped compensate for all the British scroungers who regularly visited my place. My guests dropped by most nights for a free drink – every time promising that they would see me all right on their next trip (when they had money).

Of course, I never saw any money from any Brit sponging off me, so it was just as well they were drinking my profits. I would have made a healthy profit if it weren't for the British consuming my alcohol almost every night.

The Dutch, Italians, Canadians, and French all paid their way, but not a single time did any of the British pay me anything other than compliments to encourage the free flow of alcohol.

I left Iran in February of 1993, and I met my first wife just a week later. I'd just bought a new soft-top Vauxhall Astra, which was probably what caught her attention. She asked around until someone gave her my number, which she used to call me first thing the next day. I was vulnerable after being alone for over two years in Iran, so I was an easy target.

I won't go into the details about her, but I'll say that the valves in her heart would have complied with the engineering requirements for cryogenic service. Her heart would have had no problem passing the toughness tests, either – even at temperatures as low as minus 150 degrees centigrade (engineering talk).

After doing another nuclear power station shutdown – this time in Somerset – I was given a new contract for work in Saudi Arabia.

CHAPTER 5

Kingdom of Saudi Arabia

In October of 1993, I went to Saudi Arabia. I was required, by contract, to work for a three-month probationary period, so my wife had to join me later. Things were fine until then. After a thorough baggage search in Riyadh (where they looked for anything that they might find offensive, such as a *Bible,* I was allowed to enter.

I was based in Riyadh for the first eighteen months before being transferred to Jeddah for another eighteen months. My wine and beer making was soon underway and going down very nicely until the father of an Indian family – who lived on the same compound and worked on the same project – reported me to our head office in Riyadh for making alcohol.

He had never seen any evidence, but the wife of a fellow British expat from Wick, Scotland had deliberately told his Indian wife. And she had naturally told her Indian husband, and he had naturally told my head office. It was all very natural. Not!

Neither I nor my colleagues continued to speak to the Indian man after he had sold his fifteen-year-old daughter to a seventy-five-year-old Saudi for the marriage dowry. He knew the man because they went to the same mosque.

I was instructed to go to the head office and accept the consequences from our administrative and human resources managers. I had no idea what was happening at the time, and I was actually slightly excited that I was being transferred to Jeddah.

Anyway, those Saudis were rather polite about the whole thing. I was let off with a caution and told to empty any bottles I still had. That was some party. I invited a load of expats — mainly Swedish and German — to help me do just that.

After being betrayed by my fellow British colleagues, I applied to be moved to an apartment situated at the other end of Olaya Street, which passed all the way through the centre of Riyadh. One Friday morning, shortly before moving to the apartment, I began to feel a soreness in my throat. We had been invited to a barbecue that evening, so I was hoping that all I needed to do was gargle with strong salt water to stop it from getting worse.

The salt water did nothing, and I became sicker as the day went on. My wife refused to listen to me complain about the increasing discomfort in my throat. She only thought about the barbecue and which bachelors she could meet there.

Late in the afternoon, my throat became so bad that I couldn't speak — even my breathing became restricted.

Eventually, I collapsed. I tried to get up, but I didn't have the strength to move.

My wife, complaining bitterly, went across the compound to call a British nurse working in the city. She came rushing over to see what was wrong with me. Within seconds of checking me out, she went running as fast as she could to ask her husband to bring his car around to our outside entrance.

I was fading fast; I could no longer say anything at all. Her husband came rushing up the stairs to help carry me to his car while my wife just stood there, helpless. While her husband was busy bringing his car around, she called the hospital to give them advanced notice and instructions to be waiting at the side of the road with a wheelchair and an intravenous drip.

Sure enough, when we arrived at the side of the road outside the hospital, a Filipino nurse was waiting as instructed. It was a struggle trying to get out of the car and into the wheelchair. I felt totally useless as my friends did everything to help me.

I was in a terrible state. The Filipino nurse was desperately trying to get an intravenous needle into the back of my left hand, but she kept missing my veins. Soon the nurse took charge and inserted the needle into my arm in seconds. After that, she taped it securely and wheeled me into the casualty reception.

An Indian doctor soon came in to examine me. Using an instrument, he looked down my throat and wasted no time in prescribing me a strong cocktail of antibiotics and a private room for the next few nights.

Saudi Arabia can proudly boast that they have some of the very best medical facilities in the world, and everything looked immaculate as I was moved to my room. The nurse appeared a short time later to check the settings on my automatic drip.

She made a slight adjustment and told me that the machine was the very latest available. My friends asked my wife whether she'd return later because they needed to go (the car was still at the side of the road), but much to their surprise, she said she'd return with them because the barbecue was about to start.

Early the following morning, the very same doctor came to see how I was doing. He told me I was a lucky man. He had diagnosed me with ulcerated tonsillitis and explained that the ulcers had become septic and managed to poison my bloodstream. I asked him if all that could possibly happen in less than a day. He smiled and replied, "It did with you."

My wife visited me that evening (after missing the daytime visiting hour due to a shopping trip) to see how I was doing. She arrived late, so she could only stay with me for twenty minutes. She didn't seem to think it was necessary to visit me because I had nurses to take care of me. Nevertheless, people kept asking her how I was doing, so she didn't have any choice but to visit.

I was able to speak a little by the time she arrived because the antibiotics had started working. I asked her to leave some money in the drawer next to my bed so I could buy a newspaper to read. She told me I didn't need any money whilst staying in hospital because I had a TV. She coldly left without giving me anything.

I spent five nights in the hospital before being cleared and discharged to return home. Those five glorious nights in the peace and quiet of the hospital enabled me to finally get some restful sleep. Several weeks of living on the compound did not afford such luxuries.

Outside our compound, workers had dug a long trench right alongside our street. In the daytime, I couldn't get any sleep from working my nightshift because the Lorries were using the spare ground next to our compound. Every time they dumped a load of earth, the tailgate of the Lorries would slam shut, which made any sleep impossible.

At night, an ancient diesel generator with no silencer was turned on to run a long string of electric light bulbs along the trench. The noise made our entire villa shake, causing things to fall off the shelves. Driving to and from work was becoming more and more dangerous as I fought to stay awake. One time, I actually fell asleep at the office while standing. It must have only been for a split second and I fell to the floor when I woke up. I missed the hospital.

One night, while working out in the desert, something occurred that would have made it to the newspapers if the project hadn't been top secret. It was one o'clock in the morning and time to drive up from our underground workplace to head to the site canteen. As I neared the area, I found workers everywhere, all looking up into the clear, starlit sky.

I pulled over and asked one of the security officers what was going on. He said that someone had visited the site with three very bright lights that lit up the ground brighter than daylight could ever have.

Once in the canteen, it was clear that everyone was very excited and talking about the same subject. I joined a table full of Filipinos to try to find out more, but everyone had the same story to tell.

After I finished eating, I drove over to a Pakistani security friend to see if he knew anything more. He told me that something had hovered over the site with three super high-powered spotlights. The airspace above the site was restricted, so no civilian aircraft were permitted to fly anywhere near.

They had called Riyadh and were told that there wasn't anything showing up in the area according to their Airborne Warning and Control System (AWACS) defence surveillance, which was flying around the capital twenty-four hours per day. The security stressed that everyone had stopped work on the site and could still see something, so they couldn't be wrong. The air defence agreed to send two jets to fly directly over the site to get a visual of what everyone was claiming to be there.

My friend continued to tell the story with increasing excitement. Evidently, he went outside to wait for the jets to fly by with his colleagues, telling them what was about to happen. The object was still hovering silently over the very same area, but then it slowly began to move. Suddenly, it shot off at an incredible speed and disappeared into the night skies. Seconds later, two air force jets flew past at very low altitude, followed by the deafening roar from their engines.

Apparently, the jets hadn't picked up anything on their radars either.

There was always something happening out in the desert – if not a thunderstorm, a sand storm. One night, accompanied by a colleague, I drove back above ground because we heard there was a thunderstorm from hell going on. As I approached the entrance of the tunnel, I was met by a beautiful array of lightning, which fanned out like fire coral.

We drove to the highest point at the site to get a better view, and we noticed that one particular streak of lightning was headed directly for us while other streaks continued all over the place. We waited for a few moments until we realised that the lightning really was heading in our direction.

Quickly, we drove off. Just as we moved a few yards, a streak of blinding light drilled the very ground on which we'd been parked. Cameras weren't allowed anywhere near the site, so it wasn't possible to take any shots of the display, but it was an amazing show to have experienced.

Another night, the wind seemed to pick up dramatically. In just a few minutes, it had changed from a gentle breeze into the strongest wind I've ever experienced. The sand storm had come from nowhere, and I could barely make it across the open yard to my above ground office. I was practically horizontal by the time I made it to my office. Once there, I realised that the office didn't seem like the best place to seek refuge because the entire portable cabin was lifting off the ground at times and likely to roll over.

I telephoned my colleagues based underground for that week and told them to stay where they were (it was almost time for them to head up to the canteen). I remember looking up into the air to see an empty fifty-gallon oil drum flying across the yard … about a hundred feet above the ground. I would never have believed such storms existed if it hadn't have been for that night.

Driving back to Riyadh the next morning, I noticed that a huge, concealed door had been exposed by the sandstorm near our workplace. It was close by, but still a few hundred yards outside the perimeter fence. When I returned to work that night, it had been covered up again.

Ramadan came along, which I was very grateful for. Because my wife never cooked for me, I always arrived at nightshift hungry, waiting for the canteen to open. Fortunately for me, all our site security guards were from Pakistan, and they prepared special food for themselves during Ramadan. I arrived on site just in time to be invited to sit with them on the ground and share their food.

They always prepared extra so they could invite friends to join them. It's worth noting, however, that they were repaid throughout the year. We constantly supplied them with soft drinks that were freely available in the office kitchen, but otherwise inaccessible to them at their posts. Ramadan was their way of saying thank you.

After eighteen months in Riyadh, I heard I was officially being transferred to Jeddah. Being transferred to Jeddah was a good move. It meant I no longer had to see the faces of those who'd revelled in stabbing me in the back time and time again.

After just a few weeks in Jeddah, my wife insisted on going on holiday on her own instead of waiting another two months to go with me on my annual leave. As it transpired, she had secretly planned with her mother and aunt to go to Spain. And that's exactly what she did (rather than stay in the United Kingdom, as she'd told me).

It was in her absence that I found out she had been unfaithful whilst I was working shifts in Riyadh.

I called her at her mother's home number to ask how she was. Instead of reaching her mother, however, her brother answered the phone. He didn't realise that I didn't know anything about her going to Benidorm with her mother and aunt.

Thus began divorce number one.

Once I learned what she was doing while I was at work, I paid my Saudi site manager a visit. He was a prince, and his family was very powerful in Jeddah. They owned a large amount of the land. He was a very good man and keen fisherman, and we often talked about our escapades fishing in the Red Sea.

I went into his office and asked if he could help me cancel my wife's re-entry visa to Saudi. He gave me a warm, sympathetic smile and picked up his phone. After he said a few words in Arabic, it was done.

When my wife arrived back after her sleazy stint in Benidorm, her brother explained that I'd called and discovered where she'd gone. Suddenly worried that I'd found out, she became nervous and wanted to return back to Jeddah as soon as possible. She claimed that she missed me – yeah right.

With the pain I was feeling due to my newly broken heart, it was a real pleasure telling her that her re-entry visa had been cancelled and couldn't be revoked.

She didn't believe me and went to Heathrow airport to try to return to Jeddah. Only at the Saudi Airways check-in desk (when they did their routine check) did she believe her visa was no longer valid.

She wasted no time getting both my offshore and Swansea Bank accounts frozen. That was great: she couldn't continue shifting money out of my accounts and into her own as she'd done since I first left for Saudi. It was clear from the beginning that she was probably following her five-times-divorced mother. We got married on a Saturday, and she made me give her access to all my accounts that Monday!

Three days after she got access to my money, she claimed she needed to go shopping, but when I offered to drive her, she snapped at me. She said she wanted to go alone. Several hours later, she returned without any shopping bags. She told me she met up with a friend and didn't make it to the shops.

I found out two weeks later that she had had a secret abortion. When I quizzed her why she'd done it, she said, "You have to take me all over the world before we can start a family."

My friends in Saudi laughed when I told them she'd frozen my accounts because I was paid in Saudi, and the funds went directly into my Saudi bank account. It didn't affect me at all; rather, the move protected what I'd already made in Iran and Saudi.

I just looked at the experience as a blessing because it happened so early in my overseas life.

Saudi became a whole new place to live without my wife around. I was able to enjoy parties again without watching her dancing cheek to cheek with other bachelors' hands all over her.

I was able to take up scuba diving again, and I became a dive master in a few months. I was able to spend money on myself for the first time since meeting her. Life was great again!

I moved from the compound in Jeddah to an apartment that was closer to the site where I worked. I met a Filipino woman at a friend's party called Myatt, and she became my maid. She visited my apartment every morning at eight o'clock.

A few of my Riyadh colleagues later joined me in Jeddah, so it wasn't long before all the complaining started all over again. In Riyadh, we used to work twelve-hour shifts six days per week (alternating weekly from day shift to night shift). That was torture because the body couldn't adjust from one week to the next.

In Jeddah, it was set up differently. There were only morning and afternoon shifts – no night shifts. The day shift was from six o'clock in the morning until half past four in the afternoon. The afternoon shift started at four o'clock and went until one o'clock in the morning. I only needed to see the rest of the team for half an hour before having the entire site to myself.

When it came time to choose our work shifts, all my colleagues selected day shifts. Thus, I grabbed the chance and volunteered for permanent afternoons. Everyone immediately agreed. After that, I visited my favourite prince in the world's office to explain what had been discussed and agreed upon.

I already knew there were no afternoon shifts on Thursdays, so I got paid the same for working a five-day week. This left the others with six days per week (waking up at half past four in the morning and leaving at five to start at six).

It took a couple of months for my colleagues to realise their mistake, but it was too late to change things. I used to leave my apartment at 3 p.m. (Saturday through Wednesday) for my one-hour drive out into the desert. I would return home at two o'clock in the morning.

This had so many advantages: the traffic was light both ways, and I could enjoy the luxury of my home brew every night before going to bed.

Because I was the sole client representative on afternoon shifts, I could organise things exactly how I wanted them to be with the contractor. It was certainly the best move I could have made. Soon, a Swedish friend of mine (who was representing the contractor) changed to permanent after-noons, and that allowed us to scuba diving together in the mornings whenever we felt the urge.

I built up quite an impressive stock of beer, wine, and rough brandy. I was working when my British colleagues were free, so they couldn't visit me, like they had in Iran. Due to my impressive reserves, I allowed Myatt to invite all her friends to my apartment for a party every month. My quality of life couldn't possibly get better now that I was fee again.

Due to my permanent afternoon shifts, I had a lot of spare time to do whatever I wanted. I could visit my favourite fishing equipment shop in the centre of Jeddah or take my scuba tanks to be refilled with air whenever necessary.

Because I was well settled in Jeddah, I could go scuba diving every day or every night. I preferred night diving, but it wasn't without its dangers, as I discovered one night whilst diving with my instructor. That night, at eleven o'clock, we were on a corniche in Jeddah, just a ten-minute drive from my compound.

It was Friday, and I was using a new, high-pressure tank I'd just bought. It was made in Sweden, like all my diving equipment. The normal scuba tanks were made out of aluminium, and their maximum working pressure was 200 bar, which is equivalent to 3,000 pounds per square inch.

The new tank I bought was much smaller, but it contained the same volume. Also, it was made of steel. The tank was very heavy on my back, and its working pressure was 300 bar, which is equal to 4,500 pounds per square inch.

As it turned out, this dive was the last night dive I would ever make.

Once fully equipped, we had to climb down the large, hazardous rocks in the dark until we got to the water's edge. Before entering the Red Sea, we broke the glass inside our chemical lights and shook them until the fluids mixed together and lit up. I always took two underwater lamps on my night dives: a main, rather powerful light and a smaller, standby light for when my primary light would inevitably die.

My primary lamp was my new and ridiculously powerful dive lamp. It was capable of turning total darkness into bright daylight. It burned up eight D-cell batteries in just forty-five minutes, so the end of my dive required the use of my spare little lamp. In the end, the powerful lamp was what probably saved my life that night.

We began our decent to just ten meters, and we tied the red chemical light to some coral to mark our entry/exit point. And then we continued our dive, exploring the coral and placing additional green chemical lights every so often as markers to trace our way back to where we started. We wanted to have our cars close by when we finished the dive.

While underwater, it was a little difficult to stay positioned with all the weight on my back. Still, everything seemed okay at first. The wetsuit was made of lycra and polar-tech, which mainly helped protect the body from coral. It didn't need to help me stay warm however, as it was 28'C in the Red Sea.

We completed our first thirty minutes of the dive and turned to complete our second thirty minutes. We were heading back to our starting point to ensure that we both had spare air left in case of any unforeseen event.

After about ten minutes, while I was busy stroking a large, sleeping grouper, I experienced one hell of a surprise. Night diving offers a whole new meaning to the word *darkness*. The only possible view was in the direction the dive lamp was pointing.

I was focused on the sleeping fish when something caused me to roll over uncontrollably. All I could do whilst struggling to roll back over was swing my dive light around.

It is well known that sharks like to eat at night in shallow water. After all, fish also need their sleep. Coral reefs present a perfect lunch venue because most fish like to live in the first ten meters' depth. And that's exactly where I was.

As I managed to spin around and aim my powerful dive lamp into the dark abyss, I saw what had moved the water in such close proximity to me. It was the tail of a shark of enormous proportions. I had a brief but clear view of the shark's tail, which was as tall as I was making it at least sixteen feet long. It was only a few feet away, and I briefly caught sight of it before it disappeared into the darkness.

I quickly swam over to my dive buddy and indicated a big mouth by spreading my arms. I pointed in the direction the shark had gone, and we both pointed in the up direction at the same time. We wasted no time getting there.

Diving at a depth of ten metres does not require any decompression stops – which was good because we weren't in any mood to hang around. We made it to the coral drop off and clambered over it to safety.

The following weekend, a fellow expatriate stole the show. He had just returned from diving alone (which I never did) in the same place where we had night dived the week before. His scuba tank had a strong nylon net over it to protect it from getting scratched and to keep it looking like new, but the netting had been ripped to shreds.

There were teeth marks in the tank's hard, enamelled paint that covered most of his tank.

He had been attacked from behind by a large shark that shook him vigorously by his tank and pushed him face first into the sand. He was very lucky that he had been pushed into the only little patch of sand in that area. Had he been forced into the coral, the outcome would have been very different – especially for his complexion!

When he was forced into the sand, his demand valve was ripped from his mouth. He couldn't breathe. Luckily for him, the shark didn't like how the hard aluminium tank felt in its jaws, and it released him. He was able to go on an emergency ascent and clamber over the same coral as I had the week before.

I managed to go on over three hundred dives in the Red Sea whilst living and working in Jeddah, and I will always be grateful to Saudi Arabia for granting me a diving license that allowed me to enjoy its west coast reefs.

It is not my intention to deter anyone from diving in the Red Sea – quite the opposite. With over three hundred dives that enabled me to map parts of the seabed of Jeddah for others to enjoy, I can't complain. Therefore, I will only elaborate on two more instances that have remained in my memories.

One instance was when I went on a chartered dive boat fifteen kilometres off the coast of Jeddah. The day and the sea started off too perfect for my liking. The Red Sea is well known to change unexpectedly, but the Saudi coastguard allowed vessels to leave the safety of Jeddah's marina that morning. So off we went.

We did one dive in the morning, which wasn't terribly special because there wasn't very good coral to explore. But the second dive in the afternoon was something quite different. We were diving at a depth of twenty-two meters near a shipwreck. The shipwreck was nicknamed chicken wreck because it was a cargo vessel carrying thousands of chickens bound for Jeddah when it hit a reef in a storm, broke its back, and sank.

The dive started off fine. The waters were unusually calm. After just half an hour, however, the tranquil dive became a different world. I became aware of movement up above me, which caused me to look back up to the surface where our dive boat was hovering.

Due to the Saudi environmental policies in those days, dive boats were not permitted to drop their anchors (which might damage the coral).

When I looked up, I could see the ocean surface becoming turbulent and dangerous. As the dive master on that day, I aborted the dive by tapping every diver on the shoulder and indicating that everyone should return to the surface.

At the surface, the real danger became apparent. Everyone's objective was to get back on the dive boat while it bounced more than ten feet off the surface of the water. The main danger was at the transom, where we needed to climb up. That part of the boat was hammering down on the water, easily capable of smashing a skull.

Eventually, we could account for each and every diver, and we started our journey back to the safety of Jeddah's marina (which was still a long ride away).

In Jeddah's direction, all we could see was a sky full of sand. The coast was out of sight, which explained the waves we were riding on the way back. We estimated the swell to be around twenty-five to thirty-five feet.

Our dive boat was struggling to ride up the waves, and each time we got to the top of a wave, half the hull would be out of the water – only to come slapping down again on the other side. We had a Filipino skipper who was very experienced and knew what to do. He began to zigzag the waves one at a time.

It was a much slower way to get back, but it was also much safer. We sat on bench seats on both sides of the back of the boat. We all gripped the benches with white knuckles: one minute we would be high up in the air looking down towards the guys on the other side of the boat, and the next minute we would be looking up at them.

All the while, we were slowly but surely getting closer to Jeddah. We could see the battering the sandstorm was giving the mainland. It took us several hours to reach the marina, by which time the storm had calmed down a lot. We took advantage of the lull and pulled up against the quayside without being slammed against it.

It was still quite windy, though. There was a lot of sand in the air, and all the roads were a mess. We saw sand dunes piled up against buildings and other similar sights. When I got back to my apartment, there were many messages left on my answering machine from concerned friends who knew I was going out on a boat dive that day. I called everyone back to put their minds at rest.

We went on several more boat dives after that event, and they were all well worth the effort. One such dive took us far away from shore to another shipwreck. That ship had been carrying heavy duty electrical cables. Just like the previous wreck dive, the ship had broken up on a coral reef in a storm, which had blown the ship well off its intended course.

The wreck was decently intact. The tonnes of copper cables had been removed years before due to their value. As we gradually made our way around it, we found a small oceanic whitetip shark sleeping. There were seven of us, and I was the only diver without a camera. Everyone was busy taking photos of the shark until it suddenly became aware of our presence and darted out quickly, pushing straight through the middle of us.

As it did so, it hit me in my chest with its fin, knocking all the air out of me. It was too deep to make an emergency ascent to the surface, so I had to struggle to get my breath back while the other divers were busy laughing. Clouds of bubbles were pouring out of their demand valves.

When I began to start breathing somewhat normally again, I noticed something that could best be described as a submarine not too far from where we were.

The submarine moved very slowly, but it had noticed our presence. I motioned to the others to look over their shoulders to see what I was looking at. The "submarine" could have been the small shark's mother, but if so, it was a fully grown mother – approximately sixteen feet long.

This is something new, I thought. We didn't exactly know what to do. The shark slowly swam around us as we huddled against a large coral head until our dive computers starting beeping to alert us of low air. There was no more time to think – we had to go back to the surface regardless of the shark, which was getting closer every time it circled us.

We all began our ascent together and with the dive boat directly above us, it wasn't long before we were all clambering at the transom trying to get the hell out of the water as quickly as possible. The worse part was needing to make a safety stop half way up to decompress with the small amount of air we had left. We stopped at ten meters and again at five meters so I was sucking air by the time I surfaced.

Of course, nobody admitted to being afraid, but there was a strange smell among us … and it wasn't coming from me.

I met a guy from Cornwall called who also worked on the same project (managing site security). He was ex-British military – and his wife worked in a nearby hospital in Jeddah. He had a boat in the marina, so it wasn't long before we teamed up and went fishing every Friday.

They invited me to their compound every Thursday night, which was a Swedish compound. Someone was always having a party there on a Thursday night, so it was a great place to be. The idea was that we could leave together early in the morning to take the boat out by seven o'clock. We bought squid for bait and sacks of ice on the way to preserve our catch.

We always returned with a cooler box crammed full of fish at around four o'clock in the afternoon. Grouper and red snapper were always popular with the Filipinos I worked with, and I was only too happy to oblige them every Saturday afternoon when returning back to work.

Myatt opened my cooler box every Saturday morning (the ice had not yet melted) and cleaned all the fish before I got up. When I think about it, Myatt was a diamond.

I told her which fish I wanted to freeze for the monthly party and which fish I wanted to give to the Filipinos on site, and then I gave the rest to her to take home. This went on for several months until, one day, she opened my cooler box and found only two little fish.

I was waiting for her to arrive. She didn't know I was listening to her as she made a kind of disappointed moan. She could see all the shelves had been taken out of the fridge, and she was surely curious about my reasoning.

When she opened the fridge, she couldn't stop herself from letting out a little scream: there was a forty-seven kilo yellow fin tuna wedged diagonally in my fridge. That was the only way I could keep it cool – the cooler box was far too small.

I proudly entered the kitchen, trying my best to resemble a character from Ernest Hemingway's famous book (but a younger version). I found her smiling from ear to ear. She asked me how I wanted it prepared, so I asked her to cut it up into steaks. The steaks were so big that we needed to cut them into quarters which would still overhang a dinner plate.

While Myatt was busy fighting with the tuna, I went to the local supermarket and bought the biggest aluminium saucepan I could find with two handles. After that, I went to a garage to pick up a sack of ice.

When I returned, I poured some ice into the saucepan, placed the head of the tuna on top of it, and continued to fill the rest of the saucepan with ice until the tuna's head was fully covered. Finally, I placed the lid on top of the pan.

Myatt asked what I was doing, and I replied, "I'm packing the head for you to take home with you, darling."

Later, Myatt explained that she was able to make Filipino fish soup for an entire month!

One of my normal Thursday night visits to my fishing partner's compound presented me with quite a surprise. It came as a little, furry, four-legged kitten. My friends wife noticed earlier in the day that a black plastic garbage bag was laying on the ground underneath his car. It was moving, so she dragged it out to see what was inside.

There were four little kittens inside, which had been strategically placed so they would be driven over. One of the little kittens immediately bonded with me – and that was that!

I took Muffy home with me the next day and immediately went back out for cans of kitten food, cat litter, etc. Of course, I also bought her some little toys so she could amuse herself. For a litter tray, I used a large rectangular cooking tray I had found in a kitchen cupboard.

Muffy was very nervous when she first entered my apartment; she hid under the sofa and couldn't be persuaded to come out until she became hungry. The drive home probably didn't help. After she ate, however, Muffy's confidence grew quickly and soon she became a wonderful companion to have.

She was certainly a feral cat – always on the wild side. My shoulders were permanently covered in scratches and claw marks because she liked to take rides around my apartment while perched on my shoulders like a parrot.

Her favourite game was helping me when I was rigging more fishing lures. This was quite dangerous once hooks were attached, and we had many a near accident when she came darting out of nowhere to pounce on the lure I was busy rigging.

I was coming close to completing my third year in Saudi Arabia, but with all my divorce proceedings wearing me down, I decided not to renew my contract. Meanwhile, my Cornish fishing partner had been busy over the last three months entering us in the annual fishing tournament in Phuket, Thailand, which was held in the first week of November every year.

With my soon-to-have freedom, I left Saudi Arabia in October of 1996 and returned to the United Kingdom for just a couple of weeks to finalise my divorce. Myatt took Muffy to live with her and I replaced the litter tray back in the kitchen cupboard for the apartments next occupants to use.

While I was back in Swansea, I decided to get my first tattoo to prepare for the Phuket fishing tournament.

I had a T-shirt with an illustration of Ernest Hemingway's book, The Old Man and the Sea. The picture featured a blue marlin caught on an old man's hand line while on his little fishing boat. Because time was short, I just had the tattoo artist put the fish on my right calf muscle. I figured I could get the rest done the next time I was back in Swansea – whenever that would be. I couldn't have guessed that the tattooist would loose his right forefinger later so it was never completed.

With my divorce complete, I flew to join my fishing partner, his wife, and their Dobermann (Sasha) in Thailand. They had left Saudi around the same time I had.

CHAPTER 6

Phuket Fishing Tournament

Previously, we had fishing team T-shirts and baseball caps made in the Philippines by a friend who was visiting his home while on leave from Saudi. We called our fishing team "The Hot Rods and Hookers" for some strange reason?

My partner had the word Captain on his hat and T-shirts, and he arranged for mine to feature the words *Master Baiter*. Thankfully, the words were separated by a space. Our team regalia went down very well in Thailand at the bars on Patong Beach!

The tournament kicked off at 6 a.m. sharp, so we rented rooms close to the jetty to get ready for the early start every day. I met my team at five o'clock in the morning the first morning because I needed to know where the hell our boat was out of the thirty-nine other entries.

I hadn't slept the whole night because I was both excited and unsure how well we'd fare with so many other boats. I walked to the area at the entrance of the derelict wooden pier and was amazed to see how busy it was. Even at five o'clock, the Thai TV crew were already busy filming everything that was going on. The whole place was a hive of activity, and I could feel the energy in the air growing by the minute.

I had already rigged my tournament rod, which had been custom built in America by AFTCO with a heavy Penn 80TW reel. I dropped it in one of the rod holders at the port side of the stern because I felt it would be my lucky place for the three-day event. Our crew had slept on the boat all night, protecting the live baitfish that they caught the day before. These little, yellow-tailed fish were considered the best live bait for the sailfish that we were aiming for (each of which would earn us five hundred points), and they needed to be protected from potential thieves.

At exactly 6 a.m., the horn sounded to start the tournament ... and off we went in our old, Thai-style, deep-sea fishing boat.

We didn't think we had enough of the little baitfish, so we wasted the first hour of the day fishing for more of them before trolling out to the most popular fishing area where all the other boats had already gone.

Suddenly, our skipper made a sharp turn causing our lines to cross. This was disastrous because we came right alongside four sailfish, but there was nothing we could do except waste more time untangling our lines. An hour passed, and I was finally hooked up with a good-sized sail. The hook hadn't gone deep enough into the fish's mouth, though, and I only had it on the line for a couple of minutes. I kept the line tight the whole time, but the fish still managed to spit my hook out. This raised my morale – not to mention adrenalin! With no more action on the first day, we turned and headed back to the jetty; everyone had to be back before 5 p.m.

I was able to land a large sailfish on our second day, earning us our first five hundred points in the competition and putting us on the scoreboard. *Wow, the game is on,* I thought. The tournament followed strict rules, and all "billfish" had to be released unharmed. Each boat was given a disposable camera to take a photo as proof of the catch before releasing the fish, so we handed in our camera and got another to use for the third and final day.

After catching my very first sailfish, I was awake all night. My veins were still glowing with adrenalin, which made sleep impossible.

Our final day was frustrating and didn't raise our score. Our total of five hundred points wasn't enough – we came fifth out of the thrity-nine boats. We didn't qualify for any prize, but it was great meeting all the other teams (of varying nationalities).

The end of the tournament was held at the Holiday Inn, situated on Patong Beach. The Holiday Inn had organised an amazing night with food and entertainment, which I'll never forget for the rest of my life.

Each winning team was announced, and the trophies were awarded. I sat patiently waiting for mine. I knew all the prizes stopped at fourth place, but I was told to expect some kind of acknowledgement because it was my first tournament on the island. Sadly, that recognition never came.

Anyway, I was in a very nice and relaxing part of the world – so what did it matter? The glory was simply being a part of the tournament. In February of 1997, whilst chilling on a Thai beach, the same Japanese company I'd worked for in Iran called me. They asked me if I would be interested in re-joining them in Venezuela to build the very same direct reduction iron ore plant that I had been involved with building in Iran.

Venezuela? I thought. And then I thought: *salsa; merengue; tambor; hola, mi amor;* ¿qué quieres, chicas? I did not need to think any longer; immediately, I asked the following: "When do I fly?"

CHAPTER 7

First Time in Venezuela

Sadly, I had to leave Thailand to return to the United Kingdom so I could take my passport to the Venezuelan consulate in London for a work visa. The Japanese firm had already sent a letter of invitation, so the process was quick. I submitted my passport on a Monday and collected it again that Friday. My flights were arranged for the following Monday, so I had the whole weekend to prepare for the trip.

Because there were no rotational leaves in my Japanese contract, I needed to ensure that I didn't forget anything – I had no idea when I would be back in the United Kingdom.

I flew out from Cardiff towards the end of March, but again, I was delayed due to bad visibility. Consequently, I missed my connection in Amsterdam. I took a later flight, but the Japanese firm hadn't been notified – which meant there wasn't anyone to meet me at the airport in Puerto Ordaz.

I didn't know I wouldn't be picked up, so I continued waiting at the airport for someone to collect me ... all the while turning down local taxi drivers and chancers hoping to get the job. Eventually, there was no one else around. The airport was closing for the night, and it was too late to get a taxi. Thus, I began to walk.

I was in a hot country, but I was dressed in winter clothes. The sweat was pouring out of me. I wasn't aware how much danger I was putting myself in by dragging my suitcase behind me.

I must have walked over three miles in the dark before I came to a military installation where I found two guards waiting at their post. Without any Spanish, it was almost impossible to make them understand that I needed a taxi. One of the guards went off and brought back his superior a few minutes later who could speak a little English. I asked him whether he could help me get a taxi to a hotel. He understood my request and helped me out.

Because I was European, I ended up being taken to the Intercontinental Hotel in a beautiful part of Puerto Ordaz. When I got there, I checked in and went straight to bed. The next morning, I called the office to let them know I had arrived in the country – much to their surprise. I was picked up an hour later (before being charged for a late check-out).

I was first dropped off at my apartment for a few minutes so I could drop my luggage off and proceed straight to the site office.

The office was just a twenty-minute drive away, and upon entering, I was amazed at how many beautiful women the Japanese had employed. I wasn't complaining. The piping engineer (who called me in Thailand) was the only one I knew from the previous project in Iran, and he had been promoted to construction manager.

I was introduced to all the staff, including the quality manager. If first impressions count, I found him to be a rather inadequate man – someone not to be trusted.

I was later taken to the contractor's office to be introduced to the managers based there, including their quality manager called Hector. Luckily, he spoke perfect English. I was not aware at the time, but I was going to spend a lot of time with Hector because he didn't really have a clue what he was doing.

He seemed desperate for my help, so in order to make my job easier, I gave him all the help and support I could.

Nobody thought to tell me that it was *Semana Santa,* (Easter) in just three days, and everyone had to take those days off.

That same day, one of the Venezuelans in the office called Jorge came to me with a distraught look on his face and asked if I had any spare cash. When I asked him why, he explained that his five-year-old daughter needed an emergency operation or she would die. Naturally, I didn't know whether to believe him or not, but I didn't want to hear later that she had died because I didn't give her father any money. Thus, I loaned him the only money I had.

The day before the Easter holidays, I was dropped off at the apartment and told that they'd see me in three days. "Three days?" I asked, "Why?" Only then was I told about the holiday. *Great,* I thought, not knowing where the nearest ATM was, where to shop, or where to eat.

The next day, I walked around for a couple of hours in the heat and humidity before finding an ATM. I didn't know how dangerous the place was. Fortunately, I didn't have any problems – they would come later – and eventually I found a place to eat. Without having any mineral water in my apartment, I proceeded to boil water for twenty minutes and put it in the fridge.

Once the holidays were over (and I was back in the office), I heard Jorge explaining to one of the Filipino workers what a great weekend he'd had in Puerto de la Cruz with his wife and her sister. Jorge didn't have any children!

Because it was my first time in Venezuela, I didn't know that the vast majority of Venezuelans lie, have no respect, and never return money to foreigners.

After not learning a damn thing from my cryogenic wife, I met spouse number two, Carolina, while helping the contractor's quality manager. Unlike cryogenic wife, she was better suited for high-temperature service in my very first week on site. Carolina worked for the contractor on the other side of the site.

I spent quite a lot of time with her in my first few weeks because I was busy preparing all the welding procedures for the contractor. Evidently, they didn't have anyone else capable of writing and qualifying them.

Carolina explained – with help from another girl from Trinidad – that there was a riot on the site the previous year. The office had been burnt down. So many Latin Americans are hot-blooded people with fiery tempers; and it didn't take much to start them off. Apparently, the armoured salary van was late one Friday, early in 1996, so the workforce became impatient and started a riot outside her office.

Things quickly got out of control, and the office was set on fire. Everyone managed to escape through the back door, but they could do nothing but wait outside and watch their office burn down. Except for Carolina. When she couldn't be accounted for, the site safety woman told the project manager that one of the men should go and look for her. The project manager refused. He said, "If anyone were still inside, it would be too late to help them in any case."

With that said – and no time to waste – the safety woman jumped into a Toyota Hilux and reversed it straight through the wooden office wall near Carolina's desk. She found her frozen at her desk. Carolina, stricken with fear, couldn't move, so the safety woman had to physically push her into the truck and drive out, minutes before the entire office was ablaze.

The men watching her heroic action looked quite pathetic when the salary van arrived a few minutes later.

During those early days on the project, I noticed a business card left on a desk in the contractor's office. What caught my attention was that the business card had the Welsh dragon on it. First I was somewhat angry, thinking a Venezuelan had taken a fancy to my little country's flag. I told the contractor that I wanted the guy who left the business card to see me in my office.

Later the same day, I couldn't believe my eyes when a fellow Welsh man introduced himself. It transpired that Richard Jones didn't just come from Wales, he came from Swansea and the Mumbles where I was from!

Richie had lived in Venezuela for almost twenty years by that time, and he had a lot to tell me – including advice that I shouldn't fall for the beautiful women there. Richie had the contract for the underground firewater piping, so he needed to return to Puerto Ordaz regularly to check on the progress and his workforce.

Each time Richie returned, we met in a local Tasca restaurant for a few beers and a game of pool. There, we'd play pool and have something to eat, inevitably a popular dish called *mar y tierra* (that is, *surf and turf*) in true Venezuelan style.

I continued to spend quite a lot of time with Carolina. Her job was to paste her company's logo on the page headers I was busy writing. As she did that, I prepared the welding procedures. I think she pasted more than the logos because we got married in her parents' house seven months later.

At the time, my Spanish was practically non-existent, and Carolina didn't speak any English. To me it sounded like a perfect marriage because she couldn't argue or complain about anything.

All wedding plans were arranged in super-fast time (so I couldn't change my mind), and off we went to Ciudad Bolívar, where Carolina's parents lived. We spent the whole day filling up their house with more food and alcohol than there was space for.

Ciudad Bolívar was formally called Angostura, where the famous bitters originated. Ciudad Bolívar is the capital of Venezuela's south-eastern Bolívar State. It was founded as Angostura in 1764 and renamed in 1846 after the death of Simón Bolívar in 1830. Simón Bolívar was the key force behind Latin America's successful struggle for independence from the Spanish Empire. He is still considered one of the most influential politicians in the history of Venezuela.

Later in the afternoon, Carolina went to a salon to have her hair entwined with plastic strings of pearls and plaits and a few other things while I waited for her in a nearby bar.

Something kept telling me to get a taxi back to Puerto Ordaz, but I was quite comfortable where I was in the bar. There was a guy standing at the door with a sawn-off shotgun to protect the customers, so I felt safe.

After three hours of waiting for her to meet me in the bar, I was feeling wonderful. I was losing interest in meeting her family – let alone having a second wedding.

I eventually weakened and agreed to jump into a taxi and return to her parents' house. If I had remained sober, I would have returned to Puerto Ordaz, still a single man.

As soon as I arrived, her father and I took his taxi so I could buy even more ice. We arrived at the Venezuelan Polar brewery and bought two more blocks of ice. He managed to borrow an ice pick that would allow him to break it up. Amazing, really, that they allowed him to borrow the ice pick, I guess they must have trusted him?

We also found some special music CDs made for weddings. We arranged for a DJ to play for us, we bought enough food to cover the seventy-nine family only guests, and we purchased enough alcohol to knock out the whole street.

In Venezuela, it is customary for every man attending the wedding to dance with the bride (and for every woman to dance with the groom). This was not what happened at this wedding.

Yes, every man succeeded in keeping my new wife well occupied while her father kept her away from me the entire wedding night. I, however, spent the whole night completely ignored. I was left sitting all alone at a table near the road.

As I turned around every five minutes to watch wife number two having a wonderful wedding, I could only wonder why I had not taken a taxi back to Puerto Ordaz.

As I watched the family drinking, eating, talking, dancing, and having a wonderful time, my frustration and anger reached an explosive level that was about to escape into the open. Those ignorant people were finally going to get a Welsh wake-up call.

I remember asking one lady to dance with me so I could participate in my own wedding, but she flatly refused me. And then another ... and another. The only woman who could actually speak a little English took pity on my frustration and loneliness and explained to me that no lady wanted to dance with a man who didn't know how to dance salsa or merengue very well.

That was it for me. I told all of them to go back to the hell they came from. I was shaking with anger. My new wife's cousin, who was a nurse, went to his car and brought a syringe filled with some kind of tranquilliser. He had stolen it from the clinic where he worked.

The first injection had absolutely no effect on me, so he gave me a second dose. That dose did something, but only enough to stop me from physically throwing each and every Venezuelan guest into the street.

They decided that it would be better for us newly-weds to return to my apartment in Puerto Ordaz that night instead of staying the night in an aggravating environment. We went to take our wedding CDs, but someone had already stolen them.

When Carolina came back from her bedroom (where she'd kept her handbag out of sight from her family guests), she was in tears. Someone had stolen all her new make-up, which I'd bought for her the weekend before. I had hidden my wallet in her bag, which someone had also emptied. *My new family!* I thought.

A few days after we got married, her parents presented me with their electricity bill, water bill, telephone bill, and any other bills they could find. I was now family.

Another two weeks passed until I returned home from work one Saturday lunchtime, only to see my apartment's balcony full of Venezuelan's drinking!

I was together with an American and German colleague. They agreed to help cover me while the three of us went into the private club in the centre of the complex. We all figured that I wouldn't react too well to my welcome committee, so we went for a few beers with the hope that they'd have gone by the time I got home.

After half an hour, Carolina called me to ask where I was, as I was late getting home. I told her that I'd seen all her relatives and their friends all along my balcony with beers in their hands and thought it best I didn't arrive while they were still there.

I did all my weekly shopping on Friday nights, and had made several trips back and fore my truck in all the heat and humidity so I'd be well stocked for the following week, and could just relax after getting home after work. The night before, I'd bought three kilos of fresh prawns which I was looking forward to cooking that afternoon. With my fridge fully stocked with beers and a few bottles of the finest rum, I wanted to invite both the American and German to share it with me.

After seeing all the Venezuelan's along my balcony, I knew there would be absolutely nothing left to return home to.

I told Carolina to call me once they'd all gone home, but she insisted I return as they all wanted to meet me! *How would they expect me to react I thought, seeing them helping themselves to all my stocks?*

It wasn't until five in the afternoon, that they finally left. I knew that meant they'd finished everything there was to eat and drink so it wasn't worth them hanging around any longer. Anything that was left over would have been carried out with them as they left in any case. That was their style.

As soon as the last sponger had left, Carolina wasted no time in coming to the club to meet me. She knew that as there was a large outdoor pool, there was always an abundance of scantily clad ladies who were looking for a foreign man to entertain for free food and drinks. It had been on her mind all the while her visitors prevented her from leaving.

She had a worried look on her face as she knew how I would react when I saw the mess back in my apartment. I was starving hungry by that time so I agreed to go home so I could start preparing my *beloved* prawns. She was very quiet as we walked back to the apartment.

When I entered, it was just as I'd expected. There were five cases worth of empty beer cans and empty Black Label whisky bottles all over the place and all the Rum had been taken. I opened my fridge, and that too had been emptied of everything, including my prawns.

They'd made paella with all three kilos and I was left with a small amount of cold rice in the bottom of the pan and nothing else!

I went to take some cash from my bedside drawer so I could go out to eat but someone had stolen the lot. There was the equivalent of five hundred dollars which was about two months' salary for them. I told her I was off to a restaurant as I really need to eat and she told me she'd go with me. I told her to stay behind and clean all the mess and I'd return later.

I grabbed my keys and ATM card and off I went to relax and calm down after all I'd just lost.

I banned anyone from visiting my apartment after that, but that didn't always work. The following Saturday her cousins wife visited and had opened two full cases of beer cans and had just taken a sip out of each before opening another and another so they'd be cold from the fridge. I couldn't begin to understand such mentalities.

This continued throughout the first year – including a new roof for her parents' house, glass in their window frames instead of the bars they had before, a gas cooker, a refrigerator, beds with legs, an air conditioner, and even glasses to replace the jam jars they used to drink from.

I was made to visit them at least every two to three weeks, and I was like a lamb to the slaughterhouse every single time. As soon as I arrived, her father would rush me off to the local off-license to buy three or four cases of Polar beer and a bottle of Black Label whisky.

The entire street was very happy with this arrangement, because they'd pass by and help themselves to the spoils – and in many cases they returned home with a couple of six packs without saying a word.

Even Carolina's cousin (who lived next door) would walk past me without saying anything and take beers back to her house time and time again until everything was gone.

I complained to my new wife that she had to stop her cousin, but she said that we couldn't do anything because her cousin's only job was to perform voodoo on people for a small fee!

Later, voodoo played a big part in my life causing me to quit my job, sell my Chevrolet Grand Blazer (which I'd bought from a German friend), and leave the country to have the voodoo removed back in Swansea.

During that first year, we planned a long weekend on Isla de Margarita with another expat and his girlfriend. The island was quite nice, but the atmosphere changed after we walked to a tasca restaurant.

We were warned by the owner not to walk back the way we came because the locals were hanging around in door-ways waiting to relieve us of all valuables or even worse. When it was time for us to leave, the owner arranged for a taxi to meet us right outside the front door so we'd get away safely.

Working with the Japanese wasn't the same this time around. The quality manager I was introduced to on my first day hated the air I breathed and disagreed with every-thing I said or proposed. An example was my rejection of sixty tonnes of electron fusion-welded stainless steel piping, which was set to hold natural gas under a reformer (giant sixty foot long by forty feet wide cooker).

While testing the welding, we discovered that the actual pipe seams were not fully fused and leaking badly. It was unusual to use such piping for gas service, but this was for Venezuela, so they wanted to go cheaper!

I wrote instructions for the contractor to stop all work on the pipe, but the hateful quality manager told me the pipe was fine and not defective.

This was enough for me. I was sick of him doubting my professional judgement, so I chose to disassociate myself from the project and quit.

Just a week later, I joined a project just up the road called Orinoco Iron. One night, a Japanese friend saw me in my local Tasca restaurant and said, "Andy, you were right about the stainless steel piping."

When I asked what had happened, he told me: "When they introduced the gas into the piping to light the reformer the whole lot almost blew up. There was gas leaking from the pipes, the pipe bends, everywhere you said." The faulty piping put their project back over six months.

Around this time, whilst driving back from Carolina's parents' house in my Chevrolet Grand Blazer, a strange smell began emanating from somewhere in the truck. Soon, the smell got stronger. Eventually, my gearbox seized up. We broke down exactly half way between Ciudad Bolívar and Puerto Ordaz, where there wasn't any lighting. We raised the bonnet as a sign we'd broken down and waited for a tow truck to arrive – they constantly patrolled the road.

Eventually, we got lucky and were towed to Puerto Ordaz where they left my truck outside our apartment block next to the security guard – who, for a small fee, promised to keep an eye on it all night. The next morning, the tow truck returned to take my truck to the Chevrolet dealership in Puerto Ordaz so they could check it out.

Once they'd examined my truck, they gave me the bad news that my gearbox needed replacing because it had been running dry for a long time. The previous German owner had paid a Venezuelan to have the engine oil changed every month, but when the garage checked it, the oil was a thick black colour indicating that it had never been changed.

They needed to order a new gearbox from Caracas, so I rented a small Chevrolet Corsa to get around while repairs were being made.

One night, Carolina wanted me to drive her friend home. I was reluctant because it was already late, but I finally agreed if only to have some peace and quiet. We waited at a red light for quite some time before it eventually changed to green. As I began to cross the junction, there was a terrible *smash*. A drunken Venezuelan running the lights hit the back corner of my car, spinning us around. He had a jeep, so he didn't have any real damage, but my rental car was a mess.

When the police finally turned up, they weren't at all interested in the drunken Venezuelan. Instead, they took interest in me as a foreigner. They took me back to their police station and then to my apartment because they wanted to see my passport. When I returned, they took my passport off me and demanded a hundred dollars for its return. In the meantime, they let the drunk go. Once they had the money from me, they let me go – but they did absolutely nothing about the accident.

The rental car was collected the next day, and I later discovered that they'd debited my credit card for the full repair even though I'd paid for insurance (which they probably claimed as well).

My truck was ready to collect a couple of days later, and I was issued a four-thousand-dollar bill because they not only changed my gearbox, they also "fixed" a lot of other things that didn't need fixing nor were they asked to touch. I registered a complaint with Chevrolet in America, but nothing came of it.

The next trip to Ciudad Bolívar was to collect Carolina. This time, the alternator bearing collapsed, rendering it useless. We made a temporary repair just to get back to Puerto Ordaz, but I had to replace that, too.

A week later, the air conditioning pump failed. Next, the evaporator. It didn't seem normal for a sixteen-month-old truck to have so many problems.

The same problems began happening inside my rented apartment. I'd have one air conditioner fixed, and then the next would fail. Later, the refrigerator, the washing machine, and (again) the air conditioners would fail. There was no end to the problems I was having.

As I mentioned, I didn't stay there much longer because of voodoo. So many things kept going wrong, it just didn't make any sense to hang around any longer.

I met a friend who recommended I visit his mother in Ciudad Bolívar so she could check me out for voodoo.

I drove to Ciudad Bolívar the following Saturday and met my colleague's mother. She took me into a back bedroom where there were two single beds.

She sat on the edge of one bed whilst I sat opposite her on the other bed. She put an old, battered, aluminium saucepan on the floor between us and unwrapped the first of three fat, hand-rolled, Venezuelan cigars.

She proceeded to smoke the first cigar by continuously puffing on it. Her aim was to produce ash and examine the formation of it.

She repeatedly spat the tar building up on her lips into the saucepan until half of the first cigar was smoked. She looked at the ash and saw that it had divided perfectly into two halves.

She said, "A girl wants to split you up from your wife." She continued until the cigar was too short to continue, and then she gave me the girl's name. It was the secretary from the other project, the girl from Trinidad!

She lit the second cigar and started burning it down in the same manner. And then she asked me if I had been having problems with my truck.

I explained that my Chevrolet Grand Blazer's had experienced a lot of problems: the gearbox had seized, the air conditioner pump had died, and the alternator had broken.

As fast as I was replacing parts, other parts were failing. I explained that all these things started to go wrong the day I found a dark grey ash sprinkled over its bonnet. She told me to sell the truck because it would never be the same again. And that's what I did.

The third cigar burnt in a different pattern, and she said that I should leave Venezuela as soon as possible or face death. When we arrived at our rented apartment later that afternoon (back in Puerto Ordaz), the same dark grey ash had been sprinkled outside our front door.

It was impossible to enter our apartment without taking some of the ash in with us. That was an unforgettable night! The first thing I did was open the fridge to have a glass of cold water.

When I tried to drink from the glass, I instantly vomited without any warning. Later, at the dining table, my drink started moving around the table. We watched it happen with our own eyes.

Later, cigarette butts rose up out of the ashtray, floated through the air, and landed on the middle of the quilt on our bed. And then the next cigarette butt would do the same … and then the next one. Everything was done in threes.

My colleague's mother had advised me to smoke a hand-rolled cigar in each room of my apartment, which was supposed to reverse the voodoo. I did this, but when I blew smoke at a place which should have had a small cupboard and not a wall, a force threw me back. I did it again, and again I felt a force. My wife freaked out and asked whether we could stay in a hotel.

I didn't want to leave the apartment as I was made to pay four months deposit instead of the normal one month as I was from Europe. I went into our en suite to wash. In the bathroom, I felt a strong presence behind me and turned around. Behind me, I saw the same dark grey ash growing out of the white ceramic floor tiles in three piles.

I called my wife, and she had also felt something pass by her on the way to the bathroom. Again, she asked whether we could leave. We tried to sleep, but we were constantly interrupted.

I could see the indentations of fingers gripping my wife's arm. I lay there knowing that I had stopped breathing. My wife realised what was happening to me and slapped my face to bring me to my senses.

When we turned the lights back on the problems stopped, but each time we switched them off to try to get some sleep, the problems would start again.

That happened two more times, so we found a hotel at three o'clock in the morning. We stayed there for the next few days. It was only about a week before things started happening again – this time in our hotel room. After we changed hotels, all was fine for about a week … and then it started happening again.

My only option was to leave Venezuela and get professional help back in Swansea.

CHAPTER 8

Help from Swansea

Throughout my hardship in Venezuela, I kept my mother up to date with all the unbelievable events that were taking place. Thankfully, she believed me and made some inquiries with friends she knew. A doctor she worked with had heard of such goings-on and mentioned the name of a spiritualist working in Swansea.

An appointment was made before I arrived in Swansea. Therefore, the day after I arrived, I went to see what could be done.

I went to Swansea's Spiritual Centre. There, a remarkable man called Jonathon welcomed me. As I walked inside the centre with him, I couldn't stop explaining all that I'd experienced in Venezuela. Jonathon asked me to relax in a very calm voice, and he told me that he already knew everything that had happened to me the moment he laid eyes on me.

He said he could help. He told me he would need to place his hands over my shoulders, but not in contact with them. He added that it would take ten minutes, and he played peaceful music in the background to help relax me as he began his cleansing. Seconds before he began, he explained that I might feel electric, hot, or cold sensations.

Wow! The moment he started, I felt a lot of static electricity between his hands and my shoulders. And then I felt a cold feeling that quickly became quite hot. He continued for forty-five minutes before stopping. He explained that someone had done a very professional job on me, and that I'd need to return the next day – which I did. There were no fees involved.

The next day, he performed again and explained that he'd managed, together with some good spirits, to remove some of the voodoo, but I needed to return a third time.

The next day, he repeated the exercise and explained that he'd removed most of the voodoo. Once again, he informed me that I needed to return, but for a final session the next day.

The problem was, I couldn't return the next day because I had a new contract back in Venezuela!

Before I left the Wales, he added my name to a list of people who were sent healing during their Thursday night spiritual meditations. He told me that I would feel something as they helped me (or perhaps a few hours later).

Strangely enough, I did feel something was happening from time to time. I felt a new and very peaceful feeling washing over me and calming me down.

I should have listened to him when he advised me not to return because my stay in Venezuela ended up being a waste of time. Everything went wrong again. It was for a

Venezuelan engineering contractor and everything agreed and endorsed in the contract was not honoured (as expected). I needed to stay in a small Venezuelan village called Puerto Píritu.

Puerto Píritu was actually a beautiful place to be based, which was directly on the Caribbean. My new company had found me a temporary place to stay, which I still needed to rent, which was a small outbuilding of a German owned villa on the top of a hill. I was to stay there until I could find something better suited for myself. After a month I was able to find an apartment across from the beach, shops and local restaurant.

The Venezuelan house sitters were very accommodating, especially by taking me to the local supermarket so they too could get stocked up for free at my expense. They owned a scooter, which they let me use to get around, which was a great help.

They enjoyed the opportunity of being able to go away for weekends, as I was there to take care of their two boxer dogs. The dogs bonded to me the minute they sniffed me and sensed I was an animal lover. I was alone with the two dogs; the night Hugo Chávez was declared the new president of Venezuela.

The minute that it was publically announced, people from nearby houses went outside and started to fire gunshots into the air. It was the second time in my life where bullets were shot into the air! The poor boxer's were petrified of the noise and huddled tightly against me while I sat outside listening to the noise, but under a roof.

I bought the two dogs collars and leads and would take them for a run along the beach as their owners never took them anywhere. We would walk down the hill together and the dogs seemed to sense they were being cared for and never once pulled on their leads, even out of excitement.

In fact, they chose to walk either side of me, so tightly that it was sometimes difficult to walk. The open air restaurant on the beach allowed dogs inside so long as their master was ordering, so I'd take the dogs with me and order three 16oz rare rib-eye steaks, one on the table and two on the floor. I hadn't taught the dogs to sit at the table, but I was sure they were ready to learn.

Even once I had moved into my own apartment, I would still return to the villa to collect the dogs and take them out for the day as if they were family. The dog's ribs gradually became less noticeable as I fed them as much I as could. Soon it was noticed by their Venezuelan owners that their dogs ate better than they did.

I don't have any respect for people who don't take good care of their animals. For me, owning an animal is a serious responsibility not to be neglected. It always amused me in my loneliness, that when I, together with the dogs left the restaurant to return them back to the villa; that we never carried a human bag back with us for their owners.

I arranged for the local veterinary to visit to inoculate the dogs against heartworm, which was prevalent in the area, like most hot countries. It was repeated every month. The poor dogs had only lived off scraps thrown on the ground. With all the flies laying their eggs and other bugs, the poor dogs were ingesting it all out of starvation.

Whenever I took a swim off the beach, the two dogs would sit together guarding my things whilst watching my every stroke. Dodgy locals wouldn't dare to go near my things as the two dogs would turn, stare and growl at them. One day, the dogs sensed something and started barking at me while I enjoyed the warm Caribbean water. Suddenly, I felt a sudden pain as something took a bit, then another and another. The water wasn't too clear so I couldn't see what had taken a liking to me so much so I started power swimming back to the beach.

I felt a couple more nibbles before I realised I was no longer moving as my chest was on the sand in just a few inches of water. The two dogs were already in the water fussing around me, licking me profusely, checking to see if I was okay. As I stood up I found five puncture wounds from whatever had taken a fancy to me. They were only little tiny nibbles, but it was clear that something had sharp teeth.

When I returned to the villa, the house sitters told me that nobody swam in the ocean there as it was infested with baby sharks, which would go for anything that moved. Typical of Venezuelan's I thought, they only warn you after the event had taken place!

Every Saturday morning, I would meet the night fishermen as they returned to the quaint little harbour at six in the morning to have first choice of their catch. I'd take a new bottle of the finest Venezuelan Rum (Ron) with me to aid their daytime sleep, which was always a bottle of Pampero Aniversario. It was probably the finest quality Rum I've ever had the pleasure of tasting. I'd carry a cooler box full of ice and cans of Coke and some disposable plastic glasses. I normally took the little scooter, but on nights when I couldn't sleep and gave up in the early hours, I'd take the dogs by foot which took a forty five minute walk to the harbour. The dogs always got excited seeing the still alive fish flipping about.

The deal was I'd swap the full contents of my cooler box in return for the pick of their catch under five kilos. The Pampero Aniversario was worth a lot more than five kilos of fresh fish, but as I was an avid sea fisherman myself, I loved sitting there chatting to the fisherman, while listening to them telling me about the big fish that had got away! I know all about fisherman's tales, but due to my own experiences, some of them I'd believe as I had my own unbelievable stories to tell which I have deliberately omitted form this book to maintain my professional integrity and reputation!

I had been known to get lucky on some fishing trips, like the day I caught a sixty pound Wahoo along with six more Wahoo, two Barracuda and a small skipjack Tuna.

My Venezuelan company hadn't been totally honest in my contract. They promised me a Toyota Hilux to use as my own, but they hadn't told me it was only for site use and that it had to remain on site when I went home each night. It used to take me at least an hour and a half to get to the site every morning for a 7 o'clock start along the coast in Barcelona.

Taxi's were not allowed on site so once I had arrived at the site entrance, I still had a thirty minute walk through the dust in the intense heat and humidity to reach my office. The local workers used to look at me wondering why I had to walk as they did? By the time I had reached my office I was in a hell of a state. My cloths were already totally saturated in sweat. I thought this is *great* for a quality manager responsible for all the quality on a one billion dollar project! Pure *Venezuelan style* I thought.

Back at my newly rented apartment, redecorating was finished and I had bought all the usual essentials to make it move liveable. One day I saw a girl cleaning the road along the beach, so I offered her the job of cleaning my apartment once a week for extra income. She jumped at the opportunity and would also help me when I went shopping and help carry all the bags back with me.

Back in the office I continued to complain about my lack of transportation but nothing changed. I quit, gave all my recent purchases to the cleaner and retuned back to the United Kingdom.

CHAPTER 9

Pakistan

In March of 1999, I went to Karachi, Pakistan for the last half of a project, which had been going for over a year. Karachi was a hot and very humid place. We all stayed in the same hotel in the centre of the city. Sanitation was non-existent in Karachi and all the wastewater went directly into the canals throughout the city. We all went to the job site in a large coach under armed escort. Our office had employed its own local chef who was very good and the kitchen just inside the entrance of the office.

I would sometimes visit the chef to ask what he was cooking that day. He, together with his helpers would often be found sitting on the concrete floor picking weevils out of the rice, which had been poured onto newspaper. The sacks had become infested with the little six legged brown creatures from the warehouse. Adult weevils can live for two years. The females lay up to six eggs a day into separate grains of rice, which she makes holes in and later closes with a secretion. Those are the ones that ended up eaten. At least the odd ones they'd miss added some protein to the dishes. Everyone suffered stomach problems during their stay and one of the British caught hepatitis and had to leave the project.

One afternoon, our usual route back to Karachi was blocked, so we had to take a detour through a village. I had *never* seen so many children in my entire life. They were all so young and completely filled the pavements either side of the narrow street, which our large coach was struggling to drive down. There must have been tens of thousands of them and all well under the age of ten. It was a perfect place to be ambushed, but fortunately nothing happened.

Carolina joined me after three months, but that was another mistake. She had a terrible time while waiting in the hotel all day. She received several phone calls to our room every day from a man who was pimping. He asked whether she wanted to have many boyfriends.

He kept saying that he knew many men who needed a lady, and that he would arrange men to visit her! We had to have the telephone put through the hotel operator to vet each person calling.

If that weren't enough, the minibar stocker visited our room every hour to check the drink status. Of course, that was just an excuse to look at Carolina. We had five hotel employees fired due to this behaviour. There were other incidents, too, such as finding needles in our toilet paper rolls and discovering drawing pins in our room service meals.

While in Karachi, I needed a local man to work for me in the office at site, and take care of the database I'd created. The Japanese firm I was working for set me up with three guys that I could interview. The first two seemed terrified.

They only answered *yes* or *no* to all I asked them, but the third and final candidate was quite different. His name was Izhar Ali.

Izhar not only answered all my questions, but he also had many of his own to put to me! All Izhar's questions gave me an excellent impression of his professional integrity, and I asked him how soon he could start.

Izhar started the following Monday, and he immediately began dismantling the computer I was having trouble with. With bits all over my desk, he found a loose chip that was causing the problem. He put it all back together again in a few minutes.

That was probably the best first impression anyone has ever left on me. Izhar and I became the best of friends, and we still are today. Fortunately, Pakistan wasn't the last place I had the pleasure to see Izhar.

My wife's problems continued at the hotel. The best one was when we were in the elevator together with a local man who moved behind me, bent down, and tried to sniff my wife's backside! I spun around and cracked him hard on the side of his jaw, knocking him out cold! I was rather proud of myself.

When I told Izhar about the episode the next day, he recommended that I buy Pakistani clothes for Carolina. He said no one would dare look at her the same way again — and they'd leave her alone.

Luckily, there was a clothes bazaar in the hotel the very same week, so Izhar came over to do the negotiations and help us choose two outfits. Carolina looked just like a local lady in her new disguise – plus, she already had the skin tone.

Once, she was fed up with staying inside all day, so she tried to lie down by the hotel swimming pool. But that innocent action generated a reaction from the locals: they all moved in close to her. She didn't do that again.

Many taxi drivers hovered around the entrance of our hotel. One particular was a horse drawn carriage. The horse was a big boy called Jack. I'd take an apple back with me every night to give to Jack. Its owner would hold the apple with his hands cupped so Jack could nibble his way around it. Jack would eat the whole apple except its core, which I found very unusual for such a big house. I would choose to go with the carriage to look around Karachi on the weekend. It was a hot and dusty way to get around, but still better than inside some of the taxis. I always spayed a handkerchief with cologne and carried it with me each time I went out for use each time we passed over a canal for natural reasons.

I regularly visited a furniture and ornament factory. All the furniture was made from solid rosewood and could be decorated with skilfully inlaid brass. I bought many items from the factory shop including onyx carvings. The onyx was a mixture of dark green and brown and of exceptionally high quality, not to mention the brassware. I bought a rosewood captains trunk, which had my name inlaid in its lid together with the date 1999. It was ideal to store all the other items I'd bought which included a handmade silk carpet.

I continued to visit the place and Carolina also enjoyed going with me as there wasn't anywhere back in Venezuela which sold such beautiful handmade ornaments. Once the captains trunk was full, the shop arranged for my box to be crated and sent back to the United Kingdom. The box arrived in the United Kingdom while I was home on holiday. A friend was with me and able to help me carry the box into the house from the delivery van. All the items were certainly intact, but the onyx was a different colour to what I had bought. Instead, they had swapped it for the cheapest quality, which I dealt with as soon as I returned back to Karachi two weeks later.

At one of the weekly parties the German hotel manager held for expats, Carolina and I were introduced to another Venezuelan man who fully understood and sympathised with Carolina's situation. He gave us the phone number of the wife of one of his Pakistani friends who was also Venezuelan and living in Karachi.

Carolina couldn't wait to make the call the next day (the Venezuelan man called ahead and told her to expect another Venezuelan lady to call). The married lady was very excited to hear from Carolina, and she immediately drove to the hotel with her private driver to pick up Carolina.

It turned out that the lady's husband was a very successful company director of a textile company. Carolina had a great day out and came back to the hotel refreshed and excited that she had a new friend to visit. She was also thrilled that she could finally escape the confines of the hotel.

On the weekend, I was invited to the director's house. Because he'd visited Venezuela many times on business trips, we had plenty to talk about. He also owned a farm, which we all visited for a barbecue the following weekend. There weren't any animals or fields of crops, though. He had bought the farm just to have somewhere to relax outside the city – a place with some much-needed fresh air.

Because Carolina now had a friend, the shopping trips started. Her friend and her driver took Carolina all around Karachi. She bought more and more clothing for herself and her family back home. Naturally, I went crazy some days. She kept coming back with more clothing, and I was concerned about the baggage restrictions for our flight out.

Amazingly, she had already thought about that: a friend working for KLM had access to the system and made a notation that the excess baggage had already been paid! We were told to say the following when we got to the KLM check-in: "You need to look at the notes. Our baggage has already been paid." It worked!

In September of 1999, we parted company at the airport in Amsterdam. I needed to work in Habshan, Abu Dhabi. Abu Dhabi was a wonderful place, except I was a two-hour drive out in the desert surrounded by sand dunes. My time in Abu Dhabi was short-lived because I received a phone call from an agent in December enquiring whether I'd be interested in working in Venezuela again.

Shortly after getting back to the United Kingdom – while I was preparing to return to Venezuela – I turned on the TV to see some horrifying news. Continuous, heavy rains had caused mudslides in La Guaira, on December 17, 1999, where their international airport was situated. The torrential rains, flash floods, and mudslides isolated coastal towns and forced 120,000 Venezuelans from their homes. The storm claimed many lives.

Security forces patrolled the mud-filled streets of Caracas to halt scattered looting and rescue thousands of people from flooded buildings.

At least 15,000 people lost their homes, authorities claimed, and dozens of towns and villages had been cut off. Venezuela's rainy season normally finished in early November, but not this time. Venezuelan authorities claimed the rains were the heaviest in sixty years.

The disaster shut down Caracas's Simón Bolívar International Airport and closed schools and businesses in the capital. Also, parts of the subway system were closed, which normally transports one million people every day.

Mudslides raged down El Avila Mountain (overlooking Caracas), and they carried homes and parked cars with them. Mangled bits of furniture and tree trunks littered many city intersections. The country's National Guard ordered the evacuation of shanty towns clinging to hillsides and bordering gullies.

I began to wonder whether I should have stayed in Abu Dhabi. I didn't know how long it would take for Venezuela's international airport to reopen, and I was somewhat hesitant to return due to the previous problems I encountered there. Still, I decided to go so I could be back with Carolina.

CHAPTER 10

Second Time in Venezuela

Arriving in Venezuela made me wonder whether my problems were going to return. I even recognised the immigration officer who I'd dealt with in the past, so I let someone else go before me so I'd have a different guy. That immigration officer previously refused me exit unless I gave him one hundred dollars. He figured that I was working without a permit, and he threatened to have me arrested and taken to the main station in Caracas. Considering my choices, I paid the bribe and flew out.

I spent the first night in Caracas because the vice president of the company who selected me wanted to meet me in person before I began work. The reason he wanted me was because I had helped his company out so much on my first project in 1997 in Puerto Ordaz, when I first met Carolina.

I was booked into the Intercontinental Hotel and scheduled to meet inside the rooftop bar. A very tall, blonde-haired man approached me and introduced himself.

He was originally from Russia, and he had a very high-strung personality – he looked like he was heading for a nervous breakdown.

The manager of his head office in Caracas accompanied him. He was a short, weedy-looking man who resembled a ferret.

We moved away from the bar so we could speak more freely and face each other. The Vice President didn't waste any time cutting to the chase, and he started telling me that the project was in real trouble. I put my hand up to stop him from rambling on, and I asked if a certain Italian contractor was on the project. The look on his face was that of shock and horror.

He said that they were his main contractor. I replied, "I fully understand why your project is in such trouble." Without allowing him to explain any of the problems, I explained what the contractor had done in Puerto Ordaz. He was all ears, listening to every word I had to say. He knew that I understood the style of his contractor.

He asked what could be done to put things right. I replied, "You've already started putting things right because, when they see me, they will recognise me from before and know they're in for a rough ride. They won't be able to screw you anymore."

Previously, I had uncovered many of the scams the contractor had pulled over the Japanese in Puerto Ordaz, and I mentioned what they liked to do. With the aid of our corrupt procurement people in Puerto Ordaz, the Japanese had been charged two or three times the normal prices.

His face changed in such a way that I thought he would either laugh or cry. Instead, he bought another round of drinks before retiring for the night.

The following morning, we all left the hotel early and drove straight to the construction site from hell. We made one stop halfway to the site to have something for breakfast because it was going to be a long day. When we pulled up, the Russian got to hear me switch into Spanish for the first time as I ordered a chicken arepa and a coffee.

Before it was time to pull off the main road, we drove right through the middle of a quarrel between Venezuelan police officers and someone on the other side of the road. There must have been four or five police cars along our side of the road with officers crouching behind them, firing across the road into the trees. We couldn't see anyone in the trees as we passed, but we felt lucky the police paused as we raced by.

The last twenty minutes was spent driving through the Andes Mountains. In the distance, I could see the plant, which was not looking great. People in the construction industry develop a trained eye, and as we neared the plant, it was clear that it wasn't a good project to pursue.

The highly stressed vice president wasted no time showing me around. There was no opportunity to grab a coffee – or any time for introductions. I was a stranger to all the onlookers, and I'm sure they were wondering who was getting a personal, escorted tour of the mess they were trying to construct.

The job was an engineering disaster due to the two previous Eastern European quality managers. They had been fired, and quality records were non-existent during their two-year stint.

I could see signs that the contractor's style was well and truly impregnated throughout the construction project. One of their tricks was to erect steel beams the wrong way around and later charge for additional work (drilling new holes where the original holes should have been). I could see unused holes everywhere.

The project was the worst I'd ever seen; all the structural steelwork was crooked or out of alignment. After a little investigation, I learnt that the former Eastern European quality managers had no control over their Eastern European construction supervisors. And the supervisors were (foolishly) being paid a bonus for progress. Consequently, everything was basically thrown up with no regard for accuracy. Faulty bolts had been bought cheap, and they were shearing off when torqued up. They had to replace over fifty thousand such bolts, so additional work claims were totally out of control – they were re-erecting scaffolding everywhere.

The only (but expensive) solution was to bring a team of professional steel erectors to do whatever they could to try to repair what the idiots had built. We had a team of New Zealand steel erectors come over, but I thought it would have been quicker to take it all down and re-erect the entire building properly.

When the new team came in, I met an amazing man from New Zealand's Bay of Islands. Dave was a huge man whose body had been completely tattooed in the old-fashioned way, except for his face. We became good friends, and the Venezuelans nicknamed us *the twins* (like the movie).

When Dave and I walked around the site side by side, I measured up only to his chest.

This giant played the guitar and sang with the softest voice. It was like a Hawaiian lullaby.

We lodged in a small town called La Victoria. It was certainly not a place to walk around in the daytime – let alone at night. The nickel plant we were working on was deep in the Andes Mountains, which had been declared a nature reserve.

The mountains were impossibly steep, but cows managed to live where even goats would have to watch their footing. One slight slip, and that would be the end: there was nothing to stop the fall except the bottom of the mountain (over a thousand feet below).

It was a true engineering accomplishment to dig into the hillside to lay the new road, but the constant risk of landslides was a permanent reminder to drive as fast as possible. Our tires screeched almost the whole way.

It wasn't long before Carolina joined me in La Victoria, and she eventually began working in one of the site offices. We were only a one-hour drive from Caracas International Airport, so we took advantage of that fact and went for a five-day trip to a little Caribbean Island. That was my first visit to the Caribbean, but (unfortunately) it wasn't my last. An Australian and Dave also went at that time, so it was a fun trip. Inevitably, we always ended up at the bar on a beach Pier.

After several months of working on site and living in the hotel, life became more boring.

We passed a bottle store every night on the way back to the hotel. One night, when I was driving back alone, I pulled over for a quick beer. I spent some time talking to the owner, who came from mainland Spain and had just had his eighty-eighth birthday.

The next day, I invited my New Zealand colleagues to join me at the same place after work. As it worked out, everyone had a great time. Thus, the little bottle store became the new place to go every day after work. The eighty-eight-year-old Spanish owner could not believe his luck.

Word got around until the bad guys heard about the nightly event (attended by foreigners). One night, I was too tired and needed to walk back to the hotel alone because my colleagues had the truck and didn't look like they were going anywhere for a while. As I was about to start the three-minute walk, a local woman called Mary-Eva stopped me. She said that there were two local guys waiting at the corner.

Apparently, they had been waiting there every night. In the past, we had always driven back, so they couldn't do anything to us.

That particular night was different. I was getting fed up with the restrictions of living amongst the same dangers from one day to the next, so I walked towards the two Venezuelans and invited them to join us. In Venezuela, if you offer people a drink, you are expected to pay the bill – even for anyone else they bring along.

The two shady-looking characters looked at each other and walked towards me. I invited them into the bottle store, much to the owner's surprise. There, I bought them both a beer.

They didn't speak any English, so I explained to my colleagues what I was doing. They understood and played along with my plan. In short, we got the two guys very drunk.

The next morning, the muggers must have woken up with an impressive, free hangover. From there, they probably worked it out that it was better to keep friendly with us than try to rob us for a few dollars.

Word continued to spread around the small town until every scumbag in the area ended up joining the nightly event. A beer only cost ten cents, so we were not bothered by the added expense. Plus, La Victoria became much safer for us all. The funny thing was, the loco locals actually became our bodyguards.

The average attendance rose to as many as thirty locals – as many as fifty or sixty on a Friday or Saturday night. Husbands started bringing their wives, and soon, their wives began preparing food to bring along and share with us. Even my staff began to join us, which further added to the party.

Venezuelans like to spend more on their cars' music systems than the cars themselves. We were guaranteed to have at least one macho man in attendance with a car better suited to being a mobile disco, and that meant plenty of dancing.

The old Spanish man had to order hundreds more cases of beer each month as more and more people joined the party. The expats all chipped in some money so the old man could increase his security, and we made it clear to the loco locals that if his business was ever compromised, all the parties would stop immediately. Therefore, nothing happened.

Like most other places in Venezuela, there were often shoot-outs in the streets. One morning, as I left the hotel, I noticed several bullet holes in the walls of the hotel reception. We had all heard shots fired the night before, but we didn't realise the fight had continued into the hotel. Evidently, someone involved in the shoot-out had used it for shelter whilst returning fire.

I became friendly with a local storeowner, and he and his much younger wife invited Carolina and I to visit a beach he liked. I didn't know it would take over an hour and a half to drive there when we left La Victoria. Eventually, we arrived at the beach, which wasn't anything special. We hung our bags on the only tree we could find to shade us, and we went for a swim. As it happened, we couldn't risk taking our eyes off our things because a man was showing a lot of interest in them and standing nearby, just waiting for his chance to run off with them.

The storekeeper had to go back to guard everything so we could relax and enjoy the warm water. He drove back a different way, which took us through the winding mountain roads of La Guaira to show us where villages once stood until the December mudslides.

All that remained was what could best be described as dry riverbeds. Not all the roads had been rebuilt. Instead, many had been roughly cut deeper into the mountainsides. The earthen road was so dangerous and narrow in places that we had to get out of the car and walk ahead in case the car slipped over the side.

It became more unnerving when the storekeeper took a gun out of his glove compartment and explained that the area was well known for people dressing up as police officers and holding up cars that they stopped. I'm not the type to unnecessarily put myself in dangerous situations as those happened naturally, and if I'd known about the drive back to La Victoria, I wouldn't have gone in the first place.

After nine long months, we had the work in some kind of shape and it was time to erect a prototype monorail to transport the nickel into the furnaces. Though I was originally a Plater and not a design engineer, I could still see by the design that there was a major weakness. It was an accident waiting to happen.

I reported the design weakness from an obvious and practical point of view, but I was shot down every time I mentioned it.

The day came to weight test the monorail, so I instructed my people to keep well off the monorail steelwork (and safely on independent surrounding steelwork). As per procedure, my contractor followed the usual protocol and made the monorail lift just five tonnes of the seventy-tonne dead weight test, which it managed to do.

And then they added another five tonnes, which it also managed to lift. I remained on the ground standing under some concrete flooring while they loaded another five tonnes. Again, like the other times, it lifted the test weight, but this time they lifted it higher. When it was around thirty feet off the ground, it failed.

Without any warning noises, the monorail broke exactly where I had predicted. It ripped off a German technician's left arm, close to his shoulder. As the test weight hit the ground, many small stones hit me in the face. After that, I turned and ran straight into a concrete column, which didn't help my appearance. Everyone emptied out of the offices to see what the noise was all about, including my two secretaries.

They found me covered in muddy water and blood (which was coming from several little puncture wounds on my face). I was lucky – as were my staff – to be alive. Because we were in Venezuela it was very difficult for the site ambulance to help the badly injured German technician. Apparently, everyone wanted to see the blood dripping down through the open mesh flooring.

A few months later, they tried to conduct the test again. Sure enough, the next failure was the steelwork joints themselves, as I'd previously pointed out to the vice president. That time, a man was badly injured on the side of his face.

They didn't need a design engineer to point out the weakest points in the design, but two guys would never forget that project.

On one weekend, when Carolina was home visiting her parents, a friend and I decided to drive to the beach for a change of scenery. The beach we aimed for was famous for a Venezuelan folk dance called the *tambor* (meaning *drum*). We drove into a place called Maracay, also known as *Ciudad Jardín* (meaning *Garden City*), which is home to the only bullfighting school, Maestranza, in the country.

From Maracay, we ended up following a road that began at the north-western part of the city (called El Limón) and went to Ocumare de la Costa and the beaches of Cata and Cuyagua. The road is still the most dangerous I've ever driven on. It passed through a rain forest with few remaining barriers along the edge of its winding route. Due to the frequent landslides, the original barriers had long since been knocked over the edge.

Because the landslides had reduced the narrow road over the years to single-line traffic, the road was considered a one-way route with an entry timetable (depending on the direction you were coming from).

We arrived at Cata Beach, where the road first provides access to the coast, and we found a hotel near the beach. It was a quiet place that never hosted tourists due to the dangers in the country. It was lunchtime, so we ventured along the beach until we came across a very sorry looking restaurant. With plastic tables and chairs set out on a rough concrete floor and a rusty, corrugated iron roof full of holes, it didn't look very inviting. Thus, we just grabbed a cold beer.

While standing at the bar which was made from old wooden pallets, we noticed a large aquarium across the room. I went over to see whether there was anything inside. Much to my amazement, it was crammed full of lobsters of all sizes.

The barefoot waiter joined me (his T-shirt filthy and full of holes), and he asked whether I fancied one. I thought I'd make it easy for him and pointed to the lobster nearest the surface. He pulled it out alive and kicking. Even though it was too big for the two of us, we went along with the choice.

He returned back to us a couple of minutes later and asked how we wanted it cooked. I hesitated as he listed about a dozen different ways – only one of which resembled *thermidor*, which I recognised. After selecting that option, we waited well over an hour before he returned with the lobster.

He placed it on a battered, old, stainless steel tray, but the food itself looked fine. It wasn't until I tasted it that I realised it was the very best lobster thermidor I'd ever had in my life. Needless to say, we couldn't finish it and asked for the bill. For the beers and the meal, we didn't pay more than ten dollars.

The hotel was set about a hundred yards from the beach, but that didn't stop us from hearing drum beats starting at eight o'clock in the evening. We couldn't hear any other instruments, so we followed the sound until we got to the beach.

A few of the local people had already arrived and were drinking Polar beers from their cold boxes. They were still dressed in beachwear. They were already dancing the *tambor* on the sand, probably still drunk from the daytime. The dance had been invented at Charoni Beach, which was just a short distance along the coast.

By ten o'clock at night, the area was alive with local people demonstrating their very impressive dancing skills. Because we were probably the only foreigners they had seen for a long time, we were encouraged to join in. Of course, they all found our pathetic attempts very amusing, but they understood it wasn't our natural style. The tambor is a very erotic form of dancing, and couples swapped their partners every couple of minutes, carefully avoiding any physical contact to keep the knives from coming out.

We stopped a taxi and got him to take us to buy some beer and a cheap polystyrene cold box and ice. After that, we returned to the beach so we could pay back the beers we'd been given. We went to the shop two more times before retiring at four in the morning. From the hotel, we could still hear the drums beating for another four hours.

We checked out in the early afternoon, but we were told that the road back wasn't open until four o'clock. Not knowing what to do, we asked whether there was anywhere of interest to visit nearby. The receptionist recommended we go for a swim in a river, which was on our way, and scribbled a rough map for us. We found the place okay, which was downstream from a derelict hydroelectric power station just above a waterfall. The day was hot and humid as we explored the old works. We were completely engulfed in dense rainforest, and I felt the place had a very uncomfortable feel about it.

I really didn't like the atmosphere, so we didn't stay long. I felt like I was in a very small humid room with something hanging on my back. Instead, we went back to the waterfall for a hydro massage. We spent far too long sitting under the waterfall enjoying the cold water pounding down on our shoulders, however – we felt like we'd been beaten up the next day.

During this contract, Carolina began her old tricks again: demanding money to support her family. I still hadn't fully recovered from how they had abused me back in Puerto Ordaz after we'd got married. Plus, I had already rebuilt their house – practically, anyway. I grew tired of it, and I made Carolina return home. I found a Venezuelan *abogado* (lawyer) to put an end to it. He had been recommended by a friend, and he turned up at my office the same week.

He arrived in his full air force uniform, and every Venezuelan on site recognised him but me. He was the major general of the Venezuelan air force, but he was also a lawyer in his spare time. He used his influence to make his legal work easier. Eventually, he drove me to Maracay, where we registered the first step in my separation.

As we entered a building, everyone who was sitting in the waiting room queuing for their turn jumped up. *My lawyer is very famous,* I thought. We didn't queue. Instead, we walked directly to the local judge's office without even knocking on the door. The client with the local judge got up and left the room immediately when we entered. Just a few minutes later, we were done and on the way back to my office.

I met him a few more times over the following months. He came to visit me at my hotel to discuss my divorce, joined me at restaurants, and even drove me to the military base in Caracas once to show me where he worked.

When we received a copy of my marriage license, the complications started. When I signed the marriage paper back in September of 1997, the night I got married, I didn't realise I was also verifying that I was the original father of Carolina's seven-year-old daughter.

Even though I'd never been to Venezuela before 1997, he explained that it made the whole divorce process more complicated because I now had a daughter to support until she was eighteen years old.

Later that month, he picked me up at my hotel on a Saturday afternoon. He was wearing civilian clothes, and he drove me to Caracas using his wife's car to show me the military base. When we stopped at the checkpoint, the guard on duty casually walked up to his side of the car and asked for his ID. When he produced his ID, the guard jumped to attention faster than a speeding bullet and saluted him.

We drove all around the base before leaving for the centre of Caracas (I wanted to go to a bookshop there to pick up a dictionary). Everywhere we walked, people stopped and stared. They probably wondered who the little white guy with the major general of their air force was. We returned in the evening, and after he had a couple of beers, he left for home.

I only met him a couple more times before I returned to the United Kingdom to carry out my first contract there since 1989. My lawyer assured me that everything would be taken care of in my absence and that there was no need to worry.

Back in the United Kingdom, I started working at a compressor station in Scotland. I'd heard how beautiful the countryside was in Scotland, but I never imagined it could be so picturesque. While driving through the country lanes to the compressor station, I saw pheasants, rabbits, foxes, and roe deer every day.

The local hospitality was second to none, and many a good night was spent sampling some of the 366 single malts in the lounge bar. A selection, I might add, that put the pub in the *Guinness World Records* book.

CHAPTER 11

First Time in Qatar

I travelled to Qatar in October of 2001, which added to my track record of mistakes. I realised after the first day in Doha that I was being paid less than half the amount agreed upon in London. I quit the same day, but the company refused to hand me back my passport, claiming it was already being processed. I asked why it was being processed after I'd quit the day I'd arrived, but I just received a dumb look as a response.

I was staying in one of the few hotels in Doha at that time, and I demanded the return of my passport every day so I could fly home. This went on for almost a month until, one day, we all had written instructions to find a place to rent.

There was a big seminar that was going to be held in Doha, and every hotel room had been pre-booked. I was about to be homeless, living on the street. A kind Iranian welding engineer working with us offered to help me out. He showed me his rented place, but staying there would mean sleeping on the floor as he did. Out of desperation, I contacted the British consulate for their advice.

They told me that it was illegal for my company to withhold my passport, so they contacted the corrupt project manager and instructed him to immediately return my passport and arrange my flight home.

The day I arrived back in the United Kingdom, an agent called me just five minutes after I entered the house. He asked whether I was interested in a contract back in Venezuela.

CHAPTER 12

Third Time in Venezuela

On 19 December 2001, I went back to Venezuela to work on two upstream oil facilities in a place called San Tomé. It was another opportunity to see Carolina because San Tomé was only an hour drive away from Ciudad Bolívar. I wanted to know what had happened regarding our divorce. Shorty after arriving, I discovered that I was still a fully married man. As I had previously paid in full to process my divorce before I'd left the country, nothing more was processed once I had left!

Naturally, it was the Christmas season, and most expats had already flown back home. But not me: I flew *out* of Cardiff. It was the problem time of year again, and the early morning fog caused a take-off delay. As a result, I missed my connection in Amsterdam. I called my agent, and I was booked on the next flight going roughly in the right direction nineteen hours later.

I went into Amsterdam to waste some time before returning to Schiphol Airport where I'd have to wait to board my flight. My flight took me to a remote Caribbean island where I had another six – hour wait. Finally, I boarded an Italian Airways flight to Caracas.

Caracas International Airport can be a very dangerous place for those who don't know the tricks the kidnappers use to get visitors into their fake taxis. They assume a company representative is meeting its contractors in the arrivals hall. Thus, they boldly approach the unsuspecting traveller and ask for his name and company.

Next, they inform their fellow kidnappers, and they quickly write the traveller's name in big letters on a large card before walking past the traveller with the card held high. The innocent traveller would introduce himself as the person on the card, and the Venezuelan would proceed to escort him to the car – even helping with the baggage along the way.

Once in the car, a gun is produced, and the traveller is taken to the nearest ATM. If he's lucky, he might be dropped off in the middle of nowhere, or he might be retained for future ATM withdrawals, or held for ransom.

The only trustworthy taxis were the official airport taxis. Those taxis required travellers to prepay prior to departure in case something happened to them once they'd left.

For those familiar with work in Venezuela, the oil-rich areas are all high risk for expats moving around. Every week, I heard a gunfight somewhere outside. The rival mafia groups were trying to gain more territory. I was sure to keep clear of the windows during such events in case of stray bullets.

One night, there came a powerful reminder of the dangers when I heard a knock on my apartment door in the early hours of Sunday morning. It was our piping engineer, Paul, and he was standing at the door in quite a bad shape.

He had been shopping just down the road at the local supermarket (called Cada 2000). After shopping, he opened his car door and had a gun pushed against his head and another into his ribs. The muggers forced him into the passenger well and drove him off to a very remote road about three kilometres away. There were no lights on that part of the road.

It was shortly after six o'clock in the evening, and the sun had already set. They pulled over and made him get out. He was forced to remove his work boots and walk towards a small ravine. Paul knew what was coming, so he distracted the guy with the gun, punched him as hard as he could, and started running.

The other two accomplices saw him running in the bad light, and they reversed the car back down the road, shooting at Paul the whole time. Paul ducked and weaved until he was out of sight. He didn't feel the pain of all the thorns, glass, and barbed wire fence that he ran into in the dark.

He finally got to El Tigre, where he found one of the few Venezuelan police officers in the area who agreed to help him by driving him to our compound. Paul's hands, stomach, and feet were all badly cut, torn, and bleeding.

With still-not-divorced Carolina and our part-time maid, we spent a couple of hours removing pieces of wood, thorns, and glass from Paul. We wrapped his wounds the best we could. Fortunately, we had a spare bedroom for Paul to stay in because he didn't have his keys anymore to get into his own apartment in the next block.

Later in the afternoon, we went to the local police station. We helped Paul obtain a police report and loaned him the money to go to Caracas for a new passport because the criminals had taken everything.

Paul visited us again the following Saturday to invite us out to the local Chinese restaurant as a token of his appreciation for putting him up, feeding him, and taking care of his laundry.

As always, I had a fridge full of beer, so we sat there chatting and drinking for a couple of hours before Paul said that we should go to the restaurant before it closed.

Carolina didn't feel like going with us; she just wanted a take away. Thus, the two of us went out alone. When we arrived at the Chinese restaurant, it had already closed. We thought it was very strange because we had never seen the restaurant closed at that hour.

We discovered the next day that the restaurant had been raided by (probably) the same muggers. Everyone there lost any valuables they had on them – the alternative was getting shot.

We missed that, if it weren't for the beer in my apartment, Paul could have been mugged by the same guys twice in the same week, or shot, considering the fact that he knew their faces! I thought, *This just proves that beer really is good for you.*

That was the final blow for Paul. He left the project and went to live with his wife back in Trinidad. After that,

Carolina went to the supermarket with our maid to do all the shopping without me. It was too dangerous for her to be associated with me because she would become a target to be kidnapped for ransom.

During the project, life became more difficult because Venezuela underwent a national strike. The biggest problem – apart from the rise in crime – was fuel. The government limited fuel, so all public transport was eventually stopped. I was working an eight-week-by-two-week rotation.

Unfortunately, because I was reorganising the mechanical completions for the project by utilising my own copyrighted system, I couldn't take my first rotation as I was too involved at the time. We were working seven days per week, which involved an hour drive both to and from the site. Towards my second opportunity to take a break, the national strike became a real worry.

By that time, the oil refineries had also joined the strike. With limited fuel supplies, public transportation had been stopped to conserve fuel. Likewise, domestic flights were cancelled because all aviation fuel had been reserved for international flights to continue. My main concern was getting to Caracas by any means possible to fly out. For something to look forward to, I went ahead and booked my domestic flight to Caracas (along with my international flight to a little Caribbean Island).

Due to the odd flight times, I needed one night in a hotel near the airport in La Guaira, Caracas. My British colleagues took full advantage of my stress and revelled in reminding me that there was no chance I'd be able to take my much-needed break. After working twelve hours a day, seven days a week for sixteen weeks straight I was getting desperate. I'm happy to say that they were all wrong.

The very day I was due to fly out of San Tomé, the strike was lifted. The entire country was about to run out of fuel to run the power stations, so if the strike had continued for just two more weeks, the whole country would have been without electricity. With no electricity to power the freezers in supermarkets, communications, and domestic supplies, the country would have died.

Carolina wasn't going with me this time because I wanted a relaxing break, not a family shopping trip. I travelled light – very light. My luggage only consisted of a camera, a toothbrush, and a razor, so I set off for the airport in San Tomé all the same. There were only daytime flights at the single-strip airport because the runway didn't have any lights.

My flight to Caracas was on time, so off I went with a smile. When I arrived, I was surprised that nothing had gone wrong yet. I began to get suspicious – something always went wrong (normally due to the local people abusing their authority).

I passed through arrivals without any problems, and I found the official taxi office right away without anyone waiting. I was in a taxi a few minutes later and thought *this is great,* as we pulled out of the airport to take the twenty minute drive to my hotel in La Guaira.

The peace wasn't to last, however. After five minutes of driving towards my hotel, all hell was let loose. We were on a dual carriageway, and there weren't any exits where we could use to get off. We drove around a bend and came face to face with thousands of Hugo Chávez supporters.

They had filled all lanes in each direction, and they were rioting and smashing everything in their path. They were excited and angry – very angry. They were wearing red berets, and all of them had used lipstick to draw two red stripes on each of their cheeks. They were all very macho.

They were wielding machetes, iron bars, and anything else they could use, to cause havoc, death, and destruction. My new problem was that they were heading straight for us. It was too late to try to turn around or reverse; all we could do was slowly drive right through the middle of them.

My pale complexion due to sixteen weeks of all work and no play was not working in my favour, and I risked being torn apart. The driver was well aware of that danger, and he motioned to me to crouch down on the floor in the back of his taxi so it would appear empty. Fortunately, he had a newspaper that he was able to spread apart to better cover me.

Seizing the irresistible opportunity for some great holiday snaps, I managed to unzip my bag and get my camera out while continuing to hide under the newspapers. The driver noticed my hand coming up with my camera, and he quickly slapped it back down.

I noticed through a gap in the newspaper that I was trying to read, that my taxi driver had opened his window. He was slowly waving his left hand out of the window with a closed fist, which indicated his support for the riot. The noise was deafening. It brought back memories of Cape Town years before.

After a very long fifteen-minute crawl through the enraged group of Rambo's, the crowd began to thin out. Finally, we passed through the stragglers at the tail end. When it was safe to look around, I came up from my hiding place to see cars on fire, shop windows smashed, and a trail of debris from where the mob had been.

Once outside my hotel, I tipped my driver twenty dollars. In those days, he could exchange that bill on the black market for ten times its value in local Bolivars. Thus, he was happy – but he still needed to return to the airport. I wished him the best of luck, shook his hand, and walked into the reception.

I could see stains up the hotel walls from the mudslides in December 1999. They must have been over six feet high. All the walls outside were the same. The receptionist explained that the whole floor had been filled with mud. They had to close the hotel for several months to dig it all out and make repairs. She added that all the streets in that area of La Guaira were the same. On a gruesome note, when the big cleaning operation began, many bodies were uncovered.

People in Venezuela had avoided eating shellfish for over three months due to all the bodies that had been washed into the ocean and never seen again. A local fisherman in the marina had the sense to tie together all the boats moored there and take the flotilla out to sea for safety. This turned out to be a smart decision when boulders the size of houses came crashing down the hillsides. I couldn't see the full extent of the damage, however, until I got to my room on the fifth floor and looked out from my balcony.

Because I only had my shoulder bag, I didn't bother going straight to my room as usually to drop off my things. Instead, I went to the bar for a couple of cold beers to chill out after what I'd just been through. I was the only customer at the bar, so I chatted with the barman. He said I was very lucky to have got through in one piece because his countrymen were all loco! That wasn't exactly news to me, so I told him to tell me something I didn't already know.

The next morning, I checked out and had an uneventful trip to the little Caribbean Island. I checked in to the same hotel I used before with Carolina. The trip was more pleasurable the second time around because I could actually walk past the shops in the lobby and go straight to my room.

I slept well the night before and worked up an appetite, so I wasted no time going to the beach shops for some holiday clothes. I took one last trip back to my room to change into my new tourist disguise and headed back to the bar on the pier.

Because I was alone, I had a great time sitting at the bar and talking with an American. He was staying in his timeshare. He ended up joining me for the rest of the afternoon and evening. In fact, I met him and (later) his wife on the pier almost every night. They, in turn, introduced me to their friends (who owned timeshares on the beach as well).

He was the perfect guy to have around on holidays. He liked to party in true American style, making him very popular on the beach pier. Due to his timeshare, he had visited the island three or four times per year for many years. It wasn't surprising that I met him again the next time

I returned in April of 2009, which was when I made the biggest mistake of my entire life.

Totally refreshed from my singles holiday, I was greeted in San Tomé by a disappointed wife who couldn't believe I hadn't returned with arms full of presents for her family.

The reality of work hit me when I got back to the site office to find that my team of ladies hadn't really done anything during my absence. The work that they had bothered to do was all messed up, which had drove the commissioning team crazy in my absence.

The reason was clear: they had all brought their earphones to work with them so they could listen to salsa all day instead of concentrating on the job at hand. Previously, I had removed the speakers from their desktop computers for the very same reason. It was like having a classroom full of disobedient children. Anyway, I was received with a cold welcome because my presence meant the return to work as usual.

The peace after the national strike didn't last long before we encountered yet another problem on the project. The new dilemma directly involved the contractor's workforce. They could see that the work was nearing completion, so they tried to slow things down. The workforce used any excuse to strike, which was more annoying than dangerous. In short, the streets of El Tigre were crowded with construction men who didn't want to work.

This continued on and off for a number of weeks until it began to heat up. The main contractor, together with his subcontractors, started to direct their anger in our direction. A false rumour was sent around that the reason they were not getting paid was because we weren't paying their companies.

This certainly created a volatile situation, and we were told to stay home a few times because there were threats that the workers would storm the site offices. With three thousand angry Latin workers, the concern was legitimate; plus, the majority of them held gun permits and carried their guns all the time as a part of their macho image.

The situation continued on and off for several weeks. But with very little construction happening, I had plenty of time to bring all the documentation up to date. With my staff using every possible opportunity to avoid showing up for work, I carried on doing everything myself – that was the silver lining.

My staff even arranged to go to Puerto De la Cruz for a weekend, even though there was work as normal. They switched off their mobile phones so they couldn't be contacted until after their holiday weekend. They were all presented with disciplinary letters when they finally came back to work, though, which made me more unpopular.

Shortly afterwards, there was a genuine fear that the workforce would riot, so everyone was told to stay home. Only a few members of senior management risked going to the site, including myself and my immediate boss, Chris. But we didn't stay long.

To avoid any problems on the road to the site, I left my apartment at four o'clock in the morning. I had already made the coffee before Chris arrived shortly afterwards. The site construction manager arrived half an hour later. When he saw the lights on in my office, he came over and asked what the hell I was doing there. I explained that, after so many false alarms, I decided to take the risk and come in anyway. He wasn't comfortable and said that he'd keep Chris and I informed if he heard any further developments from security and also our community spies.

As it turned out, there were further developments, but by the time we found out, it was too late to evacuate down the only main road from the site. It was ten o'clock in the morning, and Chris asked me whether I knew of another way out of the area. As luck would have it, I did know of one way back to El Tigre, but it still meant using part of the main site road. We just had to hope the mob hadn't already reached it. The road I had in mind was almost impossible to navigate in anything other than a four-wheel drive vehicle, but it was the only chance we had.

I was okay because I had a Toyota Hilux, but Chris was in a Corolla, which I found very funny at the time. We couldn't waste a minute, so we each took a site radio (in case we got split up), locked the office, and hastily headed to the car park. There wasn't time to scrape off the ridiculously large yellow windscreen sticker which was for car park entry, so we left it and drove off. I figured it wasn't the time to stick to the 30km speed limit set by our wonderful HSE guys, and I floored the gas pedal.

Chris hadn't driven home using the track I was heading for, so he was close behind me as we raced down the site road to beat the mob to the junction.

I could see my left turn in the distance, but I could also make out the mob approaching it from the other direction. They had completely filled the road. Four-wheel drive vehicles aren't designed to swerve around potholes at high speed, so I flew over them instead. It wasn't so good for the Corolla, though. Chris was following close behind, and I could only laugh each time I saw him angrily flash his headlights in my rear-view mirror when his wheel hubs were almost ripped off with the potholes he couldn't avoid.

We made it to the junction with only seconds to spare. The angry mob was almost on top of us, but they couldn't make it to us quickly enough to block our escape as they were all on foot.

The track I turned into was badly broken up, and some of its potholes were over two feet deep and too wide to jump at speed. We were already out of the main danger, but we still didn't know whether the workers' unions had had the brains and organised another group to use the same track we were on. Out of sight and in the middle of nowhere wouldn't have been a good place for Chris and I to be caught.

We continued swerving around the potholes for another half hour before the road began to improve, but it was still slow going.

There weren't any signposts at the junctions out in the middle of nowhere, and I had only been along that route from the opposite direction once in the past. Luckily, I navigated correctly in the right direction which was a first for me so we didn't get lost and eventually ended up back at the village without incident. There weren't any workers hanging around as before – they were all outside our site entrance, picketing without an audience.

I was receiving death threats from anonymous emails because my mechanical completions system was reducing the project schedule. The project was seven months behind when I had arrived, but using my system I had succeeded in bringing it forward by around three or four months. This enabled the oil company to make an unplanned $millions.

Thus, I began using that old track more often. I continued working for a few more months before leaving in September of 2002 and returning to the United Kingdom.

During those last few months, Carolina had started demanding yet again, that I help her married sister, her sister's husband, her two brothers and the rest of the family. This continued until I was about to fly home. Eventually, I weakened and left her with plenty of money, including extra for a lawyer to get divorced for the second time.

Needless to say, I was given a business class ticket back to Wales and a thank you handshake from the project manager without any bonus at all. All the staff employees had received mega bonuses for bringing in the project months earlier than forecasted. It amused me to think that their project was already seven months behind due to their genius, but my unpaid for system was what put it back on track!

CHAPTER 13

Libya to Nigeria

July of 2003 was my first introduction to Melliteh, Libya. It was mainly an LNG tank farm and jetty. My stay was shortened, however, because I wore shorts in the camp canteen one evening, which offended the locals living in the men-only camp. Basically, they could see the tattoo of the Blue Marlin on my right calf which I'd had for the International game fishing tournament in Thailand, and they tried reprimanded me for having it.

Needless to say, I voiced my opinion and quit the project at the same time. My thinking was: *If I have to accept their religion, they should equally accept mine.* Was I being unfair? I always made a point to respect the local laws and customs in the countries I visited, but I wondered why they didn't return the same respect when they visited my country.

A few weeks later, I arrived in sunny Port Harcourt, Nigeria which Chris had secured for me. It was a slight culture shock, but not too different from what I'd already experienced in Pakistan and Venezuela.

I stayed just a ten-minute drive from the office, in the Genesis Hotel on old Wogi road. I enjoyed my stay at the hotel, and I thought it was much safer to spend my spare time there instead of venturing out to the local bush bars like many other expats.

The project involved attending a kick-off meeting in Yokohama, Japan, and I was grateful to have my time in Port Harcourt broken up.

I explained to my colleagues before we left Nigeria all about the important Japanese customs which had to be respected if we were to get contracts successfully signed. I guess it was ignored as we were the client for the project. We all left our Japanese hotel at the same time the day after we'd arrived to visit our proposed contractor in Yokohama. In just the first few minutes of formal introductions, I knew we could forget any contract being signed.

The Japanese respectfully handed each of us their business cards using both hands to hold their cards, their thumbs over the top of them, in their main meeting room before we seated. My colleagues took their cards using just one hand instead of taking them in the same manor with which they were given and simple glanced at them before putting them into their back pockets! They may as well have slapped our hosts in the face. I knew then that we shouldn't waste any more time and fly back to Port Harcourt.

Due to my time working for Japanese in the past I was able to return their respect and do the ceremony correctly, plus exchange some pleasant dialog in Japanese to add to the respect of being a guest in their country. After five long days spent in discussions all day in our host's office, we were invited out on the final day to a very reputable local restaurant which is also a part of the Japanese professional business ethics.

We were courteously escorted into a private room in a restaurant which could sit all of us around a large round table. Much to the dismay of my Nigerian Project Manager, I was seated in between the Vice President and proposed Project Director of our Japanese hosts, opposite him.

It is customary in Japan, as well as South Korea to pour the drinks for your guests or hosts yourself. A very warm custom to which I have maintained since. My problem was that as I had the Vice President on my right hand side and their proposed Project Director on my left hand side, I was basically kept busy the whole evening topping up wine and sake classes.

While pouring drinks, you had to touch your pouring arms elbow as if to support it with your other arms hand to show your intention was with full respect. I was swapping my arms all evening while turning to the left or back to the right. Needless-to-say, I had two sets of glasses. One set on the right of my plate and another set to the left of my plate. This was so I could drink with each of my Japanese hosts individually. I have loved Japanese customs ever since.

It was no surprise that contracts were never signed by that contractor or should I say corporation and I'm sure it was due to the total lack of respect that my fellow colleagues showed during the introductions on the first days opening meeting.

Back in Nigeria my stay was not without its surprises. Often, I encountered roadblocks, which stopped me from returning to the hotel unless I paid off the police several times per week.

One night, while enjoying a few beers in the hotel bar, I was invited to join the hotel owner and two of his local friends. I liked to smoke cigars in those days, and the owner's two friends also fancied a smoke. I went back to my room and brought some more to share. Because I was going on my rotational leave the next day, I didn't need them and gave them the box. That gesture was received very well and proved to be a good move.

One of the two introduced himself as the chief of police for Port Harcourt, and the other was the High Court judge. We had a good time, and the chief of police asked whether I was being harassed in "his town." I mentioned that it was rather humiliating being forced to stop at police roadblocks and having a gun pointed at me. I explained that I was never allowed to go on my way without giving away some Nigerian naira.

I also mentioned the risky drive to the airport when I was leaving on rotation. He fully understood what I was saying and gave me his card. He told me to call him and hand his officer the phone the next time I was stopped. *That will be the last I'll ever see of my phone,* I thought.

He also added that he would lend me one of his officers who would sit in the front seat of my car whenever I needed to go to the airport. I was thrilled because there were often community roadblocks along the airport road, and the people at those roadblocks always demanded payments for passage. Basically, nobody went anywhere in those days without money.

The Chief of Police also said that he would have a letter prepared that would give me the freedom to Port Harcourt!

In Nigeria, people couldn't be caught driving down the street when on the first Saturday of the month. That day was called sanitation day. There wasn't any real infrastructure in Nigeria, and that meant no garbage collection. Therefore, to try to reduce the garbage, they invented sanitation day. Everyone was required to clear and burn everything outside their homes or businesses.

On sanitation days, the air was thick with acrid smoke, and it was better to remain indoors until it was over. If I needed to go to the office, I left very early in the morning and remained in the office until late afternoon when it was possible to drive again.

I made some good Nigerian friends whilst staying in Port Harcourt, and I have maintained email contact with them ever since. It's no secret that Nigeria has a bad reputation, however, there are so many wonderful people in Nigeria who will be the first to come to your aid, whatever it may be. Later in my story, the true warmth of Nigerian hospital and helpful support comes to light when I really needed it the most.

CHAPTER 14

France

In October of 2004, I found myself working in Paris for a subsea company. It was an interesting change to write quality, inspection, and test plans for subsea installations for Angolan and Nigerian oil projects, rather than represent the client and only ask to see what someone else had written.

The local French adopted me the very first week I arrived. The French in Nanterre were totally different from the other Parisians. They used to pick me up on the weekends to show me Paris at night. I enjoyed it so much that I even agreed to work through Christmas and the New Year!

I will never forget New Year's Eve. The events started by meeting at noon at the local restaurant next to my hotel. We had lunch, which turned into dinner, and then we ended up in somebody's apartment in the heart of Paris. We finally battled through the traffic and arrived at the Millionaire's Club on the Champs Élysées.

We couldn't find anywhere to park the car, so we pulled up onto the pavement just before midnight. My friend (who was driving) opened the boot of his car and produced a bottle of Champagne and some flutes. A police officer came over to us and told my friend he'd have to move his car because it was illegally parked. After giving the officer a flute of Champaign, he allowed us to leave the car where it was. He said he'd keep an eye on it, so off we went to try to get into the club.

Because I was wearing white training shoes, blue jeans, and a red Welsh rugby shirt, I was stopped at the door and asked whether I had anything more appropriate to wear. I said, "No," and the girl at the door went inside to ask the manager whether I could enter. She returned a minute later and said, "No problem … as long as you buy a litre of Blue Label Vodka at 380 euros per bottle. After agreeing to the crazy price, we were escorted to a table next to the dance floor, which was just perfect.

Wow, what a place! I thought. There were Russian women everywhere and just a few French guys, all in evening dress. They couldn't believe their eyes when they saw me dressed so casually. After an hour, the Russian women couldn't hold back any longer and wanted to know who I was to be able to enter dressed in such a way. I asked them whether they'd seen me on TV, and they all said they hadn't.

I continued winding them up until I had about a dozen of them all dancing with me at the same time. By the time we left the club, it was time for breakfast. In the daylight, I could see countless telephone numbers written all over my arms. It's funny what happens when you tell Russian ladies that you own a night club!

CHAPTER 15

Tunisia

In March of 2005, I found myself working on a gas plant in Tunisia. This was a huge change. The plant had been built twelve years before, so all I had to do was set up a documented quality system that we would hold contractors against during planned maintenance and shut down operations. The contractors didn't have their own procedures, so they would need to follow the ones I'd prepared.

Because the company received its gas from its own offshore platform out in the Mediterranean Sea, I needed to obtain my offshore survival certificate to visit it legally. The closest place that offered the course was Malta, so I arranged to make good use of my time and go to Malta on my next rotational leave.

It was July – a very hot time of year to be in Malta. The Maltese were very hospitable, and my weeklong visit went too fast for my liking. The survival course was conducted on a large training facility near an old Second World War air base. It was ideal for training purposes and well organised.

Its own minibus collected me from my hotel early every morning, which made things even easier.

Because it was an international training facility, there were several nationalities taking the course. Among us were three West Africans who made everyone's day particularly interesting. They were attending so they could work off-shore somewhere off West Africa, but none of them understood a single word of English.

The course syllabus had to fully comply with international requirements for offshore survival training, and it included as much theory as practice. Part of the classroom practice entailed basic life saving techniques, including artificial respiration for accident victims. Each of us needed to demonstrate competency by using a dummy called Little Annie. The doll was developed by a businessman who lost his young daughter because he couldn't save her from a drowning accident.

To maintain the coursework schedule, all the English-speaking attendees went first – more time was needed for the non-English speakers. After two of the West Africans completed the test, the last prepared to demonstrate his competency at administering artificial respiration. He remembered the sequence, but he didn't know when to stop.

The instructor motioned to him several times that he could stop and return to his desk, but he continued for some reason. Again, the instructor asked him to stop, but still he continued, as he wanted to save the dummies life. After the instructor repeated himself several times, he left him alone to continue, which he did for another hour.

After lunch, we received practical fire fighting training, and we were taken to the changing rooms to dress in coveralls and rubber boots. Once dressed, we noticed that the same African was missing. The centre was searched, but to no avail.

He couldn't be found anywhere, so the centre took their minibus out and found him walking down the main road about a mile from the training centre. He was looking for a new career.

As a weekly break from the desert, I took the helicopter to the offshore platform early every Monday morning to check out ongoing quality activities. Up until that time I'd never really been one for routine work, so I moved to South Korea in December of 2005 for a new challenge.

CHAPTER 16

South Korea, China, Japan, Singapore, Indonesia, Dubai, Qatar

After working closely with Koreans in Pakistan (guys who were always happy to share their Kim Chi with me), I saw the move to South Korea as the perfect opportunity to see the country where that food originated and eat myself healthy.

Kim Chi is made by soaking Napa cabbage in salt water for a few hours to dehydrate it, and then after washing it, it is mixed with a large amount of finely grated ginger, garlic, and chopped onions. Then it is all mixed thoroughly together with ground Korean chillies and left at room temperature for a day, before refrigerating it for three more days.

The smell of Kim Chi doesn't appeal to all foreigners, but with its strong anti-oxidants and ability to remove toxins from the body, it is ranked as one of the top five healthiest foods in the world. There are hundreds of variations of Kim Chi and I enjoyed trying different types whenever I had the opportunity. At least living in South Korea, there were plenty of opportunities and I ate it all the time. I actually lost eight kilos in just three months due to a diet of Kim Chi and plain boiled rice.

As the Kim Chi was removing all the toxins I'd built up in my body over the years, I began to feel fitter, and more awake than ever before.

The project in South Korea was still in the engineering and procurement phase. Consequently, I had to fly all over the world to visit vendors for pre-contract award audits, kick-off and pre-inspection meetings, and factory acceptance tests. I clocked up over 480,000 air miles with one airline and another 90,000 with an Asian airline at the expense of three forty-eight-page passports in the first twelve months. Every month, I went back to Japan – sometimes revisiting a manufacturer, sometimes going somewhere new.

On one visit to Japan, I took the opportunity to visit an ancient Japanese castle that once had an army of three thousand women.

In the year of 2006 I visited China nine times. I also used to visit other places like Thailand, Singapore, Dubai and Indonesia every month. Other places, including Italy, and Qatar.

My first visit to China entailed conducting a pre-contract award audit to assess the company's ability to fabricate
structural steelwork. As I was originally a Plater and had
served a full apprenticeship in a similar fabrication facility, I
was looking forward to the visit.

I flew from Incheon airport, an hour drive outside Seoul
for the short fifty minute flight across the Bohai Sea on
the northeastern coast of mainland China to a city called
Yantai in the Shandong province on a very cold February
morning. The original name of Yantai came from lookout
towers constructed on Mount Qi in 1398, during the reign
of the Hongwu Emperor who was the founder emperor of
the Ming Dynasty. 'Yan' means smoke in Chinese and 'tai'
means tower. The smoke towers were built to serve as lookout towers to warn against Japanese pirates.

Everything was fine until we were about to touchdown on the Chinese runway. I remember looking at the runway from my window seat expecting to feel the wheels touch its tarmac at any second, when suddenly the pilot put the engines into full thrust and pulled the aircraft up as steeply as it could go. What an adrenalin buzz that gave, we were going ballistic. I had a faint suspicion as to what was going on, but didn't want to think about it while I was still in the air.

The pilot continued flying deeper into China for another fifteen minutes before making a turn to return back to where we'd almost landed. The second attempt went fine and as we pulled up outside the terminal, I could see a Chinese lady dressed in uniform bow to the aircraft as it came to a stop.

Once inside the terminal building, I took a minute to ask an airport representative if they knew anything with regard to why my flight had aborted its first landing attempt. The lady explained in very good English that we were head to head with another flight as it was taking off and we'd flown right over the top of it just before it left the ground! It reminded me of the flight I decided not to take back in Iran that had a bomb on board. I felt like a cat with a few less lives.

I was accompanied with one of my main contractor's representatives and after completing two different arrival forms and clearing the Chinese immigration we found our driver patiently waiting for us in the arrivals area.

Our first venue was to check-in at the pre-booked hotel. As I entered the hotel I was speechless! It was an incredible place and probably the most finely furnished and decorated hotel I've ever had the pleasure of staying in. With its highly polished marble floors and huge columns all highly decorated with carvings, I could have spent hours walking around to absorb its full grandeur. The contractor had booked me a corner suite which again, added to the luxury. I had views over the sea and also down, along the coast.

When I asked my contractor representative why his company had booked a suite in such a lavish hotel, he explained that I'd need somewhere very comfortable to rest after the Chinese hospitality, which would follow later in the day!

Once we'd checked into the hotel, we left to visit the fabrication company an hour drive away.

That part of China sported the most beautiful scenery. As we drove along a very straight and perfectly flat highway I observed the flowers, which were fully cared for all along the verges on either side. As I arrived at the contractor's facility I had a very pleasant surprise as I pulled up outside their office. The entire management team were all standing outside the main entrance of the building in a line saluting me with their right hands held to their heads underneath a huge cotton banner with the words "Welcome Mr Andy Lang" printed in very large red letters. I only wish I could include the photo, but my laptop was later stolen in Ghana, West Africa when I lost almost all my photographic evidence!

My driver had stopped so that my door was lined up with a red carpet for me to walk on which continued all the way to the main entrance.

The audit went fine. In fact, all seemed to be going very well until they took me for a walkabout to view their fabrication shop and the general layout of their facilities. I was taken to their 'laydown yard' where steel profiles were grouped and stored until required. The set-up was more than impressive as the facility was directly alongside the sea and they had their own quayside for ships to deliver steel anywhere around the world.

I was freezing cold, even though I had prepared for the sub-zero temperature, but not enough. The wind was slicing my throat as we walked around outside their facility until they showed me where they stocked all their materials.

There, I saw two Chinese girls standing to attention wearing only very thin (summer type) cotton pants and jackets (their working uniform).

Immediately, I questioned how long the two girls had been standing outside and why they were there, in the middle of nowhere in the freezing cold? I was told that they had been instructed to stand there from the minute I had arrived (three hours before) so I could see that their company had stock controllers in their laydown area. The company didn't have a contract at the time so there wasn't any material to control.

I felt totally sickened that the two ladies were subjected to such extreme temperatures on my behalf, and ordered the company director to send the girls back inside to a warm room for the rest of the day, and added that I would later check that they were cared for to ensure their comfort. I explained that my company had very strict health and safety policies, which included any contractor, subcontractor, vendor or supplier, and any violation would result in no purchase order being placed.

I explained that it was all part of the pre-contract award audit which I was conducting. The company director said something very fast and strong in Chinese and one of his guys ran over to the two ladies and together with them, ran back inside their main building.

I added that if I had the purchase order awarded, I would visit without any warning from time to time to ensure that conditions had been met. Later, I did visit and all the Chinese employees were sporting very nice warm clothes.

After all the formalities had taken place, the Chinese hospitality went overboard: they invited me out to their favourite restaurant later the same day. I'm not sure whether the food was meant to impress me or frighten me.

The local restaurant was beautiful, and had a private room with a table large enough to accommodate all fourteen of us. As their honorary guest, each new dish that was brought to the table was spun around until it was directly in front of me. I like sushi and sashimi, but even I have limits. The Koreans had hardened my appetite by bringing live jellyfish, octopus, and starfish to the table, but the Chinese stole the show.

One of the dishes consisted of freshly gutted sea cucumber, still moving which was a difficult mouthful – not to mention the white, milky soup with a baby octopus swimming around in it. The method was to slurp back the soup using both hands around the little white bowl until you were able to catch the little octopus in your mouth and crack its head between your teeth. It was not a nice experience as its little skinny legs were over my bottom lip while I needed to murder the poor little thing. But what really stole the show was a plate of grilled, black snakeheads. They were crunchy – I almost broke a tooth!

All the while, I was trying to be polite and maintain some sort of smile on my face. Frequently, they would shout *gam bei* (meaning *dry glass*), and we all had to knock back a small glass of 24% Chinese wine. Each time I put my empty glass back on the table, a waitress standing behind me would fill it back up.

There is a Chinese proverb that goes as follows: "If you leave a social meal sober, you did not truly enjoy yourself." As far as Chinese proverbs go, I had a great time. It was difficult to maintain anything like sobriety with the waitress standing behind my chair!

Traditionally, Chinese people believe that it is impolite to talk too much while eating. A good meal was regarded as too special to be spoiled by conversation. Keeping reasonably quiet during the meal was easy for me because I didn't understand anything they were saying, plus some of the dishes left me speechless in any case. (Their interpreter made things even worse.) Plus, I was quietly worrying about what dish I would be presented with next.

The Chinese had employed the services of an interpreter, but her version of English was new to me. I could even understand some Scottish, but almost everything I said got lost in translation. Some normal things I wanted to say got wrongly translated into phrases the Chinese thought were hilarious. After that, they shouted *gam bei* even more. I decided it was best not to say anything that could possibly be misinterpreted, but that didn't always work.

Once we'd finished the food (for want of a better word), I was driven back to the hotel. But instead of being allowed to retire for the night, I was invited to a Chinese massage place, which I thought was a neighbouring hotel. It was four stories high, and we had to remove our shoes and use their flip-flops to enter. After that, we went downstairs to change into clothes closely resembling pyjamas.

I was given their largest size, but they still pinched a bit in all the wrong places, which made them not so comfortable after all. We were each given a private massage room and the cutest little Barbie to do the work. Mine kept trying to talk to me, but my Chinese was as non-existent as was her English. Still, she never stopped trying to chat while beating the hell out of me with incredible speed. She did that for a solid hour without even breaking into a sweat. Amazing, but so very true. I should have married her!

Once my massage was over, my little Barbie took me to a huge room with large, reclining leather chairs in rows from one wall to the other. I arrived a little late due to my intense conversations and the other guys were waiting for me. I was given an ice cold Chinese beer whilst I watched a Russian show that entailed girls in bikinis simply walking around and doing nothing else. It was as boring as it gets. A new Barbie proceeded to give me a foot massage, and then later a head and neck massage.

I thought to myself, *This is all part of my job. I shouldn't fight it; I should just take it like a man until three o'clock in the morning.*

The next day, I needed to visit another company that would galvanise much of the steelwork being fabricated by the first company. Again, they took me to a restaurant after I had concluded my appraisal of their premises. This time it was to a different restaurant, but every bit as good as the one the night before.

Just like the previous night, everything I said was lost in translation, and some of the dishes were very difficult to swallow whilst trying to maintain an appreciative smile on my face. Fortunately, I was taken directly back to the hotel this time, so I could catch up on some much needed sleep.

I took the early morning flight back to Seoul in time to collect my tickets for Singapore the following day.

I spent the night in my usual hotel on Orchard Street and the following day, I travelled to Batam Island, which is a part of Indonesia to release a shipment of storage tank wall plates for the refinery we were constructing in Qatar.

Unlike visits to China, I was able to buy a visa on arrival for just ten dollars and as reliable as ever, my Japanese contractor had his driver waiting for me at the ferry terminal on the island.

The driver took me straight to their fabrication facilities, about half an hour away. The roads on Batam Island left a lot to be desired. They didn't have curbstones along their edges, so it didn't take long for the surface to break away – especially during the rainy season.

At the office, the Japanese director welcomed me in. He wasted no time completing the formalities before taking me to a Japanese golf course for lunch. He did this every time I visited him, which was every month. Several big Japanese companies owned the private golf course, and the restaurant had been built in true Japanese style: both the director and I had our own personal waitress waiting behind us.

To make it more comfortable for foreign guests, they had built a floor well under the table (like many of the South Korean restaurants had done) so patrons didn't have to sit cross-legged. After we ate, the director had his driver take him back to the office. But before he left, he instructed his personal driver to drive me anywhere I fancied on the island. My first stop was my hotel, and then I went to get a foot massage. After driving around several beautiful island beaches, I was taken to an outdoor seafood restaurant because I wanted to try their famous chilli crab.

The restaurant was built half on land and half over the ocean. Inside, there were concrete tanks with everything imaginable to choose from. I was escorted around by an Indonesian guy who explained what was on offer. I chose a mud crab, and I invited the driver to choose what he fancied to take back to his family before returning to the office with perfect timing so it would still be hot before bacteria had stated to work.

The restaurant had washbasins dotted all over the place. The general idea was to eat with your hands and make as much of a mess as you wanted. Once we had finished, the driver dropped me off at my hotel so I could catch up on some much-needed rest (due to the Chinese hospitality a couple of days before).

To help me with my permanent jetlag, I called the hotel spa and asked if Diana was available to visit my room. Shortly afterwards, little Diana entered my room to give a very professional massage. Half way through her massage she had to wake me up to roll over and later wake me up again to tell me she'd finished! I guess I didn't need the massage after all.

My return trip to Seoul was interrupted by an unplanned visit to Dubai to meet one of the suppliers we had there. Once I got off the ferry in Singapore's harbour, I had to wait six hours before my flight to Dubai on Singapore Airlines. I decided to pay the Raffles hotel a visit and have a Singapore Sling in their famous long bar.

The hotel is a beautiful place to walk around, and the long bar was up a couple of flights of stairs close to the elevator. Entering the bar, I could see monkey nut shells all over the floor where customers had been. (It is customary to drop the shells on the floor.). I ordered my Singapore sling but it was simply poured from a pre-mixed jug. I complained and asked why as I wanted to see the usual cocktail performance. I was told that they only did that for television cameras.

I arrived in Dubai the next day which was a Friday and took a taxi to my pre-booked hotel. I always chose to stay in the same hotel for its comforts, convenience and large choice of restaurants. At the reception desk, a message was waiting for me from my office in Seoul. They detailed a flight to Qatar that Sunday. My wonderful project controls manager thought it would be a good idea to visit the construction site in Ras Laffan because I was so close in Dubai.

With the Saturday meeting complete, I made my way to the Mall of the Emirates. I liked the huge restaurant on the ground floor at the base of the ski slope.

The menu covered most types of cuisine from around the world, so there was something to please everyone. Then came the spice and gold souks (marketplaces) to occupy the rest of the afternoon. After that, I prepared for my flight to Doha the next day. I had learned to fly very light and just travelled with a carry-on case. As soon as I arrived in a hotel room, I would call laundry service and sign for the executive service so my clothing would be returned to me in just two hours. That way, I flew around from country to country with just a change of three sets of cloths, plus my toiletries in a zip locked bag for the airport security checks.

I spent three nights in dusty Doha before returning to Dubai. From there, I headed back to Singapore first due to my flight tickets and then on to South Korea for two days. After that, I took a fourteen hour flight to Amsterdam to wait another six hours to fly back to Milan, Italy for a meeting and one night stop-over and then head back to Seoul with another six hour wait in Schiphol airport.

In February of 2007, a new wife entered my life. I met Wi in a salon in Bangkok on Sukhumvit Road, just a five minute walk from the well-known Nana Plaza on Soi (street) 4. I got to know her while on so many business trips to Thailand in 2006.

Wi was the one I always chose to cut what was left of my hair each time I returned to Bangkok. Most probably due to her smile and personality, not the fact that she was the best stylist in the salon. With my crew cut, there wasn't anything to style anyway.

Every five or six weeks, I'd meet her when I returned to Bangkok and stayed in the Landmark hotel on Sukhumvit road just across the street from her salon. The purpose of each trip to Bangkok was to visit a very large fabrication facility that was very experienced with fabricating equipment for the oil and gas industry near the Cambodian border.

Again, I travelled with a representative from our main Korean contractor, and I always endeavoured to make time to visit Wi – I was due for another haircut by that time anyway. I always remembered to bring Wi little presents from the airport duty-free shops, and we became very good friends.

Whenever possible, I'd steer away from the usual restaurants my contractor invited me to so I could take Wi out after she finished work (often with one of her salon friends). That wasn't always so easy with the hospitality of my contractor as there was millions of dollars at stake, depending on their performance.

I had to cater to Wi's work schedule, though. One week she'd work from nine to nine, and the next week she'd work from eleven to eleven. To the Thai people, holidays seemed to be something that only tourists had.

Wi took me to traditional Thai restaurants outside the usual tourist venues (and as far away as possible from the smutty places in Bangkok). Being the daughter of a rice farmer, Wi hated bars with a vengeance. She wouldn't allow me to pay the usual prices tourists became victims of. She scrutinised every bill before I got to see it, and she didn't hesitate to question any entry she didn't understand.

I learned not to take a Bangkok taxi to a well-known restaurant because the driver could order takeaway food from behind the scenes and have his meal added to the final bill.

This was especially the case with the Tuk Tuk drivers who persuaded unknowing tourists to go to particular restaurants. Later, they'd return for their commission of whatever the tourist spent. Many shops offered Tuk Tuk and taxi drivers a commission just for bringing prospective customers, even if they didn't buy anything.

For those who travel to Bangkok to take advantage of the sex industry, travelling from one venue to another by Tuk Tuk would result in a bill that's at least twice as high as it should be. I have a love/hate relationship with Bangkok, mainly due to its darker side, which it is so popular and famous for.

Nothing disgusts me more, than seeing a hugely obese man proudly walking down the street with a tiny, skinny little Barbie doll holding his hand that he had recently rented. I am very well known in Bangkok to interrupt such romances and pay the girl to go home. That's better than imagining what she'd have to endure later in the evening. The customer would often take personal offense and sometimes become aggressive, but the Thai doormen in the street (Soi), all knew me very well and what I liked to do, and would have jumped in to protect me, should the need arise.

In February, I decided to leave the project I'd been flying around so much for because I had only contracted for the detailed design and procurement phase.

CHAPTER 17

Thailand

I returned to Thailand so Wi and I could get married in her family's house in Sakon Nakhon, near Laos. It took about an hour by plane to reach the area. It was a very green area, like everywhere in Thailand. There were miles and miles of rice fields.

I was still officially married to Carolina in Venezuela, however, so we couldn't formally get married. Instead, we married Buddhist style by having the all-day ceremony without signing anything. Wi knew all about Carolina, and she longed for the day I would finally be free so we could get married officially.

We were well received at the airport by Wi's brother and one of her sisters. We drove for almost two hours before we got to Sakon Nakhon where her mother and father were eagerly waiting to meet me for the first time.

Wi's father had already started cutting very fine sticks (very much like tooth picks), which were needed to form part of the flower arrangement that would later become the centrepiece of the ceremony. Other ladies in the village joined in to help with the plaiting of banana leaves, which would also become part of the flower arrangement.

Wi, one of her sisters, and I went out into the rice fields to a place where a certain type of white flower grew. We collected all we could find to add to the arrangement. Hidden inside the final flower arrangement was a small bottle of Thai whisky and a small bowl of sticky rice (offerings to Buddha). To drive around the rice fields, Wi's father had handed me the keys to his brand new Toyota Hilux, purchased with his life's savings.

As I reversed out from beneath his house everyone was watching me. This freaked me out a lot and as I reversed very slowly, I backed into a concrete lamp post, which caused a little dent in her father's back bumper. I could see the lamp post, but just as I touched the brake and changed into the first gear there was a little bump.

I felt terrible as everyone rushed over to see the damage, it was so embarrassing. A few minutes later, Wi and one of her sisters jumped into the Hilux so I could drive them to where the flowers should be. As I was still in shock and total embarrassment for denting Wi's fathers pride and joy, I drove over a little puppy, which was sleeping in the middle of the road. I love dogs so much that it ruined the rest of my day. I felt two little bumps and a squeak and that was it, poor little puppy.

It must have taken a full six hours to complete the flower arrangement. Strands of white wool completed it, and it was my job to carry it up the stairs of their house, which was built on tall wooden legs. That was, by tradition, my job. I nervously picked it up and was surprised to discover how heavy it was. I couldn't see the steps in front of me as I slowly made my way to the first floor. Luckily, I made it without any incidents. I believe the flower arrangement weighed around fifteen kilos by the time it was finished.

The last job was for Wi. She had to arrange the three hundred thousand Thai baht wedding dowry in a pattern on the floor in front of the flower arrangement. She rearranged the money three times before she was satisfied. After that, she added the finishing touch: a necklace and bracelet made of pure Thai gold. The jewellery also became part of the ceremony (along with the rings).

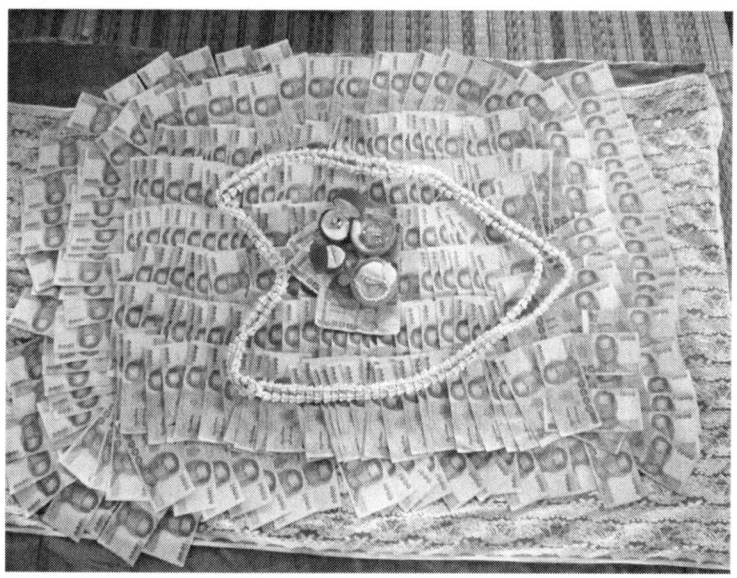

Everyone in the little village was welcome to visit the house to see the dowry arranged on the well-polished wooden floor, which I thought rather patronising for the poor rice workers. Sandals and flip-flops filled the entrance outside their house as guests went to see my offering to join the family.

With all preparations complete, it was time to change into traditional clothes, which was highly amusing. I had to wear a sarong, which was new for me. I caused a lot of laughs when the garment ended up around my ankles in front of Wi's mother and sisters.

Making and hand-printing sarongs was Wi's mother's profession, and her sarongs were well known in that part of the country. She still had many left from when she used to make them, and the patterns and colours were beautiful. To wear it, I had to pull the loop (which was all they were) tight against my waist and fold the spare material back against myself and then fold the whole sarong down over itself. Because my first attempt failed miserably, they decided to cheat and allow me to wear a belt underneath the fold of the sarong so it couldn't be seen.

I also needed to borrow a white, long-sleeved shirt. I could have bought one back in Bangkok, but I wasn't told in time. They went all around the village collecting white shirts until I finally tried one that almost fitted. It had to do. The finishing touch was a silk sash that rested on my right shoulder and draped down to my left hip.

We were ready to start the ceremony. I was taken away from Wi and made to walk to the entrance of the village. There, I was joined by quite a congregation of family, relatives, and friends who were waiting outside for me. Once we got to the entrance of the village, we turned to prepare for the *slow walk* back the way we had came. I was made to hold three pampas leaves and three tiny candles, like the type you'd find on a birthday cake.

The music started, and the *slow walk* back to the house began. I was shaded from the sun by an umbrella held above my head while others played instruments: harmonica, guitar, panpipes, and bongo drums. I felt like all eyes were focused on me, which they were. I tried to walk a little faster. Each time I tried to speed up, I was made to slow down. The walk back to Wi's parents house felt like hours instead of around twenty minutes.

Finally I made it back to the house. There, I found one of Wi's sisters waiting at the entrance to the house. As part of the ceremony, she had to traditionally hand wash the dust from my feet before I stepped onto a banana leaf to enter the house. I had no idea how much trouble Wi's family had gone to, to make all the professional arrangements. I've often thought how good they'd fare on Oil and Gas projects!

As I made it back to my starting place, I was surprised to see so many people already sitting around on the wooden floor. I was ushered through the crowd and made to kneel down alongside Wi. She looked more beautiful than I could ever have imagined. She was in full national costume, including a slim-fitting hand made silk dress and a Thai orchid in her hair.

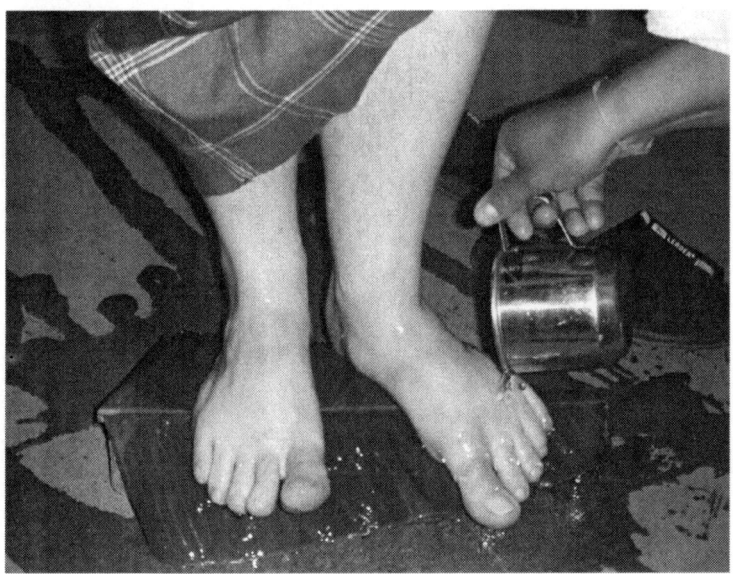

It is very bad manners to show the soles of your feet in Thailand, and I found it almost impossible to kneel down normally because there were people behind me, sitting against the wall. I had to try to sit to the side, but because it was such an awkward position, my ankles hurt against the wooden floor. Whatever position I tried, I felt pain, so I decided to cross my legs. Unfortunately, I couldn't maintain that comfortable position for the following four hours.

Wi's uncle began reading from a thick, handwritten book while everyone kept quiet.

I don't think I've ever kept quiet for four hours in my entire life, but I was afraid to breathe at times. Towards the end of the ceremony, I found out the purpose of the white wool that had been draped on the flower arrangement.

Everyone in the room began to place money in our hands and securely tie a strand of wool around our right wrists. I felt guilty about accepting the twenty Baht ($.0.65c) donations from all the poor rice farmers, but it was all part of the ceremony – a bid of good luck for our future together. With our rings exchanged, it was all over (thank you Buddha!).

After the four long hours on the hard wooden floor, I managed to pass through the pain barrier several times until I lost most of the feeling in my lower legs and feet. When it was time to stand up, I couldn't. The Thai people understood and found the situation highly amusing.

They all helped me to my feet and kept me steady until the blood rushed back into my muscles. The pins and needles feeling didn't take long to disappear and I was able to go back outside (where we spent the rest of the evening). I kept myself active slapping mosquitos and swatting the flies as there were many chickens amongst us, not to mention Wi's father's cows next to the house.

Wi's father had only seven cows remaining from his herd but I was to add to them later.

Wi was the only one who could speak English, so she regularly joined me to ask if I was alright. Everyone else was speaking Thai to me, to which I could only nod my head, smile, or laugh.

The next day involved the final part of the wedding ceremony. We went to the local village temple to give the three monks an offering. I couldn't believe my eyes when I saw the size of the village temple. It was big enough to house the entire population of the village and still have plenty of room to spare. It looked beautiful.

Again, it was time to kneel down and cover the soles of my feet for yet another hour. Fortunately, the time passed quickly, and I welcomed the time to go to the three monks and make my offering. The congregation of onlookers joined us, which was very comforting. They were there for me.

On the walk back to the house, I called Carolina to tell her what I'd been up to. Carolina was more surprised than upset, and she seemed understanding. She knew there was no point in waiting for me; she had to continue her life. I explained that my Thai marriage did not include signing any documents, so no laws had been broken. I later learnt that my Venezuelan wife has posted photos of her new-born daughter on Facebook from her live-in boyfriend!

She said she'd pursue the divorce that the second lawyer had initiated in Venezuela. Two days later, she called me to let me know that the second Venezuelan lawyer, as expected, had done nothing. Thus, the second three thousand dollars had been another waste of money.

Wi's place in Sakon Nakhon was the main area of Thailand where they ate dogs, but thankfully, that was made illegal by the King. In order to stay close to Wi, I got a staff position in Kuala Lumpur to work on a 138-kilometre subsea pipeline.

CHAPTER 18

Malaysia

After arriving in Malaysia in February of 2007, I found myself back in Italy after just ten days and back in Japan two weeks later. I could only stay in the company provided hotel for a week so I needed to find an apartment quickly. It didn't give me enough time to get to know Kuala Lumpur so I chose the first apartment which was high enough away from the mosquitos. Mosquitos don't normally fly higher than the fifth or sixth floor and the apartment I chose was on the twenty fourth floor.

Once I had bought all the usual accessories, which were rarely found in a rental apartment, Wi quit her job in Bangkok and joined me. Wi didn't need to use the air conditioners in the daytime while I was busy working, so she kept them off all day to save expensive electrical bills! Even though we lived on the twenty fourth floor, it was still too hot and humid for me, even with the windows opened to have a *through draft*. Wi would close all windows and switch on the air conditioners half an hour before my return every day.

Wi was also an amazing cook. A great friend of mine Terry would always join us when we went down the road to a local bar and Wi loved to cook for him. Terry was already in his middle sixties and Wi called him uncle Terry. One time, Terry's son docked in Malaysia off a nuclear submarine and Wi invited both her uncle Terry and his son for lunch, one Saturday afternoon. It was a really relaxing afternoon.

I, together with Terry and his son sat watching an action movie while Wi remained in the kitchen all afternoon producing courses of Thai cuisine. Wi brought many little dishes each time so each time we would have hot food to nibble on. All in all, we went through at least twelve courses and ended up *well stuffed*. At the time of publishing my story in 2013, Terry is seventy years of age, fit and thankfully healthy and working in China!

Wi was not just the best choice of wife, Wi was also my closest possible friend. She never stopped fussing around our rented apartment in Mont Kiara, just up the road from Sri Hartamas, just twenty minutes from the centre of Kuala Lumpur.

Wi was forever putting things away in drawers so I couldn't find anything. I'd arrive home from work and look for my telephone charger so I could simply plug my mobile in before doing anything. My charger was never in the wall socket where I'd left it. I needed to ask Wi every day where my charger was, and Wi would reply, "drawer darling, in draw. Charger must live in draw, not floor".

Laundry was another issue. My clothes from the day before were always washed, dried, ironed to perfection and aired every day, even though I could have waiting a week.

During our time together in Malaysia, I discovered that *Wi* wasn't actually her real name. I knew Thai people liked to be called by their chosen nicknames (such as *Nok, Lek,* or *Hoy*) because their original names were often too long.

When I originally asked Wi to write down her name and phone number back in the salon she worked on Sukhumvit road, she wrote Wi because *W* and *I* were the only letters she knew in English. Her real first name was Vipaporn, which she has since changed to Narawadee because her favourite monk told her it was a luckier name. The monk was no ordinary monk as I later discovered.

Through Wi, the monk would send warnings to me of events that wouldn't be good for me and also ways to avoid them, when possible. For some strange reason he knew all about the voodoo in my life before. He warned that voodoo would repeat itself in my life with very dangerous consequences if I wasn't careful and warned me about a black woman. I really believed in him as he was the personal monk for the King and Queen of Thailand and travelled overseas a lot explaining Buddhism.

He had explained to Wi, my past which I could never have done due to the language barrier that existed at that time before Wi later took-up English lessons to add to her vocabulary.

Wi had accompanied me to Kuala Lumpur, which was the best move for me, but Malaysia was not a good move for Wi.

Wi couldn't walk down the road to the local gym without cars pulling up alongside her trying to proposition her, and Malaysian, Indian and Indonesian construction workers used to follow her along the road until it got so bad that she remained in the apartment like a prisoner the whole day.

As a product of all the flying I had done, I had found that I had vein thrombosis in a most personal place just near the head. Whenever the vein filled with blood, the vein would become like a hard piece of plastic, raised and terribly uncomfortable. I went to the local doctor who was a lady who looked most impressed with my problem, or something similar. It was too big for her experience to handle and referred me to a surgeon just three days later. The local clinic was actually a part of my apartments building so it was perfect being on the ground floor.

I met the surgeon three days later and he prescribed a course of blood thinning drugs just to see if they would clear the suspected blockage in my vein. A week later I returned in just the same condition, so he informed me that I needed to have surgery.

I took a friends taxi and went to the hospital in a very beautiful part of Kuala Lumpur where the surgeon practised and they were all very professional and prepared me for the surgery under just a local anaesthetic! I couldn't believe my best friend was going to be cut while I was still conscious! I was prepared for surgery and left to wait in a very cold area. The air conditioners must have been on full as I was freezing cold for at least an hour.

Thankfully and eventually a very nice old nurse wheeled me to the operating theatre where I would next meet the surgeon. It was badly timed as Wi was doing her visa run back to Thailand, so I was alone, but thankfully in very good hands. He had previously informed me that he had qualified in America so I was in safe hands. With the job in hand, I was worried about friendly fire, blue on blue and have a nice day! The surgeon fitted an intravenous needle into my left arm instead of one of the two nurses. He injected something before he injected something else which he told me I would enjoy.

He had a pleasant smile on his face and to cut a long story short, I never stopped talking the whole time he performed the necessary surgery, much to the amusement of the two nurses swabbing blood. I wasn't encouraged to lean up to see what was going on, (nor did I want to), but I was presented with the end result in a test tube full of some kind of clear liquid. The vein which was removed was the whitest possible white I had ever seen. It was like chewing gum, but so super white.

I left the hospital still enjoying whatever the hell they had injected me with and took a taxi to a shopping mall in the centre of Kuala Lumpur. I wanted to buy another suitcase, or so I thought at the time whilst still under the influence of the drugs I was given. While I walked to the shop I noticed everyone looking at me. I didn't know at the time, until I got home, that my blood had managed to soak through my dressing and also my jeans leaving a large wet, red, patch for all to see going down my leg.

I was instructed to return after fourteen days to the clinic, to have my stitches removed, but due to the itching, I couldn't wait that long. Instead I bought a razorblade, a tweezers and some surgical spirit and decided to become a surgeon for the first time since I was circumcised at the age of five years old, when I performed a similar procedure in a well salted bath my mother had dropped me in.

Everything went perfectly as I cut the knots and plucked out the rather course stitches. Perfect until I cut the final stitch and pulled it with the tweezers in the wrong direction. I left it until last as it was caked in hard dry blood so I soaked it will surgical spirit to soften the blood thinking I was being sensible – not.

Like a perfect idiot, once I had cut the last stitch, I pulled the stitch in the wrong direction due to the blood, which caused its knot to pass through the first side on my skin, but ended up stuck inside my wound.

I was bleeding quite a lot, but felt so content that the operation had been done so things would only get better; I continued to finish the surgery. I pulled the problem stitch but it ended up in disaster. My wound opened up half way alone the cut and I needed to quickly stand up so my blood wouldn't make a mess on my lovely soft leather sofa. It wasn't a nice night as I spent the rest of it with my friend in a mug of strong salt water, just like the baths my mother had prepare for me when I was five years old.

Once my surgery was complete, I needed to collect Wi from the airport as she was returning from her visa run. All was fine until we started to drive back to Mount Kiara. As we were driving on the highway, I checked my rear view mirror and noticed the front window of a five series BMW. The car was practically touching my back bumper as I couldn't see its lights. I pulled over and it went past my car and then swerved across my lane forcing me to brake heavily, until I was only going thirty kilometres an hour. It had blacked out windows so I knew it was a government car, which were licensed to shoot! Guns were permitted in Malaysia if you were security, but law did not permit you, to hold a loaded weapon. Security guards outside supermarkets etc., held guns but their shells were not permitted to be loaded unless they encountered a problem! Fortunately the government car pulled away, but both Wi and I were quite shaken by the event for the rest of the night.

With the people above our apartment dragging furniture all day and most of the night, the twenty-four-hour construction of new tower blocks being built all around us, and the terrible driving in Kuala Lumpur, we decided to pull out of Malaysia whilst we were still both in one piece.

The company I worked for still owed me over four thousand dollars in expenses from several months of business trips, but despite many complaints, there was no sign of it being paid. Thus, we jumped ship and returned to Bangkok without giving my contractual (sixty day), notice as I felt they had already broken my contract by not reimbursing me.

I left my four-month-old Volkswagen Golf which I had bought in Kuala Lumpur with a 'so called' British friend living in Kuala Lumpur to sell on my behalf. Unfortunately, he fell for the oldest trick in the book and handed over my signed logbook to a Chinese garage owner who sold my car and kept all the money. I lost everything. The garage owner had done that to numerous clients before bankrupting the company (which meant nobody got their money). So that was a loss of another thirty thousand dollars.

Wi went back to working in the same salon on Sukhumvit Road, but her personality began to change because she was worried that I was not working. Tensions continued to rise until I was able to start a new contract in Qatar as the consortium quality manager of three companies. As I left Thailand, I had no idea when I would ever see Wi again so we decided to break up.

As it happened, this wasn't the last I'd see of Wi as I discovered five years later in December 2012.

CHAPTER 19

Second Time in Qatar

The Qatar job came at the perfect time. Plus, I got the opportunity to see Izhar again. I was longing to see him again so I was able to contract him for his unique computer database skills.

The company I was working for were struggling to create a mechanical completions database that they had committed themselves to in their contract, so the only chance they had of completing it was Izhar. They had turned my offer down to rent my Q-Pack database from me which was already a well proven system.

The first few weeks were spent sleeping in our assigned apartments in Doha, before our rooms were ready on the site camp in Ras Laffan. We needed to leave very early in the morning to start work at the side office which was an hour drive, out into the desert. It was a boring drive as there was nothing of interest to see along the only road to and from the area.

The social life in Doha was fine with its Rugby Club, European Club, and very nice hotel bars and restaurants. Out in the desert was nothing. Senior management had made all the usual assurances, much like politicians, but nothing ever materialised once you were out there. With no television channels, no internet and no other facilities, time went very slowly. The canteen didn't cater for Europeans, so it was curry three times a day, or starve.

Soon the summer came along so all the mosquitos left due to the daytime temperatures, but the flies chose to stay, so you were never left alone! We were all required to wear orange coveralls all the while we were inside the sites perimeter fence, including the office. As we returned back to the camp all dressed in the same colour to the rows of white containers, we realised it was an exact resemblance to the prison at Guantanamo Bay, Cuba. Razor wire was also included on the top of all the chain-linked fences which prevented anyone getting in, or us getting out!

Soon, the day came when Izhar walked into the office reception just as I was passing by. "Hey, brother," he said. "Don't waste time standing around there." I said. "Go and get the coffees," I replied. All the office staff started laughing because it was obvious Izhar and I were the very best of friends.

Again, Izhar made me proud. In return, I got him the maximum salary the budget would allow. I lost my temper with the project director because I am a firm believer that salaries should be based on capability, and not where you came from. I don't agree with exploitation.

During our time living out in the desert camp, someone had mentioned that an Indian restaurant had been seen somewhere outside the sites perimeter fence. One lunchtime, together with Kenny, the construction manager, I ventured out of the back security entrance of the Ras Laffan Industrial complex and went to see for myself. Sure enough, in the middle of nowhere, someone had opened a restaurant.

It wasn't much to look at from the outside, and even less from the inside. The food was prepared to order as they had no idea when they would ever have a customer, so the wait was quite a long one. The outside temperature was around fifty degrees Celsius in the shade and the restaurant didn't have any air conditioning. We had checked inside the kitchen before ordering and found the temperature was intolerable with the added heat from the gas cookers.

We were sure that much of the salty flavour was from the chefs own sweat! The curry however, was very good despite our surroundings. We arranged for the restaurant staff to have site entrance badges and deliver to our office once a week so everyone could enjoy their food under the comfort of our office air conditioning.

I organised a desk for Izhar in my office because we had a lot of catching up to do (it had been quite a few years since Karachi). As part of my demands to my company, Izhar got his own private unit on our desert camp, like every manager had.

Managers were also assigned an apartment in Doha so they could escape the desert and enjoy city life whenever they wanted. Needless to say, there was a spare room for Izhar in mine. Izhar joined me in Doha a few times and made me proud to have him with me every time. Beer was not cheap in the hotel bars in Doha, but Izhar always insisted on paying his way even though I wanted to cover his turn.

I took a break after four months of living in the desert camp six nights a week and went to Thailand to meet up with two British friends in the same business.

They both lived in Pattaya, which was an hour and a half drive east of Bangkok. I'd always avoided going there up until then as it was a bit too much with its thousands of bars. I preferred the quieter and more cultural areas of Thailand.

I met Neil on my first night at a bar we'd arranged. The last time I'd seen Neil was when we worked together in Tunisia on a gas plant. Neil entered the bar with one of his friends who he promptly introduced me to. His name was Mark, and he was an electrical engineer in the oil and gas business and also lived in Pattaya.

Together, we were later known as the three Alan's. This is how that happened as per Neil's request for my story to be more complete!

One night we met up together and proceeded to go down Pattaya's 'walking street', for a change of scenery. We had walked half way down the notorious street before deciding to take on some fluids. There wasn't anywhere quiet down walking street so we walked into the first bar that looked okay.

The moment we entered the bar, the lady managing the establishment came hurriedly over to us and spoke to me first. In true Thai bar fashion she said "Hello, what your name, where you come flom (from), please sit down, what you want to drink?" to which I replied, "My name is Alan, I come from England and I'll have a beer please". Next she turned to Mark and asked the same question. Mark replied, "My name is Alan, I come from England and I'll have a beer please".

The lady looked at us and said "two Alan's from England?" The best was yet to come. She turned to Neil and again, asked the same question. Neil replied, "My name is Alan, I come from England and I'll have a beer please". The poor lady looked somewhat distraught at our responses; hence, this night was the beginning of 'the three Alan's' and we consequently rode into the sunrise.

Returning back to the bar I was staying above in Soi 13, I walked past a tattoo studio, which was still open at that time in the morning, whatever time it was? The same day, but in the afternoon, when I woke up, I faintly remembered something about promising the Thai tattooist that I'd return later to have the Chinese dragon and tiger tattooed on my back?

Not to disappoint the man, I returned to ask if I had seen him in the early hours that same day? As I entered into his studio he quickly showed me the artwork he had spent hours preparing for my tattoo!

If I was thinking more clearly I would have paid him for his time and trouble preparing the artwork and left, but instead, I wasn't thinking at all. I blame the two other Alan's for that!

Instead, I removed my T-shirt and lay face down on his tattoo bed. He started by shaving the hairs off my back and applied a thin film of gel before placing a tracing of his artwork on top of it. He then pressed it down firmly to transfer the ink from his tracing onto my skin as a guide to the pattern he had developed.

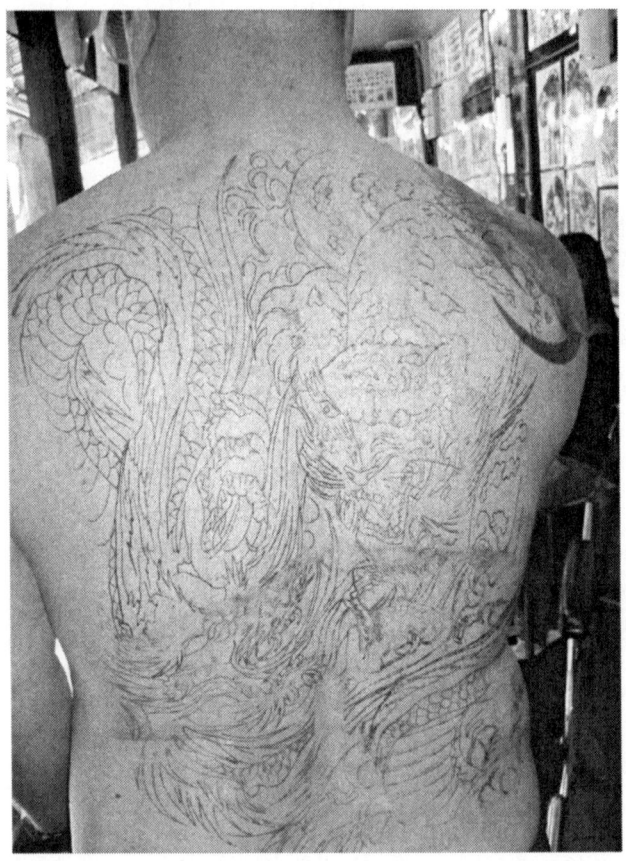

I was already thinking that it wasn't too late to pull out, but instead, I fell asleep! Again, I blame the two other Alan's, and still do to this day!

I woke up suddenly with the most gut wrenching pain, similar to someone cutting through my side with a blunt chainsaw. Alan's I thought; wait until tonight! As it worked out, I didn't leave the studio for ten hours, which took me past midnight so I went straight to my room with my back feeling like I'd slept on a BBQ. After two days the tattooist had finally finished the outline, so the next step was to colour it all in.

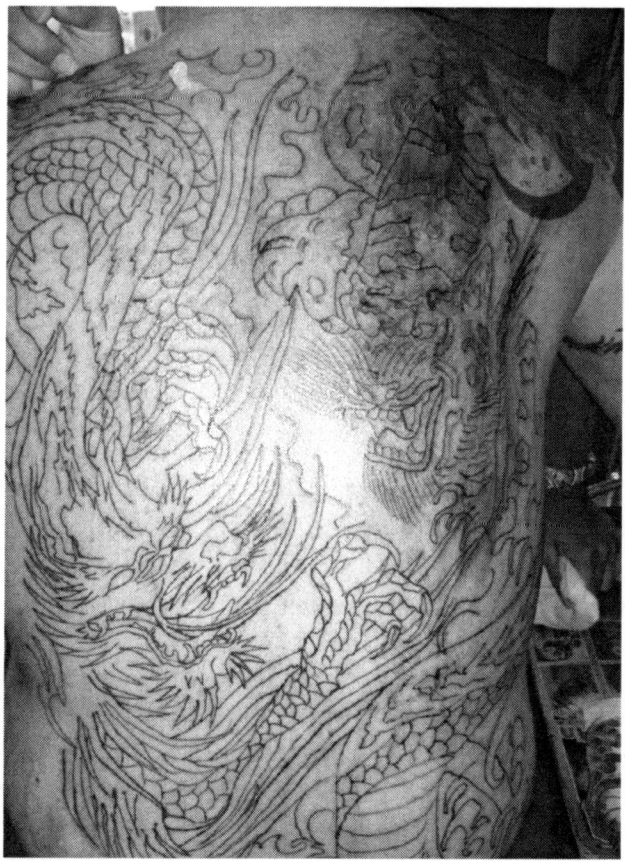

When I tried to return the next day, I couldn't get out of bed as my blood had glued me to the sheets. Together with the soreness I couldn't move. Luckily, the room maid entered to clean my room and helped to painfully peel the colourful blood stained sheet from my very sore skin. After I'd enjoyed my traditional Thai breakfast consisting of rice, chillies with some vegetables thrown in, I half-heartedly returned back to the studio for some more voluntary agony. Alan's I thought, again!

After another nine hours of unadulterated torture, I stopped the tattooist, as I really couldn't take any more pain for that day. The following three days were much the same until his not so handy work was finally over. I thought my friends were joking, when they informed me that the tiger's eye on my back was poking out of its head until someone took a photo to show me! Nobody could locate the end of the dragon's tail either? Maybe that explained the tiger's eye?

I often thought, if Wi had been with me, she would have prevented the entire escapade from taking place.

Back in Qatar, I wasn't too happy with how the project was going because we were getting badly let down by our procurement department back in Paris, but taking the blame for them on site. One afternoon, I was called by an agent to ask whether I'd be interested in a lead quality manager position back in West Africa.

My curriculum vitae was submitted and accepted, and I said goodbye to Qatar. I felt a little guilty for taking Izhar from his family to work for me and then leaving him alone, but I had a hidden agenda, which I couldn't explain to him at the time, as I didn't want him to endure another disappointment if my plan didn't work out.

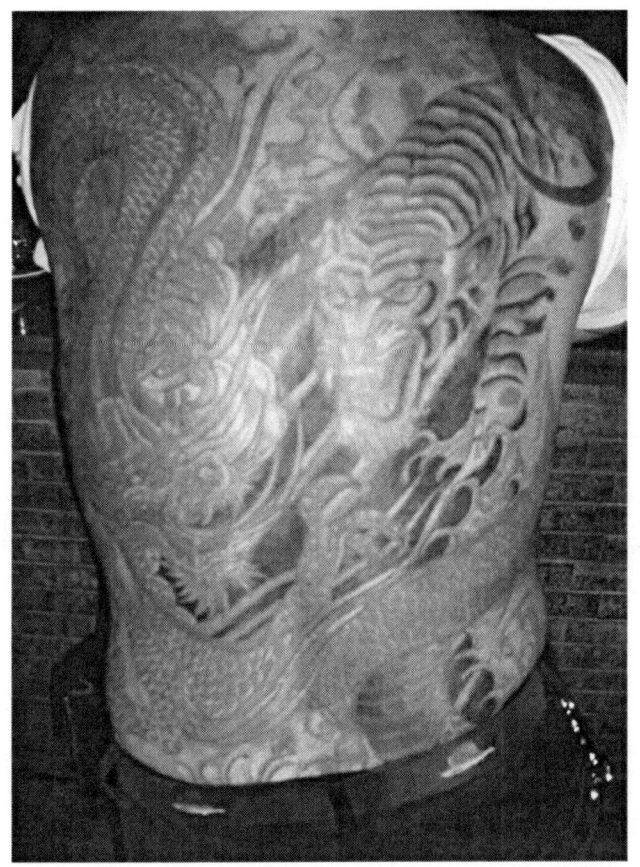

CHAPTER 20

Ghana, Togo, Benin and Nigeria

In August of 2008, I moved to sunny West Africa to take care of the quality assurance and quality control in Ghana, Togo, Benin, and Nigeria on yet another project.

Apart from the usual security problems in Nigeria; Ghana, Togo, and Benin were all fine as locations for work and visiting whilst taking the usual precautions for that part of the world. The people were friendly, and it was reasonably safe to walk around, especially Ghana – nobody really bothered me. English speaking Ghana was really rather safe to walk around, French speaking Togo needed some precautions, French speaking Benin additional precautions but it all stopped at the Nigerian border where my heavily armed escort would be waiting for me.

After settling in Africa once again, I could see the need for formal control over the contractor's activities. I managed to rent my own Q-Pack ©copyrighted mechanical completions database, which I had pioneered back in 1991. The only requirement I built into the rental contract was that Izhar would administer my system.

My database rental contract was approved, so I called Izhar. My first words as he answered his mobile phone in Qatar were, "Hey, brother, it's Andy in Africa. Quit your job and come over here. I have a contract for you." After I explained everything, Izhar handed in his resignation and joined me a few weeks later.

Izhar went directly to Nigeria to start his assignment, so I needed to drive from Ghana, through Togo, through Benin to Nigeria to meet up with him, which took me three days.

Izhar is the only man in the world I trust with my unprotected database. Izhar will always be the man to set up my database on location and add users and passwords as needed. Once done, Izhar converted the database so nothing could be changed – even if thieves copied it onto a USB memory stick.

So on the 14 September 2008, I started to drive from Ghana back to Nigeria. All was fine until I reached the Nigerian border. My armed escort was late arriving, and I needed them to safely escort me through the seventeen road blocks to Lagos Bay. Once on the road, I always checked my rear view mirror to see if they were close behind me as they were instructed to be.

In Lagos Bay, the contractor's quality manager who I needed to meet with, was delayed by a few days, which forced me to stay three weeks in the hotel complex. The hotel complex was a great place to stay for anyone who liked sand, malaria and dengue fever carrying mosquitos and watching out for black mamba snakes, *which were killed on a daily basis.* There were also green tree snakes, so we avoided standing under the trees in case a snake mistook us for a chicken and dropped on us.

After three weeks passed, it was time to return the way I'd come. I also needed to visit our Benin and Togo sites en route to Ghana. My driver and armed escort arrived late as usual, but we left eventually.

Once on the road to Benin, every car that came near my Land Cruiser was considered a threat. My escort would sound their siren to keep them away from me. One of our guys was shot in the head and chest on 17 March 2008 on the same road. He was ambushed and sprayed with bullets just ten minutes from the Nigerian / Benin border.

With that in mind, I always became tense as I approached the same border. It seemed too easy: all seventeen road blocks opened up when they saw my truck approaching at high speed and heard the escort's sirens. The flashing blue and red lights were also a visual deterrent that I had an armed escort.

Once past the last checkpoint, we were home free, or so I thought. We had just a few easy kilometres to go before arriving at the Benin border.

I didn't hear the *bang*, but my driver suddenly grasped his right arm with his left hand and almost rolled the Land Cruiser when he realised he'd been hit. I grabbed the steering wheel, but it was too late: we ploughed into the skinny trees at the side of the road. At least my driver managed to stamp on the brakes.

My escort was too far behind us to provide any protection, but they could see what was happening ahead. They were actually quite brilliant − even if they were late. They pulled over, positioned their Toyota Hilux to block any direct fire in my direction, and proceeded to return fire.

My driver only had a flesh wound. The shooting match didn't last long. Eventually, the escort had succeeded in controlling the situation. There weren't any additional casualties on my side, but I can't say that for the three ambushers.

Just another ten minutes took us to the Benin border, which was as far as my escort could go. Their instructions were to wait there until I had cleared both the Nigerian and Benin border police kiosks before returning to their camp, back at Lagos Bay.

I gave the last of my Nigerian naira to my armed escort and got back inside the Land Cruiser for safety. My driver took my passport to the immigration officers as he usually did whilst I remained out of sight due to my skin colour as I must have been the only white man for miles around.

Five minutes later, my driver returned with a worried look on his face. He told me that the immigration officer wanted to see my yellow fever vaccination card. Surrounded by locals, I went over to the immigration officer and explained that my yellow fever card was still in Ghana. I told him that I didn't know I was required to show it when exiting the country!

And then the big act started. The Nigerian officer shouted at me and told me he could not stamp me out of the country without the card. I tried arguing that I was leaving the country, not entering it, so a yellow fever card shouldn't matter anyway.

Arguing with him was fruitless. He told me I had to "dash" him something or I would be stuck in a kind of limbo. I wouldn't be allowed to leave Nigeria, nor re-enter it! All I had on me, after giving the last of my naira to my armed escort was British twenty-pound notes! I walked away so I could discretely take a note from my wallet, which I never, *normally* carried at the border crossings and folded it up and placed into my hand and returned to his little wooden desk.

Still totally surrounded by locals who were all looking for commission I approached his desk trying to maintain a false smile for him to see. He ordered all the people waiting to move out of the way so I could go directly to his desk. I said to him, "you are a lucky man as you're going to get a thank you handshake to stamp me out of *your* country!" I shook his hand, and that was that – or so I thought.

Another five minutes had passed as I waited inside the safety of my Land Cruiser; my driver came back saying that the chief immigration officer wanted to see me. Evidently, there was a problem with my passport. I got back out of the car and (surrounded yet again by beggars) went back to the same immigration desk.

A new guy wanted to speak with me this time, and he took me behind the scenes where he explained that I had over stayed in Nigeria for seven days too long.

That time they were right. When I'd entered Nigeria three weeks before, the immigration officer had stamped my passport for just a two-week stay, *even though I'd asked for a month to be on the safe side*, and had dashed him accordingly. Like an idiot, I hadn't checked the stamp he'd given me.

The immigration chief had one of his police officers hold an AK-47 to my head while he shouted at me. He said I was an illegal alien in *his* country and that he'd have to have me arrested. He continued to shout at me, and he informed me that the penalty for being illegal in his country was a twelve month prison sentence. He said that my embassy couldn't help me because I was guilty.

By that time my stress level switched to overload and I couldn't contain it any longer. While a gun was held to my head with its safety off I started laughing. I could see the remains of the red paint on the left hand side of the AK-47, which indicated the safety, had been disabled and the gun was ready to fire.

I'd got to the point where I didn't give a damn anymore and wanted to put up a final protest. I had a feeling that they wouldn't squeeze the trigger so with my left hand I grabbed the barrel of the gun pointed against my head and held it firmly downwards. This infuriated the immigration chief and he demanded to know what I found so funny and instructed me to release the weapon.

I was tired and way passed caring by this time so I said, "in the entire history of your country, I must be the first white man to have ever over stayed a minute, let alone seven days!"

His expression changed as he realised that I had already been pushed to far and I noticed a slight grin on his face in respect of my defiance and will to fight back.

Even though he was technically correct, I knew all he wanted was to be dashed some money, so I cut to the chase while still holding the AK towards the floor and asked to speak to him without an audience. He took me to a tiny little office while he continued to shout at me, asking me what he should do with me.

I admitted that I hadn't checked the date written in my passport and that *I was glad he was there to help me.* I said that whilst taking a British twenty pound note out of my wallet. His expression changed to a friendlier, more relaxed grin, and he said, "Dash me two more, and I will make sure you are fast-tracked and your passport stamped immediately."

I did as he asked, and my stress levels began to drop as I walked back towards the Land Cruiser, but suddenly the immigration chief came running up to me. He said that I was his brother now, and he asked for my phone number. I asked him why he wanted my phone number, and he explained that when I needed to pass into Nigeria in the future, he would meet me and get me fast-tracked every time!

Fine, I thought, *it will cost me, but at least I'll have easier crossings in the future.* I gave him my number and he also gave me his before I got back into my Land Cruiser to wait for my driver to return with my stamped passport. Minutes later, my driver returned with my passport together with an immigration form to enter back into Benin.

I completed the form, and we drove off just a few meters and parked again at the Benin border post, and off my driver went to the Benin immigration counter, which was just thirty meters from the Nigerian immigration counter. Like the Nigerian border, my driver took my passport and completed form to the desk while I waited in the car for safety reasons.

A couple of minutes later, he returned and said that the immigration officer wanted to see me. *Oh not again!* I thought. I asked what the hell the problem was this time, and I found out that the officer wanted to see my yellow fever card, which I knew was not required for Benin. All the trouble started yet again.

After dashing more money, I had my passport stamped and continued back to my Land Cruiser. On the way back to my car, I was accompanied by a very angry (acting) idiot who tried to tell me he was the chief immigration officer. He demanded to see my yellow fever card in order to let me enter Benin.

I already had a Benin stamp and was already on Benin turf (dust), so I told him to procreate off.

The rest of the drive was relatively normal – just a few accidents and a couple of dead bodies in the road, which was quite normal for that area. It was always such a relief to finally get across the two borders, probably the worst twenty meters I've ever travelled in my life. The downside was that I had to go through that very same process every four weeks.

The good part was getting to the hotel bar in Benin just in time for happy hour.

There, I met a colleague by the name of Tim. He was our company site representative in Benin, who found my border experiences highly amusing. I hate Tim!

The next day was Sunday, and Tim had planned for us to leave the office a little earlier to show me "The Point of No Return." It was the very first place where slaves left Africa over three hundred years before, and it was appropriately named because the Africans would never see their home land again.

We drove for about half an hour down a very long, sandy road with weird-looking voodoo statues alongside the road every twenty meters. When we got to the beach, I saw the large arch built in memory of all the Africans who had left from that very same place. I couldn't help thinking that the slaves had walked all the way along the same sandy track wearing ankle shackles that would have been cutting deep into there ankles.

Voodoo statues protected each side of the arch, and they were decorated with images of snakes and lizards and other creatures. The place did have an ambiance about it which didn't feel too comfortable.

There were still the remains of the buildings where the slaves were documented before boarding the ships, which would take them away permanently. The buildings were being swallowed up by the sand over the years, but still poking up on the sandy beach.

Further down the road, we saw a voodoo temple, which I didn't want to get to close to after my past experiences in Venezuela.

As we continued driving along the sandy beach road, we passed many people going about their daily routines until we passed by their beachside tribal village that lived off the ocean.

Because there were no stones, bricks, mud or straw for miles, all their little houses were built entirely of woven palm leaves.

The tribes used to take out huge fishing nets using a flotilla of small wooden boats, leave the nets overnight, and work together to pull the nets back to the beach by hand the next morning. There could be a group of up to fifty to sixty men and women pulling one end of the net and another group pulling the other end. They sang all the while to a rhythm so they'd all pull at the same time. Sometimes there was excitement when they'd find a shark trapped in their nets.

Further along the sandy road, we turned left into a narrow, sandy track in the middle of nowhere. I asked Tim where we were going, but all he said was, *"You're not going to believe this."*

After a short drive down the track, we came to a rough sort of car park in the sand where a few other 4x4s had parked. I still couldn't see anything though. Tim took me down yet another little path by foot while we watched out for snakes until we came across a jetty at the beginning of a mangrove swamp. We were constantly on the lookout for snakes the whole time. That was why I chose to follow Tim!

A small wooden boat appeared through an archway in the mangroves, pulled up to the rickety pier, and allowed us to jump in. It took about ten minutes to go through the mangroves, and we often needed to duck down when the branches were too low. Eventually, it opened out into a huge, inland lake which no roads led to.

We went across the lake and found a very secluded bar and restaurant owned by a retired French graphic artist. With good food, cold beer, and a good choice of French wines, we decided to call it a day.

The next day I continued to drive on towards the Togo border and saw a terrible accident in the road. A lorry had driven over a small motorcycle with two people riding it. There wasn't much left of them in the tangled wreckage and many people had gathered around causing a blockage for all the traffic. We eventually passed by and it wasn't a nice feeling, but after seeing such events so many times in that part of Africa, it made you build up a slight emotional resistance. I arrived in the hotel in Togo and went directly to my room. I had no idea at that time that there was a cholera epidemic going on and that seventysix people had already died that week.

My body had built up quite a high resistance to the usual hygiene problems in that part of the world so I had become complacent and didn't take the usual precautions like use bottled water to brush my teeth. I was soon to regret that simple little precaution. The next morning I continued to drive for the last few hundred miles to Accra in Ghana. During my journey I began to feel sick. I had stomach pains and just put it down to the food I'd eaten the night before. Later, my guts began to ache and then my muscles. By the time I arrived back in Accra my whole body was feeling affected. I met the contractor's new quality manager that I'd travelled hundreds of miles to be introduced to, and went back to my room.

I decided not to eat anything when I arrived at my accommodation, but instead went straight to my room with a few bottles of mineral water. I needed to return back to Togo the next day and Benin the day after to carry out an internal audit! Actually it was totally ridiculous being called back to Accra just to shake a new contractor's hand and then need to travel hundreds of miles back to where I had just left. It just showed the pathetic mentality of my so-called British colleagues who were both too damned lazy to get off their own asses and also afraid to do such journeys themselves.

My condition deteriorated rapidly during the evening and each time I drank water, I had to rush to the bathroom where it would come back up. I became more and more dehydrated and drank more and more water, each time resulting in the same way. Eventually, every single muscle in my body ached. It became almost intolerable, but I knew I needed to travel again the next morning. After a sleepless night, I packed fresh cloths and started my way back to the Togo border.

It took almost a whole day to reach the Togo border and the last eighty miles were spent on a badly corrugated dirt track in the middle of nowhere shaking you to pieces. Once I'd left Accra I asked my driver to look out for a pharmacy, as I desperately needed medication. He asked me if I was sick to which I replied yes. He became concerned and explained to me that there was a cholera epidemic in Togo which we had only left the day before. Actually, with every single muscle in my body screaming at me in pain, it didn't take much to self diagnose what I had contracted brushing my teeth with tap water!

I was feeling terrible and deteriorating by the minute as we drove down a road with nothing at either side of it. To my amazement, after twenty minutes my driver pulled over to a small wooden shack, which was set back from the main road and stopped outside it in the dust. He lifted his right arm and pointed to the tiny little shack and said that's a pharmacy. The shack didn't even have a sign outside it, but I was getting desperate and hurriedly got out of the Land Cruiser and quickly made my way to it.

Working in remote countries you learnt the basics of self preservation so I asked if the pharmacy had an antibiotic called 'Flagyl', as I was previously prescribed it for something I had picked up in Iran. 'Metronidazole' is used to treat a variety of problems. It belongs to a group of antibiotics known as nitroimidazoles, which works by killing the growth of bacteria and protozoa. Surprisingly and very thankfully the pharmacist stocked it! I also bought all the rehydration power sachets they stocked and a few more bottles of mineral water.

I was in a really bad shape by this time so I swallowed three Flagyl tablets in one go, together with drinking mineral water with four rehydration sachets mixed into each bottle. I continued to drink the mineral water heavily mixed with rehydration powder and took another Flagyl tablet every three hours. After only three to four hours I began to feel a little more stable and slightly better.

I eventually passed through the border into Togo and arrived at the hotel an hour later, still very weak and went directly to bed. I continued taking the Flagyl all through the night, but still felt awful the next morning. It took five full days before I returned back to normal and wondered what would have happened to me if it weren't for the little wooden shack of a pharmacy? I have since regretted not having the opportunity to return to the little pharmacy and explain to them how grateful I was to them.

I conducted my audit the following day in Benin, in its capital 'Cotonou', stayed the night and again returned back to Accra with a one-night stopover back in Togo in the usual hotel in 'Lomé' which is its capital city. The hotel in Lomé had a nightclub in its basement down a huge marble spiral staircase and the doorman was a great friend of mine. He spoke perfect English and would accompany me to the bar and keep the local ladies away from me so I could simply relax and chat with him. He arranged for video CD's to be made by the DJ and presented them to me as a gift. They was music videos of the local tribal music which I really liked until they were stolen among other possessions later in the Caribbean. I still maintain email contact with him to this day.

I needed to make another trip back to Nigeria on 26 October of 2008. I was tired of the border crossings, though, so I decided to fly into Lagos from Ghana. On arrival in Lagos airport in front of the immigration desk, I saw a Nigerian official who was pre-checking visas before allowing travellers to proceed to the immigration desks.

He was a very big man, and he towered over me. He said he needed to see my passport. I handed it to him, and he began flicking through its pages, looking for a valid visa. He finally came to my visa, which had been issued in Ghana and was good for a number of entries. Strangely, it was unconditionally rejected. *Here we go again,* I thought.

He told me that my visa had to be issued from my country of origin, not from Ghana. Actually, he was perfectly correct as I later discovered.

I asked why the Nigerian embassy in Accra had issued the visa if it wasn't any good. I also explained that it worked on several previous visits, which he could clearly see by the stamps but my words fell on deaf ears. I knew exactly what he wanted, but I was not in the right frame of mind to dash him as his mannerism was too abusive for my liking.

After being made to wait there for one and a half hours, I was escorted back through the departure immigration area to be deported. I was then held in police custody in their office for another four hours before being deported back to Ghana.

There wasn't any air conditioning in the police office, and after a short time, I was completely drenched due to the high humidity. When I asked for a drink of water, I was refused and told it was not a cafe.

I was seriously dehydrated by the end (and in quite a bad state), but I was eventually escorted by a different immigration officer to the departure gate of Virgin Nigeria. All the seats across from the window were occupied, so I had to sit against the glass windows with the sun beating down on my back through the glass for around another hour.

Finally, I was able to board the flight. The flight attendant noticed the state I was in and gave me four bottles of mineral water, which I downed in record time. I'd also asked her for a lot of salt and sugar which I poured into the bottles to help with my rehydration.

My company contacts were tracking my progress from the moment that I was denied entry, and they were quite relieved to hear I'd landed back in Accra, Ghana. They booked me into the African Regent Hotel so I'd have a little luxury to recover from my ordeal.

The following day, I returned to our head office and told everyone what had happened. I mentioned that I needed another visa – and that it had to be issued from London as the United Kingdom was my point of origin.

Preparations were made, *together with my agent back in Liverpool*, and my passport was sent to me via courier. After a few weeks passed, my shiny, new, London-issued visa was safely in my hands for any future visits to Nigeria.

Feeling quite confident on 15 February 2009, I drove up to the Nigerian border immigration zone from the Benin border, armed with my new visa.

As a further precaution, I carried my yellow fever vaccination card to reduce the reasons they might name for not allowing me into the country. I thought *what can they possibly do to me now?*

All was fine when I reached the Nigerian border crossing. I waited in the safety of my car as usual, out of sight of the Nigerian immigration officers whilst my driver took my passport to the Nigerian immigration desks for processing.

After a few minutes, he returned and said the immigration officers wanted to see my "yellow card," as they called it. Feeling rather pleased that I had remembered to bring it, I handed the card to my driver. I figured that would be the end of my troubles – wrong!

My driver returned to the car after just a couple of minutes telling me that they wanted to see me. I knew the fun was about to start all over again.

I approached the desk, shook the immigration officer's hand, and asked whether there was a problem. He explained that there was a big problem, and that he couldn't process my passport because my yellow card didn't say *yellow fever.* I found where the words were written, and I showed them to him. I explained that my card was issued in the United Kingdom by a competent tropical clinic.

Not to be outdone by solid facts, the immigration officer asked me for my meningitis card. I told him that no such card existed, that such information was simply recorded on a normal vaccination card with other inoculations.

He wanted to see the card on which my meningitis data was recorded, but that was back in the United Kingdom with my other records (such as hepatitis A and B, cholera, typhoid, tetanus, and polio). I called the immigration chief who had given me his number before to ask where the hell he was? He told me he was home in his village four hours away and therefore couldn't get to me.

Here we go again, I thought. It was dash time all over again.

Carrying all those cards would have been a total waste of time in any case because it would just prolong the agony and force me to listen to excuse after excuse before I resorted to dashing them.

The only amusing part of the whole fiasco was winding them up to see just how far their excuses and imagination could stretch. Those guys had the patience and the power ... and all day to abuse it.

My new brother of an immigration chief was useless, he didn't want to deny his fellow brothers from making a score in his absents.

After I proceeded to dash, I returned to the safety of the car before saying something that I might later regret. The car was locked, so I had to wait outside in the direct sunshine. I was surrounded by bogus salesmen that resembled the old Robinson's Jam labels which British will understand. They all wanted to sell me fake watches and used clothing – or beg me for money and cigarettes.

Five minutes later, I was called back to fill in immigration forms, which the driver normally did. Later, I was again called back so the officer who was sitting in a wooden kiosk could compare my face to the one on my passport.

Eventually, my driver returned with my passport, so we buckled up and started rolling towards the borderline. *I'm sure to proceed to my destination now,* I thought. Wrong again!

Another Nigerian police officer stood right in front of my car and held an AK-47 directly towards my head to stop us. An official asked my driver to get out of the vehicle so he could show him my passport, which he promptly did. As soon as the official looked at my passport, he approached my window and signalled for me to roll the window down. He introduced himself as a Nigerian Drug Enforcement Agency officer.

I'd just about had enough yet again, so I asked to see some ID. He produced his DEA card, which looked official enough, so I asked what he wanted. He ordered us to put the car in reverse, park up and bring my entire luggage to his shabby, wooden desk so he could search through everything.

Everything he saw he liked, and he asked whether it was his present. I replied no, so he continued going through everything until there was nothing left to search. Surrounded by local onlookers I had to cover my back pocket where my wallet was, plus keep an eye on everything in my small case.

He particularly fancied my shiny, new UK mobile phone, which I had just replaced after the previous one was stolen two weeks before (along with my laptop, wallet, and a lot of hard cash), from the guesthouse I stayed in Accra.

I was also carrying a couple of dozen large Cuban cigars, which he was sure were a present for him. Luckily, I managed to hold on to those, too.

Finally, after repacking my things, we proceeded to cross the borderline and then another Nigerian appeared. She was a rather arrogant police officer who demanded to see all the papers for the car before we went another yard.

Fortunately, all the papers were in order, so we were finally permitted to cross the border. My armed escort had been patiently waiting for two hours to escort me through the seventeen police roadblocks so I could reach my destination.

The problems I encountered are everyday occurrences for westerners trying to cross the notorious Benin/Nigerian border. My British colleagues in the head office in Ghana refused to go that way because it was becoming way too dangerous.

They had formed quite a corrupt little click and as I was the new guy, I had to go where they were *too afraid* to go, plus they were quite comfortable sitting on their butts in the head office waiting for their 'brown envelops' which I wouldn't and didn't fit into!

I do think, however, that I may have brought the wrath of the DEA upon myself by wearing a particular T-shirt. I bought the shirt in Amsterdam a few days before, and it had a large marijuana leaf on the front. The text of the T-shirt read as follows: "Don't Panic, I'm Organic." I told the officer, "Honestly, I only bought it because the colours went well with my jeans."

But one thing is for sure, I have much more respect for the Nigerians who liked to put the knife in my front for money to subsidise the pathetic salaries than so many of my former well paid expatriate colleagues who preferred to stab me in my back for free as I don't accept bribes as they like to do. If they read my story, they'll know exactly who and what they are.

I left the project in West Africa in March of 2009, basically as I didn't fit in with the corrupt click and stupidly
decided to return to a certain Caribbean island to visit some
friends I'd met there years ago when I worked in Venezuela.

CHAPTER 21

Caribbean

My intention was to visit the island in the Caribbean for three weeks and then fly to the island of Cebu in the Philippines and look for an apartment to buy there.

Because I was on a sort of holiday, I had a great time and went deep-sea fishing twice a week. On my first fishing trip, I caught a ten-foot blue shark. It was quite a fight which lasted over three hours. During the fight, a huge container ship was heading directly for us as we were reversing our boat to regain some line that the shark had practically stripped off the reel. It was my first sunshine for a long time so I kept myself covered up while fighting the shark.

The ship was contacted by radio and asked to divert its course because we had a big fish on the line. To my amazement, the ship did exactly that. It was also the first time I'd gone deep-sea fishing for a few years, so by the time I got the shark to the boat, every one of my fingers had a large

blister ready to burst. The shark was spinning like a crocodile on the side of the boat while the deckhand grabbed a
gaff to drag it on-board. The boat was far too small to take
the shark, however, so I instructed the deckhand to cut the
line and let it go.

Seeing the Island through the eyes of a tourist, I enjoyed
the place and moved my return flight back another month.
British tourists were only permitted to say on the island
for a maximum of thirty days, so I had to do a visa run. I
decided to stay on an island called Curaçao for the weekend,
and my hotel receptionist joined me for a break.

Because I was having a nice time and making new friends
– or so I thought – I changed my mind about buying an
apartment in Cebu and started to look at condos on the
island I was on.

My original plan was to buy a condo with some security guards, so I could just lock the door and fly off overseas to work. I was deterred when I found out I had to pay a maintenance fee of over five hundred dollars every month, which I thought to be ridiculously high.

In the meantime, another thirty days was about to be used up so I needed to make yet another visa run. I chose Havana, Cuba or Habana as it is spelt in Spanish this time. There were no direct flights to Cuba from the island so I needed to change flights in Panama. Panama airport was quite impressive but I only had two hours there before boarding my Cuban flight.

At that time, bird flu was an international concern so waiting at the airport in Havana was a line of doctors waiting to question everyone entering the country prior to being allowed to proceed to the immigration authorities. After passing through immigration was the drug sniffing dogs and then the wait at the carousel for my little case. Drug sniffing dogs were also paraded all around the hall and even over the baggage as it went along the carousel, all very impressive. I was only planning to stay in Havana for four nights, but regretted not booking the hotel for a full week.

Upon arrival at my prepaid hotel, I was made to pay the full amount again. The hotel manager was called and presented with the receipt, which included a *paid in full* stamp. That didn't make any difference as the hotel manager claimed they hadn't received anything so I went to the ATM and withdrew the cash and paid them. I thought I'd reclaim my booking costs when I returned back to the island I was on.

I loved it in Havana and went everywhere as a regular tourist. Of course, my first places to visit were the cigar factories of Cohiba, Partagas and Monte Cristo (my favourite three brands.) They were all just walking distance from each other and I hired a Cuban guide to show me around for the four day visit.

I had met her at a salsa club on my very first night. She spoke perfect English and took me to places a normal tourist would never find. Due to the communist rules existing in Cuba, she really wasn't allowed to be with me; so many times she had to avoid being noticed by the police as we went from venue to venue. It wasn't possible to mention Fidel Castro's name anywhere. I once made that mistake at the hotel pool's bar and the manager immediately closed it for the day!

One of the places I desperately wanted to visit was a bar called "La Bodeguita del Medio." It had been Ernest Hemingway's local bar while he stayed in Cuba. When I entered, I could see a wall full of his 'scribbles', which had been preserved behind glass picture frames. La Bodeguita del Medio was also the bar, which was famous for inventing the mojito cocktail, or so it was believed. The mojito was a particularly refreshing drink in the heat of the Caribbean. It consisted of sugar, lime, mint leaves, rum and soda.

The Mojito's exact history is still arguable to this day. It did originate in Cuba and is one of the most popular cocktails like the Cuba libre (libre meaning free). Some historian's believe it was invented in the fifteenth century when Sir Francis Drake landed on the Island, to get everyone drunk to steal the city's gold. An associate of Sir Francis

Drake, named Richard Drake, had tried to make a version of the mojito called " El Draque" out of an early form of rum, which didn't really make it into popularity. Some people believe African slaves working in the sugar cane plantations invented it. Mojito is believed to come from the African word Mojo that means to place a spell on someone. Wherever it came from, it's delicious in any case.

One day I went for lunch with my guide and listened to a live group playing and singing in the background. They were so talented I sent them a round of drinks in appreciation. In return they all came over to my table and presented me a gift of their music CD, which they normally sold. They had taken the trouble to sign its cover, which made it an extra special gift, but was sadly stolen from my island house later. I loved Havana and the people living there, but my four nights went like a flash and before I knew it, I was sadly back on the island.

I was advised to buy a house, which I eventually did. But that turned out to be an even bigger mistake. On the island, there were two types of property: lease hold and property land. With property land, you fully own the land, and there is no planning permission as such, required for building, altering, or extending the property. That seemed like the best option.

A Colombian girl, Lisa, who I'd met in a bar where she worked, offered to help me find a house, as I didn't know any of the areas on the island. Lisa was great company and also the lead dancer for the island dance group.

The real estate company was owned and run by a Dutch man and his Colombian wife. His wife drove Lisa and I around a few properties until I saw a house that interested me. With just a three-minute walk to the shore, I thought it would be a good choice. Wrong!

I chose to live away from the main tourist area because prices were too high in that region. Plus, I wanted to get away from all the noise and bar culture. After viewing several more properties, I decided to buy the three-bedroom house on property land, which was about a thirty-five minute drive from the tourist area down the southern end of the island towards Venezuela.

Once a deal had been agreed upon, I negotiated with the owners to include the entire house contents as it stood to make the place liveable until I was able to buy things that better suited my taste.

The Colombian woman from the real estate company was supposed to return later the same day to take photos of the contents of each room so that all the main items would be left there as agreed.

She didn't return to take photos for five days, so it gave the Colombian wife plenty of time to remove most of the furnishings before any photos could be taken. The Colombian wife was going through a divorce as her Island husband was in jail for being a paedophile.

As my luck would have it, I needed to return to the United Kingdom for a month, so I had a Dutch waitress (who was recommended to me) to house-sit while I was away. She was also going to continue living in my house when I returned to work overseas, and she told me she'd take care of things whilst I was away.

After transferring funds to the local notary, I was told it would take around five or six weeks to complete all formalities and receive the keys.

The first thing I noticed when I eventually received the photos of inside the house was that there weren't any photos of the bedrooms. When I asked why, I was told that the rooms had all been emptied, so there was nothing to take photos of.

I didn't make too much of a fuss because even though I'd paid for the beds and other contents, I would have replaced the beds at the earliest opportunity in any case. I later discovered that the washing machine had also been taken, along with the stereo system and all the contents of the kitchen. The owner's excuse was that those items didn't belong to them – but they didn't mention that when I bought everything. So typical of the people on the island.

I gave the house sitter money to buy new beds and a few other things so I would at least have a bed to sleep on when I returned.

The Colombian real estate company informed me that their surveyor had been to the house and found everything to be fine. They told me that the house had even been rewired. I later found out that it had not been rewired and still had the original, eighty-year-old wiring throughout.

The purchase took ten weeks to complete, so I waited in the United Kingdom to avoid the expense of staying in a hotel room for the final few weeks. When I returned to the island as the new owner, the horror story really began.

In addition to the money I left with the waitress to buy a bed, I supplied more money for her to continue buying bedding, kitchen utensils, and other necessary items. I also provided the funds to pay for the electricity, water, gas, and cable TV.

After just the first two days of living in my house, the waitress started to make me feel terribly unwelcome, which created a really bad atmosphere. She shouted her objections to my plans to build a fourth bedroom with en suite at the back of my house. She also rejected my idea to add an additional air conditioner to cool the kitchen … as well as many other plans to improve the place.

She was taking over as the owner of the house, and she started dictating what she wanted. One such demand was a twenty-foot container from Holland, which would be permanently parked on my back patio.

She told me I had to help her by paying for its shipping, and that she would pay me back later. I knew what that meant – as until then, I had never met an honest person on the island – so I denied her request. We went shopping for all the new things, and each time she took me to a shop, she spoke only Dutch. Without me realising, she had every receipt made out in her name when I handed over my money.

Even the food I bought from supermarkets was considered "food for the house" in her eyes, and she began helping herself. She took whatever she wanted down to the beach and shared with her friends. That was the typical culture on the island: whatever you have is automatically taken as if it were there for the entire island, just like my time in Venezuela!

I also had to buy a couple of split air conditioners because the ones I had bought with the house were broken. They hadn't been used for years, but the previous owners kept that quiet, too, like many other things that I later discovered. The surveyor and real estate agent failed to check those issues and so many others when I was in the United Kingdom.

After having the girl in my house for a week – and being tired of how she was speaking to me – I had had enough. One morning, she started shouting at me because a couple of my friends had visited me the night before. She told me she would not stand for people visiting the house, so I reminded her of who owned the place and kicked her out.

That night, she went back to my house with some of her friends and emptied the place of everything I had bought (including things that came with the house).

The next day, a friend picked me up, and we went to the electrical and water companies to transfer the bills into my name. I didn't want the waitress cutting me off.

The gas company was closed by the time I got there, so the waitress who had already visited was able to cancel the contract and get the deposit back for the bottles which my money had paid for. She also went to my house insurance company and tried to cancel my house insurance and get the money from that too! Fortunately, they refused to comply with her.

When she moved out of my house, she stole all the warranties for the new air conditioners and other appliances.

The majority of people I had so far met living on the island are among the most vindictive I've ever met, regardless of where they'd come from.

She also stole the original deeds to my house. It took a threat to bring the police to the Spanish Tapas restaurant where she worked for her to return them.

Yes, they smile and joke with the tourists to increase their tips (which they have to live off), but if they ever had the chance to rip you off, believe me they would.

A few weeks later, I signed contracts to work in Kazakhstan. I was worried about the house being left empty because crime was escalating dramatically on the island. Out of pure desperation as time was short, I agreed to rent the two spare bedrooms to two young girls, one from Surinam and the other from the Dominican Republic.

They had lived on the island for several years. Not to be ripped off yet again, I had the same real estate agent (idiot), write up a formal rental contract that allowed the girls to rent their rooms for just five hundred dollars per month.

I knew it was a mistake but I just wanted someone living there to prevent thieves from breaking in whilst I was away. Due to the short notice, I gave the real estate agent the five hundred dollar deposit on behalf of the girls. I was thinking I would eventually get it back. Wrong.

Anyway, the girls moved in that weekend. I explained that my only rule was that no men were allowed in the house. Naturally, they helped themselves to everything in my fridge, freezer, and cupboards. They also started bringing a baby to the house once per week, and that baby thrived on my cans of soups, desserts and ice creams.

I found myself shopping every two or three days to restock instead of once per week. I complained, but I was totally ignored. Once, the pizza delivery guy delivered a large pizza for me and my girlfriend.

I went out, paid for the pizza, put it on the table, and went to wake up my girlfriend. When I returned, I found both girls with half a pizza each, watching TV as if nothing were wrong. They said, "We're hungry. You can order another."

I was flying to Kazakhstan soon, so I didn't let it bother me too much – I'd be gone, and they'd have to shop for themselves. I made the girls sign the rental contract and took off.

CHAPTER 22

Kazakhstan

In September of 2009, I flew to Kazakhstan to start working with Chris again as he'd made sure I had the contract as his senior quality assurance engineer. I hadn't seen Chris since working with him in Nigeria several years before. I still had outstanding issues on the island, however … and a few more horrifying surprises in store for me on a scale I could never have imagined.

The Colombian real estate agent never bothered to collect the signed contract, nor did she bother to collect the monthly rent or ensure that utilities were being paid. Actually, the real estate agent never visited my house at all. Because she already had the deposit (which was equal to the annual commission), she didn't bother.

As a backup plan, I paid a marine to be my house caretaker. He was paid to go to my house every week to ensure everything was okay. The very weekend I flew out, the two girls had a big party. My house was still full of guys sleeping on my sofa and chairs the next morning when my caretaker walked in. The girls had invited all their friends to drink everything I had built up in my bar!

He threw all the guys out and gave the girls a strong warning, but people on that island don't care about warnings. They live for the day just like the majority of Latin Americans did. I also had a lady drive past my house every morning (on her way home from working at a hotel all night). She sent me emails indicating that there was a different car in my drive every morning.

The girls never paid any rent – or any of the utilities – and they were eventually kicked out. My electric bill was incredible because they had every air conditioner on twentyfour hours per day. All my food and cleaning liquids were taken as well – I suppose they stole them for their families.

My bar had been totally emptied by all the guys, and they even managed to break the toilet (but they continued to use it without any water).

The Colombian real estate agent refused to return my deposit because she said it was the first month's rent, which had never been collected in any case. I lost out again.

A few months after arriving in Kazakhstan, I had all my belongings shipped to the island from the United Kingdom. The United Kingdom removal company was totally professional. Everything went fine until my box arrived on the island.

The pre-paid island removal company wouldn't go to the port to collect my box and deliver it. They just gave excuse after excuse until, after seven weeks; they drove ten minutes to do what they were paid to do.

Because I had Colombian builders in my house renovating it, it wasn't difficult to get my box inside.

The builders began tiling the entire house. All was going well until they broke through the bathroom floor tiles and were greeted by millions of cockroaches. They escaped from under the tiles and ran up the bathroom walls and across the ceiling. Lisa was there supervising for me at the time and had to run out of the house. Lisa would visit to take photos and later email to me so I could see the progress.

They were living under the house because all the waste water pipes had totally corroded. No wastewater was getting to the septic tank alongside the house. The surveyor had failed to find that problem; he didn't even wonder why the septic tank hadn't needed to be emptied for several years. The wastewater had eaten deep into the walls, so those had to be completely removed and rebuilt.

While all this was going on, a Colombian electrician (who had already rewired my house and been paid in full for doing so) wormed his way back into my house to rewire it again for another fee. As I was off the island, he had told my caretaker that I had asked him to return!

The first time, he had just fitted a breaker box and pretended to rewire the house. The second time, he lied to my caretaker and said it was the second part that he'd come to finish. Therefore, he got paid two times for doing the same job. Both times I was ripped off for four thousand dollars!

At the time, three quarters of my house was still without electricity because he wouldn't finish the job unless he got paid more money. I had to pay him or risk returning to a house without electricity.

Another thing the islanders liked to do was visit. When they visited, just like when I lived in Puerto Ordaz, they came empty-handed by taxi. After they arrived, they told me I had to pay the taxi for them. Later, once they had consumed every beer in my fridge, they left – but I still had to pay the taxi. In the beginning, I needed to put up with a lot just to get to know people and find my way around the island.

Once I was in a position to stop all that, I was totally ignored by the islanders ... unless I invited them for freebies, which they'd never refused.

In the bars, they adopted the Latin American culture and get familiar with tourists and invite them to other bars. If the tourist agreed to going, they'd telephone and bring more of their friends, and the tourist would need to foot the entire bill, which could reach a thousand dollars! The islanders never had any money on them, or so they claimed. They'd order take away food and drinks to supply their entire families and have it added to the bill!

When I first got there, I needed to be driven around because I had no idea where to go for things. Each time, I was forced to fill their petrol tanks, tip the pump attendant ten dollars, and feed them before getting dropped off at home.

I knew I was being financially milked, but I didn't have much of a choice at that time, and it was the island way!

It would have been a lot cheaper to fly in a builder from the United Kingdom or the States. That way, I wouldn't have had to deal with the locals. Plus, I'd have the reassurance that the work was done right and at the correct price.

I strongly advise people to forget about buying a house in that area unless they are going to be there the whole time to supervise any work being done.

If someone really wants a place there, they should go for a new place with twenty-four-hour security and keep well away from locals so they won't get drawn in and ripped off as I was.

The island in that part of the Caribbean is a wonderful holiday destination, but it has nothing else going for it. In short, the locals are not what they seem. As for me, I'll sell the house and find another overseas destination – but with different nationalities and mentalities than those found on that island just off the coast of Venezuela and its terribly corrupt magistrates. I have not mentioned the islands name not to discourage tourists who would have a nice time. Sadly, vacations are all it is good for, and nothing else.

My worst fears were confirmed when I got back to the island on the 31 January 2010. It was clear that I'd been ripped off by the caretaker. I paid ninety thousand dollars for a levelled and tiled floor, new kitchen, and new bathroom.

There were many other jobs that needed to be done, but I wasn't willing to foot the bill. With fully tiled kitchen walls and fitted units (including mirrors under wall units), they'd only fitted one visible electrical socket in the entire kitchen. Totally brainless in my eyes.

All double vanity taps and shower taps in the bathroom plumbed into the single cold water supply, as there was no hot water boiler fitted. There were "stay-bright" brass door handles fitted with plain carbon steel hinges on all the doors.

They had even installed a new inside-type bedroom door for the back door (with matching bedroom door handles).

Visitors thought I had another bedroom from the inside. The Colombian builders blamed the caretaker, and he blamed the Colombians ... but someone had bought the fittings.

The first time using the shower was another surprise: the water quickly filled the drain pipe and flooded out of the bathroom and out the back of the house. The new wastewater drainpipe didn't lead to the outside septic tank. Instead, it was buried under concrete.

The Colombian electrician robbed me of everything I'd bought, including clothes, shoes, Mont Blanc pens, DVDs, Ray Bans, tools, and even my bedroom door keys. He'd also stolen 5,200 dollars of holiday cash.

It was a nice start to the carnival month. Not even the island police could help because the Colombian Electrician had somehow heard they were on their way to visit his place and moved all my things he'd stolen out.

They found a few trivial things, such as my baseball hats, but they said that wasn't enough to arrest him. He flew to Colombia the next day, before my local mafia friends could do the vigilante thing to him.

The carnival festivities were in full swing, and they were leading up to the carnival's grand parade on the 14th of February. I had waited a long time to see it, so I was excited. *This time,* I thought, *nothing will go wrong.* Not!

I'd stuck it out in Kazakhstan for five long months to ensure I would see my first carnival, which would surely be worth the wait. I followed my caretaker's instructions regarding the grand parade day. I stayed in my house, ready to be collected in the morning (before all the roads were closed off around the island's capital).

Anyway, after taking it easy by staying home for four nights and declining the Friday night/Saturday morning pyjama parade (to ensure I wouldn't be tired for the grand parade), I was wide awake and rested for the big day.

I got up early that Sunday morning. My camera was fully charged, and I ate a good breakfast to soak up the day's beer intake. I was ready to be collected, as promised by my caretaker. *What could possibly go wrong?* I thought.

After waiting a couple of hours to be picked up – and called my caretaker several times to ask when he was coming – I dozed off on the sofa. I woke up a couple of hours later and quickly called all the local taxi companies, but they all told me the same thing: "You've left it too late." All the roads were already blocked off for the grand parade, and there was not any chance of getting anywhere near the carnival unless I was prepared to walk for hours.

Therefore, I spent the entire carnival grand parade day home alone with no food or drinks. I just kept imagining all that I was missing. With nothing else to do, I decided to walk to the nearest Chinese supermarket, which was a twenty-five-minute walk away. In the heat, however, it felt like hours. Of course, nobody thought to warn me that all the shops would be closed until Tuesday. *Even more good news,* I thought, *I can lose even more weight than I've already lost due to the renovation problems and robbery.* The island did have its advantages, I supposed.

By Monday I was starving, but nobody was picking up their mobiles because they were asleep the entire day after partying until five or six o'clock in the morning. Eventually, a friend, Marina, called me to ask how I was doing.

She spoke the usual: Spanish, Dutch, English, and Papiamento. She was horrified that I had spent the day alone at home with nothing to eat, and she immediately rushed over with some traditional island home cooking.

Marina was always the first to come to my aid and solve any problem I encountered on the island – but not without making a profit.

Marina worked permanent nights at the reception of a beach resort hotel that was just a three-minute walk from the beach and close to all the most popular bars and restaurants.

Later that day, Lisa woke up from the carnival asking where the hell I was Sunday. She was angry that I hadn't been at the roadside to take photos of her leading the grand parade.

When I told her that my caretaker hadn't picked me up as promised, she went crazy. Lisa is a professional Latin dancer, and as I've mentioned, dances for an island dance group. They entertain tourists by performing on stage at hotels, and were very popular.

The Friday before the carnival, we had spent all day shopping for materials (such as ostrich feathers for her blue and silver costume). She wanted me to take a lot of photos of her while she and her dance group were leading the entire grand parade. Because her group was the first along the road, my job would have been very easy … if I had made it there.

I spent the following two weeks winding down from all the bad news and horror I had discovered when I first arrived on the island. I deliberately kept myself away from all the people who had ripped me off and let me down. I stopped all building work; and just took things easy.

Marina continued to help me as always, and she even drove me around so I would be spared the heavy taxi fares. Plus, she kept me company whenever she could. Lisa also visited me whenever she could, so it wasn't too bad in the end.

During this period of time, I met some locals at a bar near my house. It was nice to be far away from the tourist area.

They were horrified to hear how much trouble I'd had with my house just up the road and what my house renovations had cost me. They told me what they had paid using local, professional, and (above all) honest island builders. One taxi driver explained that he had an excellent island builder build his 2,000 square foot house for the same cost as my renovations!

It really does come down to who you know. The more desperate people are for work, the more convincing they seem to be that they're the best choice. Anyway, it seemed that, from that point forward, things would be easier – and certainly a lot cheaper.

In June of 2010, my mother visited the island for the first time, and it was my first incident-free visit. Having a better imagination than I had, she explained what she'd do to my house if it were hers. So the next three months of my life were filled with local builders.

I arranged to have a very high wall built across the back of my place, mainly for security reasons. I wanted vented blocks to allow the breeze to come through. In the front, I requested a mix of walls and fancy railings with a rolling gate.

Work had just started when I left the island to return to Kazakhstan, so I relied on photos being emailed to me so I could control the payments. During the construction, they called me to let me know that my house was being inhabited by Colombians.

Apparently, the new tenant had invited his friends over from Amsterdam for free holidays, and his Colombian wife had done the same thing with her family. My friend told me there were people sleeping outside on my swing, on my sofas, and even on the floor.

I got them out after giving them thirty days notice as per the rental agreement, which I respected and they kindly left the place in a disgusting condition. Plus, they failed to pay all the utility bills and stole everything they could carry.

The solution was clear: I invited two local people out of pure desperation – I will call them *Haitian* and *Ronnie* – to live in my place rent free. All they had to do was pay the utilities. This proved to be the biggest mistake of my life, and almost cost me my life!

Haitian was from Haiti, and she had lived on the island for twentyfive years. Ronnie was an islander who had not completed his schooling.

I didn't know at the time that Haitian was a voodoo queen and practised voodoo all the time. People I had never met went to my house in my absence to pay her to carry out voodoo ceremonies there. I had no idea that was going on whilst in Kazakhstan.

During September of 2010, events occurred that changed my plans in a way I never imagined possible. On September 25th in Atyrau, Kazakhstan, the resident security guard knocked on my door at 6.50 p.m. to present his friend.

All his friend could say in English was, "Want lady." I told him no and closed my door on the both of them.

I continued to get ready to go to a wedding party that night, but ten minutes later, I heard a noise coming from my living room. I looked around my bedroom door and found the same young Kazakh man in my apartment with a young girl. I ordered them to leave immediately, but he was extremely persistent and wouldn't leave.

My camera was sitting on my kitchen table, as was some money, and my solid gold Rolex Yacht Master (which he kept looking at).

I could not turn my back on them and go to my apartment telephone to call reception because they would be able to help themselves to my things.

He insisted I keep the girl, and he still wouldn't leave. Finally, he agreed to leave after I took his name and phone number. Of course, the number was from a stolen mobile phone, as the police later told me.

After they had left, I finished getting ready and went to the wedding. After just two hours at the wedding party, I began to feel very sleepy for some reason, and I decided to leave much earlier than planned. I arrived at my apartment at around eleven o'clock at night.

I left my camera on my kitchen table, took off my Rolex, and left it at the side of my bed. I woke up early on the Sunday morning, and both my Rolex and Nikon pocket camera were missing.

I told the receptionist and called my company's security. My security was very quick off the mark and came to my apartment to view the security video footage from the closed circuit television cameras. Unfortunately, they had already removed the discs.

They arranged an identity line up with the Kazakh police so I could point out the guard who brought his friend to my apartment, but he wasn't among the men. Apparently, they'd already fired all fourteen guards who worked that Saturday night, so I couldn't identify the guilty guard either. It was a shame because some of the guards were quite nice people.

On Tuesday, along with a licensed translator and a security company representative, I went to the local police station. The building was in a terrible state – a leftover from Russian times.

The entire incident had been hidden from investigation, and I didn't have any chance of recovering my losses. Both the Kazakh police and my company's security did what they could, but the cover-up made it impossible to make any progress.

I was introduced to a lawyer who accompanied me and continued to represent me throughout the proceedings.

Her name was Antonina, and I had no idea at the time that she was about to turn my whole world upside down and inside out.

Antonina and I soon began living together. Because we had become involved with each other, Antonina explained to me that she could no longer represent me as my lawyer – it was not professional, and it wouldn't look very good in court.

Antonina recommended two male lawyers whom she'd known for many years. Evidently, they both had a well-proven track record. In the background of all the enquiries, Antonina was still leading the process, but the two new lawyers were representing me. Antonina had an unusual amount of power, but the alarm bells came too late. She had the local press and television cameras go to the apartment block to put on national television her initial inquiries.

Later, I discovered that the receptionist was also in on the robbery. She had entered a girl's name in the visitor's book at the reception by using correction fluid and covering someone else's name. Thus, it looked like I was at home the whole evening entertaining someone I'd never met.

The police assumed that the girl who I'd never met must have been the thief. Because I was at the wedding party all evening, it was easy to prove that it was also a part of the cover-up.

Because I was a European working in Kazakhstan, I didn't have the normal Kazakh police working on the case. Instead, I had an internal affairs police investigator, who was very keen to do all he could to help – especially for some extra earnings.

He came to the quick conclusion that because my residence had deliberately hidden the security camera footage, fired all guards who had worked the night of my robbery, and added a false visitor to the visitor's book, they were clearly covering up the whole incident and therefore responsible. I guess it didn't take a genius to work that out?

Under Kazakh law, my residence's administration had to compensate me for the full replacement value of both my watch and the camera. Antonina, together with the internal affairs police, organised a full criminal investigation.

Three more Kazakh police investigators came to my apartment to interview the deputy director of the company who owned the apartments and the administration manager. The presidents daughter was the main owner so they didn't want any bad publicity!

The actual director wasn't in Atyrau that day, so his deputy had to answer all the questions. Antonina questioned him with regard to the missing security camera footage, and he explained that the technician had accidentally switched off the cameras for the entire weekend. Supposedly, they only realised on Monday (after my things had been taken) that nothing had been recorded.

The police took the staffing logbook so they could find out which guards were on duty that night. After a few weeks, they were able to find the guard who had been fired in a distant village. They brought him to the police head-quarters in Atyrau and kept him detained until I was able to visit whilst he was questioned.

I'd never seen the guard before because he was always on duty at the rear of the building (at the entrance of the car park). Apparently, the reception guard needed to take his break, so he had someone stand in for him just as I was returning from the wedding party (somewhat drugged).

He noticed the gold watch when I walked past him to the elevator. I was with a friend from Uzbekistan who worked at a local hospital. She had accompanied me to the wedding party and just wanted to see me get home safely.

Actually, she left my apartment after just five minutes, but she decided not to return home. Instead, she hung around for a while for the drug she had slipped into my drink to take its full effect. She spent quite some time talking to the security guard regarding my watch, just long enough for me to be fast asleep. After that, she, together with the security guard returned to my apartment to take my watch and camera.

Once she and the guard had my things, she wasted no time leaving Atyrau and returned to a town called Aksai, which was near the southern Russian border. The police needed to interview her because she was the last person to be seen with me while I still had my watch. This delayed the investigation by a few weeks, though.

When she finally returned to Atyrau, the police invited her to their headquarters for questioning. For a while, she claimed she was innocent, but after several days, she admitted that she organised the robbery with the apartment security guard and receptionist.

The receptionist was also involved as she had entered the false visitor name in the guest book that evening and loaned them a master key so they could get in my apartment.

After the receptionist saw the police visit and revisit the building, she took ten days off. Later, she became sick and quit her job. She was not seen there again.

I was advised to leave my apartment and move to a hotel where I would be safer. I moved to a hotel just behind my office, so I was only at risk for the five minute walk to and from the office.

During that time, I had made the mistake of telling Antonina about Haitian and what she was doing in my house. That caused Antonina to want to speak to Haitian practically every night of the week, despite what it was costing me. Conversations lasted for a ridiculous length of time, and soon Antonina demanded that I give Haitian everything she needed.

Haitian was renting a small bar just down the road from my house, which is where I had the misfortune of meeting her. One night, Antonina called her, and Haitian was in a terrible state. She claimed that someone had broken into her bar and stolen all her stock. She needed to borrow two thousand dollars from me, which she promised to return when she made it back.

Antonina demanded I help her so I sent the money, but I really was not comfortable with the decision. Just four weeks later, Haitian begged me for another two thousand dollars. She said that if she didn't pay the Chinese owner the rent, she would lose the bar.

I thought about the request and sent another two thousand dollars. I figured that, if she lost the bar, I would never see my original two thousand dollars.

As it all worked out, Haitian had to leave the bar because the Chinese owner obtained legal support to evict her. Haitian promised to return my second loan if it wasn't accepted for her rent payment, but of course, being the same as the other island types, I never saw that money again.

Because Haitian was now out of work and Ronnie was only earning a tiny salary working as a barman in a beach hotel, they asked for more money. They claimed they couldn't afford to pay the utility bills each month. I learnt why later.

In the beginning of January 2011, Antonina demanded to go on holiday with me to the island to see my house for the first time. There was a lot of paperwork required for her one-night stay in Amsterdam and her longer stay on the island. Finally, she was granted the two visas, and I bought the flights.

All seemed well until we encountered the Kazakh border police in Atyrau airport.

The previous year, Antonina had her handbag stolen while a man held a knife to her throat. She reported that the bag contained her passport. Later, she found her passport but forgot to inform the authorities. In the meantime, they had cancelled her original passport.

Because she was not permitted to leave for the flight, I decided that I would also stay behind – idiot. We had our luggage removed from the aeroplane, and we went behind the scenes with the Kazakh border police. They kept us there for another two hours to write statements in triplicate (they had to be handwritten) just like in the internal affairs police station.

There was no alternative; we had to get a new Passport for Antonina before I could take my much-needed holiday. It wasn't as simple as all that, though, because she was in possession of a supposedly stolen passport.

She had to return to northern Kazakhstan, very near the Russian border, to apply for a new passport. Several people had to be bribed because her "not stolen" passport had caused so much confusion. After all, it had been cancelled, but it was still in her possession. It cost over two thousand dollars in bribes to get her a new passport that would allow her to fly a week later. Plus I had the expense of a private driver to take her on the nine hour drive north to Aksai.

When we finally got through the border control police a week later, it was a great relief. Or so I thought.

Without any reason, Antonina started performing the minute we boarded the flight to Amsterdam. Upon arrival in Amsterdam, she became worse. And the minute we got into our hotel room, she started screaming at me to open my laptop and sign into Skype before I could even take off my coat.

Once she had spent two long hours talking to her mother, daughter, brother, and others, she closed the computer and started threatening me with the Kazakh KGB. She demanded my mobile phone so she could have the KGB in Amsterdam collect her and fly her home. I was convinced she was going insane. And that was just the start of her crazy behaviour on the way to have a Caribbean holiday.

The next day was wasted with shopping all over Amsterdam for her entire family. She made me buy so much that I had to buy two extra suitcases to carry the lot to the island (and then back to Kazakhstan). If I ever refused to buy something, she would start screaming in the middle of the street for all to see.

The next day, we flew from Amsterdam to the Caribbean, which I hoped would improve her behaviour. I could not have been more wrong. I bought myself a new laptop in the airport so I could leave it in my island house (to save myself from carrying my old laptop back and forth through airports). As events worked out, I never got to use that new computer.

Haitian and Ronnie, who were still housesitting, were both at the airport waiting for us. They didn't have a car, so all four of us (along with four suitcases) had to squeeze into the same taxi.

The minute Antonina saw my Caribbean hideaway, she became even worse. Haitian stirred up as many problems as she could until things were completely out of control. It was the worst holiday I could ever have imagined possible.

I rented a car so I could take Antonina around the island and show her how beautiful the place was. I also let Haitian and Ronnie use it so they could go out and give us a little time to ourselves. That didn't work. Even with the car keys on the table, Haitian refused to leave the house.

I became so desperate to get them out of my house – even for just a few nights – that I even offered to pay for their hotel and give them daily spending money. But Haitian still refused to go. I could not get her out, not even for a couple of hours.

What it boiled down to was that Haitian was protecting her free lodging by doing everything she could to split Antonina and me up. That way, they would always need to housesit and never leave my house. I certainly didn't have any plans to marry the crazed Kazakh, but just needed to be patient until the court case over my watch was over and leave Kazakhstan permanently.

Because Haitian was a voodoo queen, my tiled floor was always a mess with candle wax. I could feel a strong presence in the house almost every night. I was finally introduced to the spirit. He liked to be called *Brave,* but he is better known in voodoo books as *Elohim.*

Antonina was very much into voodoo, and she encouraged Haitian to continue performing voodoo ceremonies (despite my strong objections). I became an outcast in my own home even though they were all living off my back. I even took them all deep-sea fishing which was also a waste of time and money.

Antonina kept promising me that when I was back in her country, she would create a very big problem for me. At the time, I ignored all her threats.

During my holiday from hell, my mother came for a day visit. She arrived via one of the many cruise liners that stopped off at the island and other island destinations.

Antonina insisted in joining me when I went to collect my mother from the port terminal for her five-hour stop off to make sure I didn't have the opportunity to explain all that was being done to me. My mother arrived on time, so we first drove her back to my house, where Haitian and Ronnie remained, to continue depriving me of any privacy.

It was therefore impossible for me to talk to my mother about the events that were taking place all day, every day. That was frustrating to say the least. I wasn't even left alone in the kitchen to make my mother a soft drink.

I went outside with my mother thinking I might have the opportunity to talk freely with her, but that was also a waste of time: Antonina, Haitian, and Ronnie followed us out.

While we were sitting outside on my veranda, a wild pigeon flew in and perched itself on my outdoor swing. The swing was large and could seat three people. It had a canopy above to shade its occupants or shelter them from the rain.

The pigeon landed on top of the canopy and looked like it was quite at home. While there, it just looked at us. After about half an hour, Antonina reached up to the bird, picked it off the canopy, and brought it to meet everyone.

The bird remained completely calm and undisturbed while we all took a turn stroking it. We put it on the green table below my kitchen window, and we gave it some bread and a little bowl of water. It wasn't interested in such things, though – it just watched our every movement.

Because my mother only had five hours on the island, we couldn't spend any longer at my house. We returned to the Capitol, just a twenty-five-minute drive away.

On my mother's first visit, she bought some wooden ornaments, which were made in the Amazon rainforest (from the Mopa Mopa tree). She was very fond of her last purchases, and she wanted to return to the shop to buy some more. Of course, we were not permitted to go alone: Antonina insisted on tagging along with us.

By the time we had parked and my mother had been to the shop, we only had enough time to stop for something to eat before taking her back to her cruise ship.

That was the last I would see of my mother until April of 2012, due to my overseas work and life. It took a serious medical problem to stop me in my tracks. But when I next saw my mother, she was there to help as usual. The moment we waved goodbye and walked back to the car and out of sight, Antonina started performing again.

Antonina was in a worse state of hatred and jealously after she had seen I came from a respectful and loving family and that I was living in the Caribbean. Haitian and Ronnie continued to worry that my 'so called' girlfriend would spoil their living situation. The voodoo, lies, and harassment were never going to stop until I was either dead or a single man again.

Haitian had made Antonina agree to a voodoo ritual that was supposed to protect us. I, as always objected strongly to the ceremony but I was aggressively out numbered. Haitian had already arranged for her cousin from Haiti, who was on the island to visit my house to help perform the ceremony.

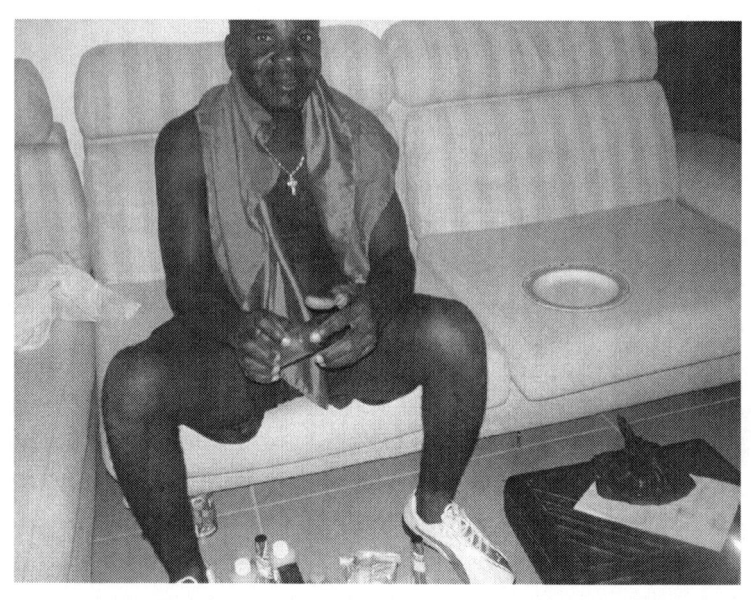

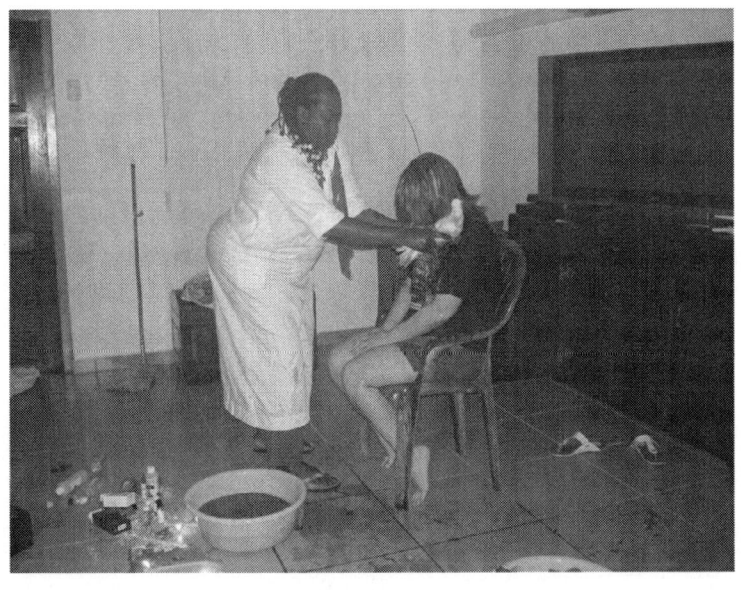

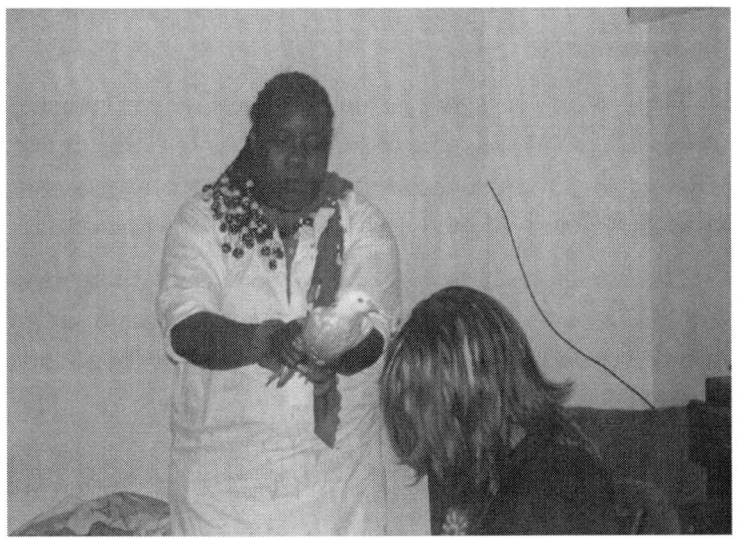

Haitian remained in my house twentyfour hours per day and spent her time just eating and sleeping. I did not have my house to myself for a single minute. Haitian ate a huge fried meal five times per day, and then she went to bed to sleep it off.

My house was always filled with the smell of fried garlic and onions because that was the base for everything Haitian cooked – she didn't know any other recipes. If I ever tried to sit outside to smoke one of my Cuban cigars, Antonina would come out and start screaming at me for the entire street to hear. I became a prisoner in my own house … *some holiday I was having.*

So many times I wanted to go out and do the usual things people did whilst on holiday (go out for a beer, eat out, or visit friends on the island), but I was denied everything. I couldn't wait for the two weeks to come to an end so I could put some distance between Antonina and my house-sitters.

There wasn't anything I could do because, on the island, it was illegal to make anyone homeless. It didn't matter whether they were misbehaving or homeless before moving in, so there was nothing I could do about the situation.

The strangest thing was the pigeon came back regularly just to see what was going on. It used to stand on my outside table and just look at me. It was totally relaxed and I could pick it up anytime I wanted.

Each new day, my holiday became worse and worse until the two weeks were finally at an end. When the time came to haul all the suitcases back to the airport, I knew it would take a few months to make back some of the money I had just wasted.

We eventually arrived in Kazakhstan without stopping over in Amsterdam because I was damned if I was going on any more shopping trips. I planned to attend the court hearing in Atyrau for the theft of my Rolex and avoid Antonina for the rest of my life.

Thinking my agonising days would soon be over, I was yet again very mistaken. Unbeknown to me at the time, they were just about to begin!

Antonina went to visit her family in Aksai the day after we arrived back in Kazakhstan because she couldn't wait to take the two extra suitcases full of presents back to them.

That was quite a relief because I was finally alone and able to relax. I tried to forget about all that had happened on my holiday to hell. A friend of mine, Andy Taylor, visited me in the evenings because he wanted to know all the grim details of my hellish trip.

But my relaxation was cut short. Antonina called me screaming, and she demanded that I open my laptop and sign into Skype so she could see I was alone in my hotel room. I did what she ordered, but seeing me alone with Andy was still not enough for her.

She instructed me to carry my laptop all around my hotel living room, bedroom, and even bathroom so she could see I didn't have any lady visitors with me.

I did what she wanted, but she still screamed at me and said she didn't believe me. She was threatening me with the police, the KGB, and some of her Kazakh mafia friends. She warned that they would go to my room and arrange it so I would never be seen again.

Andy, 'listening to all this', offered to let me stay on the sofa in his room for my own protection, but I declined his offer. Antonina returned to Atyrau three days later, and she immediately wanted to speak to Haitian to tell her how terrible I had been behaving. The lies were blatantly obvious, but Haitian enjoyed hearing them and encouraged Antonina to call her at least once per day.

Life, *as usual with this Kazakh* was totally out of control. I didn't have any idea what to do. Antonina, Haitian, and Ronnie had wasted thousands of my hard earned dollars, and I needed to make it back before contemplating quitting my job and getting the hell out of Kazakhstan.

As it happened, that was already a part of Antonina's sick and disturbing plan. It materialised that there wasn't going to be any court hearing over my stolen watch because Antonina was a friend of the girl who had organised the robbery. The two male Kazakh lawyers were just a pretence to make me think the proceedings were going along as normal, plus they were out of work at the time.

I believed I would have all my losses covered after winning the court case *because I paid for transportation, food, and accommodations for the two lawyers*, but that was never going to happen either.

Antonina became increasingly aggressive until the night I told her she could not waste any more money phoning Haitian every day. I was sick of that woman making the hell I was already living in even worse.

That didn't go down very well. On March 13th, I was on the phone with Haitian in the evening. I explained that, after the enormous cost of my holiday from hell, plus all the damn shopping and the money I had *loaned* her for her bar, it was time for me to start looking after myself.

As I continued to explain that I was sick and tired of everyone's problems, the unforeseen happened.

I didn't see Antonina coming over to the sofa I was sitting on when she attacked me from my left side. She smashed a white soup bowl into the side of my head, just behind my left ear. The bowl shattered under the power of her blow.

I felt a terrible stinging and burning sensation, which caused me to drop the telephone and fall back on the sofa with my head on a cushion.

I remained conscious, but only just. I felt a cold tingling coming from where Antonina had hit me. I opened my eyes, but I could only see green for several minutes. Finally, I forced myself to lift myself up, and I did so just before Antonina attempted to try murdering me again, but with a kitchen knife.

The cushion my head had been on was saturated in blood and I could feel it running down my back.

After an intense struggle, I removed the knife from Antonina and threw it out of the window and it landed in the snow.

I reached for my mobile phone and started to call my company's emergency number. Antonina screamed across the room that if I went to hospital, she would call her friends in the KGB, and I would be taken away long before any help arrived.

She told me she would explain that I was attacking her and her daughter. She said I would go to a Kazakh jail, which I would not survive more than a few hours.

Knowing that she really did have powerful contacts, I closed my phone, went to my bedroom, and wedged a chair under the door handle for safety.

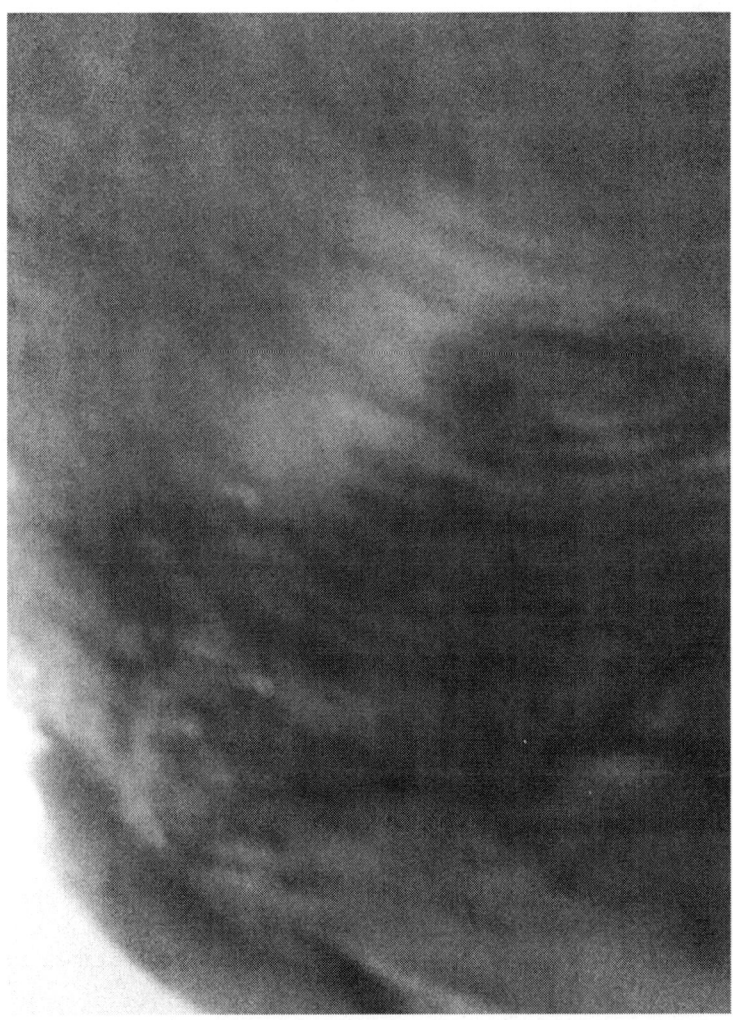

That didn't work. The crazed woman kicked and kicked the door until she had smashed her way through. She was holding another kitchen knife, and she intended to stab me to death yet again. I struggled with her while my blood was squirting all over the white bedroom walls until I managed to take the second knife off her.

I was sure by that time that I wasn't going to survive the night. Antonina returned to the living room, and after a few minutes, I started to hear thumping sounds. I looked out of the bedroom and saw her throwing herself at the kitchen table trying to hurt herself so she could blame me.

When she looked at me, I could tell she had hurt herself, but there weren't any marks on her, which was a relief. After that, she called a medical team to come to her aid because her heart problem had started again. That problem surely saved my life that night.

A paramedic team arrived and took her away for observation. I was finally alone and safe – at least for the rest of the night – or so I thought.

At four o'clock in the morning, I was woken up with a loud banging at my door. *What could possibly be happening now?* I thought. I opened the door only to find my company's security staff – they claimed there had been an official and documented complaint made about me by a Kazakh woman called Antonina.

I couldn't take any more, so I told the Kazakhs to get out of my room. I didn't want any more problems from them. They refused to go and made me accompany them to their office. There, they interrogated me and made me take a breathalyser test because Antonina had told them I was drunk and tried to kill her and her daughter.

Fortunately for me, I hadn't been drinking and passed the alcohol test, which convinced them that her story was certainly not true – at least the part about being drunk.

They could see the blood seeping from my fractured skull; it completely covered the back of my T-Shirt and stained my jeans. At least the waistband of my jeans helped slow down the stream of blood.

I told the security staff to take the shattered pieces of the soup bowl so they could take Antonina's fingerprints, but someone had already been to my room and removed all the shattered fragments before the staff could retrieve the evidence.

I then realised that the KGB was now involved because I couldn't imagine anyone else getting into my room and cleaning up the evidence.

The sun was already rising, and I had just an hour to clean myself up and make it to the office. I couldn't stop the bleeding, so I tried to cover it up with a thermal neck tube I used in cold weather.

I got to the office, but instead of taking off my coat as usual, I kept it on to conceal the continuing flow of blood. Chris didn't notice the look on my face as I approached him.

I went straight to his desk so he could see what Antonina had done to me. The look on his face was one of horror when I partially opened the collar of my coat and pulled down my neck tube which was soaking in blood by that time. He said I had to go to hospital immediately, but I told him I couldn't due to Antonina's threat.

I explained to Chris that I needed to leave the country as quickly as possible because I would not survive much longer. I was supposed to give thirty contractual days' notice to terminate my contract, but Chris explained to the senior manager that there was no time to waste because my life was in imminent danger.

I didn't have much time to pack, so I didn't bother: I left all my things behind. Soon, I was at the airport with a one-way ticket out of Kazakhstan.

To ensure some support getting through the airport border police, 'some of whom were Antonina's friends', I arranged for a representative from my Kazakh agent to accompany me. My agency was also my sponsor and visa holder, so it was in their own interest to escort me through the airport. I also asked the representative to wait until I had successfully passed through the border police.

It was probably the most nerve-racking time of my entire life because Antonina's uncle was the chief of the border control police for the entire country, and I didn't know what she had told him.

Luckily for me, my friend Andy Taylor was also on the same flight. I asked him to pass through the security and border police just after me.

That way, if the KGB were around waiting for me and I was detained for any reason, he would be there as a witness and could alert my company that I had been taken and hadn't succeeded to leave the country.

If Antonina knew about my escape plans, she would most certainly have instructed the border police, the Kazakh

KGB and also her uncle – to prevent me from leaving the damn country. If they had picked me up, she'd have me held behind the scenes until she could arrange for her KGB friends to take care of me – permanently!

I think the speed with which I left Kazakhstan was what spared my life, as Antonina didn't have the chance to make any arrangements.

Once I was successfully through the border control, I walked as far into the departure gate as possible so I would not be clearly visible. Andy, 'who was following close behind me', deliberately stood between me and the border police for additional cover.

After the longest nerve racking hour of my entire life, it was finally announced that we should proceed through the gate. A battered, old Russian bus was waiting outside the door to take us to the aircraft.

Still needing to carefully conceal the deep wound to the side of my head, which was still bleeding, I followed all the other passengers and approached the doors. The freezing cold wind was howling past at minus fortyeight degrees centigrade. The police sergeant, 'Antonina's friend and ex-colleague of Antonina's KGB brother', spotted me just as I was entering the bus.

I thought, this is the end of me; they've got me, and there is nowhere for me to run. He had a startled look on his face because he had seen me entering the country only a few days before with Antonina.

He immediately took out his mobile phone and started looking for a number to call – all the while keeping an eye on me. Surely, he was calling Antonina to ask why I was leaving so soon after arriving. I can only imagine that he couldn't get an answer from her phone, so he had no other choice than to let me proceed to board the aircraft.

While I was seated in the aircraft, my heart was pounding heavily due to my continuing worry about being taken off the aircraft. I was sure the policeman would still be trying to call Antonina for instructions. Due to the runway being covered in snow and ice, the aircraft needed to make one slow pass down it so its engines could blow it away while controlling its speed with its brakes on.

The entire aircraft was shaking with the powerful thrust from its engines while it cleared the snow. This made my wait for freedom even more intense. The aircraft could have been ordered to return at any second, if the policeman had succeeded to make contact with Antonina.

It was only when the aircraft finally left the ground that I started to relax for the very first time in so many months. I finally started to believe that my nightmare was over and began to wipe the memories of Antonina and Kazakhstan from my mind for good.

As far as I was aware, the only cloud left on the horizon was the fact that Haitian and Ronnie would be waiting at my house when I arrived home. I began wondering how they would react after seeing me so soon after all the hell they had caused for me under my own roof. I wondered which excuses they would use to try to lessen the bad atmosphere. I wondered what they would try without the support from a crazed Kazakh psychopath.

I didn't have the time to call *my house sitters* to announce my sudden return to the island. But I was fine with that because I didn't intend to give them any warning in any case. As far as they were concerned, they finally had my house to themselves and would never see me again. They would claim it as their own, *as planned* if Antonina had succeeded in murdering me, per the island law.

I arrived in Amsterdam airport after sleeping for most of the flight. I was totally exhausted from the lack of sleep from the recent days, and I had lost a lot of blood. I spent the night recuperating in a hotel before continuing to the island the next day.

I stayed in my usual hotel, which happened to be the same place where Antonina created so many problems for me just three weeks before. The second time around felt like heaven, '*which I had just avoided visiting earlier than planned!*' I felt like I had won against all the odds, like I had survived the impossible and that I was still alive to tell the tale, which inspired what you're now reading about – Andy's Story.

I went to visit some friends of mine as I knew I could always find them at my favourite Irish bar. Sure enough, they were all there. They were surprised to see me again so soon, and they were delighted to see me without the strange Kazakh woman who had blatantly refused to be introduced to them just three weeks before, *which had been so embarrassing at the time.*

I showed them the gash on the side of my head, which was still weeping blood because I hadn't had any stitches. They were all horrified after I explained how I got the wound. I didn't feel like explaining all the latest events because I was so desperate to put everything behind me, and permanently.

I returned to the hotel early and covered a part of the hotel pillow with tissue paper to protect the starched white cotton case from blood and went to bed very early. I was still quite weak from all the stress and lack of sleep, and I needed a relaxing start to the next day's long haul flight back to the island. I was quietly excited that the next day would be the first day of a new kind of life. A life I had always dreamed of having.

It was no surprise that I fell asleep the moment my head touched the pillow. I didn't wake up until eight o'clock the following morning, and I felt better than I had felt for several months.

I arrived at the check-in desk with three hours to waste. I enjoyed walking around the airport with the thought that I didn't have to buy anything for anyone.

The duty-free area felt so different and relaxing. I casually made my way in the direction of the business class lounge, and I realised that I was standing right outside the Rolex shop where I had bought my watch back in 2006.

I looked at the watches on display and wondered whether I would ever dare to replace my beloved watch in the future. I already knew the answer which was yes, if only to reinforce my private defiance for those who had taken my last one and caused me to meet Antonina.

I arrived at my departure gate in good time, and I couldn't help thinking about what had passed through my mind when I last proceeded towards the last departure gate just the day before. The second approach felt like a renaissance. I walked slowly and reminisced about the horror I had just been through – all the while trying to conceal the big smile that was trying to spread across my face.

I sat down in the very same seat number that I had sat in just three weeks before. And much to my surprise, the seat next to me, *where Antonina had sat before*, remained empty for the entire flight.

Reality set-in and I finally began to believe that I really had survived. Shortly afterwards, I was served a complimentary glass of champagne, and I made myself comfortable for the ten-hour flight ahead.

Soon, I was airborne and wondering when I would next touch down on European soil. Then I started thinking about what reaction my troublesome house-sitters would have when I returned unexpectedly, and very much alive!

I decided not to start thinking about what lay ahead until the time came. Instead, I tried concentrating on relaxing and enjoying the view from the upper deck of the Boeing 747 400.

The skies were clear and blue as I passed over the United Kingdom, but we were at cruising altitude by the time we passed over Wales, so I couldn't see the place where my mother lived. *She is probably worrying herself half to death,* I thought. I had called her from Amsterdam to let her know I had slipped through the Kazakh authorities and avoided the KGB so she at least knew I had survived the murder attempts.

She is an amazingly strong lady, which I guess came from having a son with my kind of luck travelling from country to country.

CHAPTER 23

Back to the Caribbean

My flight touched down half an hour early on the island, and for the very first time, I wasn't really happy about it.

I had my usual window seat during my flight back from Amsterdam, so it wasn't difficult to keep the wound to the left side of my head out of site from the flight attendant and other passengers.

I was still the first to pass through the customs control. Due to the Caribbean heat, I carried my jacket over my arm, not thinking about my wound. As I handed over my passport, I was given a strange look and asked if I was okay? I realised what the policewoman had noticed and said I was fine and would get checked later in the day at the hospital. I passed through all the people waiting at arrivals, and fortunately, I wasn't recognised by anyone (for once).

I passed through the gate and out into the heat and sunshine. There, I lit my first cigarette since the business class lounge in Amsterdam. I could see the long queue of taxis a few yards away, and I began to imagine my reception when I got back to my house just a twenty minute drive away.

Reality brought me back to earth firmly when I walked over to the line of taxis and jumped into the one in the front. The driver, Tristan, was a friend of mine, and I hadn't seen him on my previous visit. Thus, he had no idea what had happened to me.

When Tristan asked how everything was going for me, I began to explain why I needed to return so soon. He was totally dumbfounded and suggested we go for a beer before he took me back to my house. He suggested that I would be better prepared that way.

We stopped off at a Chinese bar called the "Hoi Sing," which was managed by a Chinese family. I always visited them when I was left to my own devices. The Chinese manager was in bed and sleeping as usual as he worked the evening shift.

I was glad he wasn't awake, though, because I was in no mood for an audience. Tristan planned to finish work early that day to take a rest, so it suited him to sit and listen to the most amazing story he had ever heard from a friend. I was sure everything I told him would be all over the island by the next day, so I was careful with regard to the details I gave him.

After a couple of hours, Tristan dropped me off at my house. He wouldn't accept any payment because I'd paid our bar bill and entertained him like he'd never been entertained in his life. I knew he couldn't wait to get home and tell his wife.

The front door to my house wasn't locked, so I let myself in. I was expecting to catch Haitian sitting on my sofa in front of lit candles and peering into a glass of water. I was right as it happened and she nearly fell off my sofa when she looked up and saw me standing there. She was busy performing a ritual for someone she knew or maybe a ritual to bring more trouble into my life.

"Oh my precious brother," she screamed as she rushed towards me to hug me. "I thought I'd never see you again," she cried. The false and nervous tears came gushing out.

I said with a serious look on my face, "With no thanks to *anyone*, I am alive, and I'm *back to stay* for a while, or at least until my next overseas contract." She immediately began examining the side of my head, which was still in a rough shape.

She said that death was waiting for me at my hotel room door the night Antonina tried to kill me. Because I avoided going through the door, I had survived. I told her to stop her nonsense and to shut up.

Strangely, she knew all about the white soup bowl that Antonina had smashed into my skull. She explained that *Brave Elohim* had been with me to protect me, and that it was Brave who had caused the soup bowl to shatter into pieces so the *weapon* could not be used again. I told Haitian I didn't want to listen to any more voodoo; I just wanted to relax and return to a normal life.

Later that night, Ronnie came back from the hotel bar. He wore a false and forced smile on his face. The disappointment that I was alive was clearly obvious. I couldn't stand the fake and uncomfortable atmosphere, so I freshened up and took a taxi to the capital. I wanted to get away from them and talk to a few locals I knew while listening to typical Caribbean music played for the tourists.

The next day, I got up late in the morning. As I walked out of my bedroom, I found Haitian sitting at my dining table. She and Ronnie always chose to eat and talk right outside my bedroom. It was meant to be a constant reminder that I didn't have any privacy in my own home.

She was using the new laptop I had bought three weeks before. She was listening to music when, suddenly, my bathroom door slammed shut at the other end of the room. It closed with enough force to shatter the opaque glass in it, but miraculously nothing broke.

All the doors and windows were closed, so I had a good idea what had entered my house. I asked Haitian if she was expecting anyone, but she didn't answer me. Just seconds later, she jumped up from her chair, almost turning my dining table over. My new laptop flew across the table and almost landed on the floor.

I knew exactly what was happening, and then she came over to me with an all-too-familiar expression on her face. Haitian was no longer Haitian; it was *Brave*. As impossible as it sounds, there is no mistaking the difference between the two in terms of their expressions, voices and mannerisms.

Brave approached me with his usual greeting with his arms crossed for a sometimes painful two handed handshake. I had to cross my arms and also join the two handed handshake. Brave's handshakes were normally a painful experience, but not that time.

He welcomed me back. He was happy to see me alive after *warning* me about what would happen on March 13th. He was pleased that I had survived certain death.

He claimed the fame for protecting me that night, and he also declared that he was responsible for ensuring that the soup bowl shattered when Antonina smashed it into my head. He told me to take his advice seriously the next time he gave it.

He didn't stay long. He left after just ten minutes, and Haitian became her usual, obese self again. Every time Brave used her to communicate with me, she was left lifeless. She always used his visits as an excuse to go back to bed.

Two nights later, Brave returned as himself at the usual time of one o'clock in the morning. There was no doubting Brave's presence – he always made it very clear that he was passing by *to check out my house*. On such nights, I heard noises that eventually woke me up. The sounds became annoying, and I usually walked outside my bedroom and into my living room to see what all the commotion was about.

The moment I walked out of my bedroom, I instantly felt his presence. After some time, I could locate exactly where in my house he was. As unreal as it sounds, it was very real for me.

At my house, there was a pair of plastic parrots on a shelf, probably made in China. They belonged to Haitian, and they had a motion sensor. Every time someone walked past, the damn things would start singing.

One night, the parrots were making such a noise that I got out of bed at half past one in the morning to take the batteries out of them. To my total disbelief, the parrots continued to sing after I had removed their batteries. Consequently, I carried them outside and trashed them.

I got angry and opened a bottle of Gold Label whisky my mother had given me when she last visited. I proceeded to sip glass after glass of it without getting any benefit whatsoever. Brave loved whisky, and he had the ability to take the full effect from me.

Without using Haitian's body to communicate to me, I got an unmistakable feeling that my problems were far from over. It felt like I was being sent a warning, and as it turned out, my instincts were right.

Two days later, Antonina called me from Kazakhstan. She was crying on the phone and saying she was so in love with me and so sorry for trying to murder me. *I guess Brave did have something to warn me about after all.*

I told her that I never wanted to hear from her again and that I would block her from calling me and emailing me, which is exactly what I did. It was no surprise that that didn't work – *she still had Haitian's number!*

Antonina called Haitian, and as expected, Haitian took her phone call in private so I couldn't listen to the conversation. Haitian was still intent on protecting her free accommodation, and she wanted Antonina's help to continue destroying my life.

Haitian promised Antonina that she would talk to me and repair all that *they* had done to me. I knew by the way

Haitian came to me with a pathetic look on her face what she was about. I turned my back and went outside to wait for a taxi to town.

After my holiday from hell, I was not going to except any more bullshit – especially from a voodoo queen with a hidden agenda.

The island has many strange laws. One of them states that if somebody can prove that they were taking care of a house when the owner died, they automatically became the new owner.

Haitian saw the phone call from Antonina as another opportunity to make my life totally impossible all over again and she encouraged Antonina to return to the island.

Though I wouldn't deal with the crazed Kazakh, Haitian maintained contact with her whilst smiling sweetly and calling me *precious* for some pathetic reason.

Three weeks later, Haitian warned me that Antonina was returning to the island to visit us. I told her to stop her nonsense – it was impossible for Antonina to get a visa without being sponsored by someone living on the island.

Unbeknown to me, Haitian had helped sponsor Antonina. Plus, the woman who worked in the travel agency in Kazakhstan still had my credit card details to debit for Antonina's trip back!

A week later, Haitian informed me that Antonina was returning to the island to make everything right. Naturally, I freaked out. I couldn't believe what was happening all over again! I remembered the hell I had endured the last time …

and the murder attempt. I felt that I was no longer strong enough to go through any more of it.

There was no way in hell I was going to allow her back into my life. I asked Haitian how she knew Antonina was returning to try to destroy my life yet again?

Haitian, the evil woman that she was, lied. She claimed she didn't know the details. I, however, knew exactly what had been going on behind my back. Haitian was so obsessed with getting rid of me permanently; she wasn't going to stop until she'd succeeded.

Eventually, I started to believe Antonina was going to get a visa and return to the island. I unblocked Antonina on Skype to tell her she was not welcome in my life or on the island or in my house after her last visit.

I could see her in a hotel room in Astana, the capital of Kazakhstan, as she waited for the Dutch embassy to grant her a visa. I heard her room telephone ring, and I knew it was a man from another room who required *servicing*.

She told me she had to go to the hotel's reception to pay the room charge from the previous night, but I knew that was a lie. Bills aren't settled until departure.

She didn't think I could hear her customer entering her room or telling her customer not to say anything because she was talking with me via Skype.

I certainly did hear everything because her bed was very squeaky. Plus I heard her speaking words of encouragement to her customer. After a very noisy hour, I shouted through my laptop to turn the lights on immediately. Naturally, she took her time doing that.

She had covered herself with one of the bed sheets, but she failed to instruct the asshole who had just finished using her to keep the hell out of sight of the laptop's camera. I could see a skinny Russian man in the background putting his clothes back on. I told her again to forget ever returning to the Island.

Unsurprisingly, the next day Haitian informed me that Antonina would be arriving on the island in two days' time. When I asked her how the hell she knew, she just put on the usual pathetic expression and said the spirits had told her.

Two days later, Haitian and her boyfriend went to the beach to see a festival going on there. They told me Antonina was arriving on the Amsterdam flight and that they would drop me off to welcome her!

I still didn't believe a word she had said, but I agreed to go to the airport to prove them wrong. I really shouldn't have done so.

The flight came in on time, and I waited for half an hour before turning towards the taxi rank only to see Antonina! I could not understand how she had been granted a visa. My nightmare was about to continue on a grander scale than before.

I asked her where she was going to stay because I wasn't letting her anywhere near my house or myself, for that matter. Antonina followed me to my taxi and threatened me with the police – just as she had done in Kazakhstan.

I totally ignored her and proceeded to get a taxi back home. I realised that Haitian was the instigator of my continued hell, and that she had gone to the beach with her inadequate boyfriend to stay out of the way.

When I arrived at my house, Antonina was full of apologies about the attempted murder, but I wasn't having any of it. I went straight to my bed with the intention of pulling Haitian aside the next morning to ask her what the hell she had been doing behind my back.

Of course, Haitian denied everything, and of course, Haitian protected Antonina … just like before. The next morning, I wanted to go downtown to buy some more Cuban cigars, and Antonina insisted on joining me, or she would arrange for the KGB to go to the island and make a big problem for me. I just laughed in her face.

Naturally, I was way past caring at that point. I just laughed at all of her threats. I kept thinking to myself, *What the hell made me deserve it all? I hadn't done anything wrong to anyone – unlike the three of them.*

I took a taxi downtown and went directly to the cigar shop in the Renaissance Mall to buy my favourite brand of cigar: Cohiba Siglo VI. Because I received a warm welcome in the cigar shop, Antonina started to perform again.

Before things got too out of control, I cancelled my plans for visiting other venues and took another taxi straight home. That was just the beginning, though. Soon after we returned to the house, Haitian and Ronnie arrived and started to make things much worse.

Of course, they sided with Antonina, as always. She made sure she had Antonina all to herself, but I didn't care – I just went to my bedroom and watched TV. After a while, I realised that the house was quiet, and I ventured out of my room to see why.

To my surprise, the place was empty. I was all alone to soak up the peace and tranquillity. It didn't last long: Haitian and Ronnie returned just half an hour later looking quite pleased with themselves.

I didn't see Antonina anywhere, and I asked where she was. Haitian said she had helped protect me and dropped Antonina off at a nearby hotel where she would be well taken care of.

She wouldn't tell me which hotel because she claimed it was better that way. She hadn't considered the fact that if anything happened to Antonina, she would be held responsible as her sponsor.

After two days, I demanded to know where she was. Haitian told me which hotel, and off we went. I had never seen the hotel before even though it was just a ten minute walk away. Haitian and Ronnie had lived there for many months because the cockroach-infested rooms were only ten dollars per night.

It was also where all the island refinery workers chose to stay due to its low cost. The whole hotel was full of illegal Venezuelan and Colombian men, and no women … except Antonina.

Of course, Haitian and Ronnie had shown Antonina around when they dropped her off. The bar was the first place they showed her so she could be seen by all the workers as being a lonely woman staying there. We found Antonina's room and went straight in as a Venezuelan man was leaving. It looked like she had not had any sleep since arriving.

Naturally, she refused to leave with us because she was making money from all the Latin Americans there. We went back to the reception and threatened the guy working there. I told the man at the reception that I would have the police raid the place if he did not help me by kicking Antonina out as most of the workers staying there were illegal on the island. He agreed to help.

She came back to my house so I could get her visa revoked in the morning and have her deported before she could cause any more problems.

In the morning, I left for the authority's office to cancel her visa. I planned to go to the police for help after that. That plan also got spoiled because Haitian knew what I was going to do and advised Antonina to stay with me.

When we got to the capitol, I tried to buy her a coffee, but she just continued walking. Because I had not invited her back to the island – and because I never wanted to see her again – I stopped trying to reason with her. Instead, I walked off in the opposite direction and took a taxi straight home.

I should have grabbed the opportunity and continued to the authorities, but my mind was scrambled with all the stress that was rising by the minute.

An hour later Antonina, called me and asked where the hell I was. I calmly replied, "At home. Where else?" I actually had my house to myself because Haitian was out as she wasn't expecting me to return for several hours.

Thirty minutes later, Antonina turned up in a taxi. She walked into my house to collect her things because she had already made a deal with the taxi driver that she would see him all right if he helped her.

I encouraged her to get the hell out of my house by throwing her little case out of my front door. I thought that would be the end of the hell I was living in. But I couldn't have been more wrong!

An hour later, the police visited me. They demanded to know why I had brought a poor Kazakh lady all the way from her country only to abuse her and sell her off to the highest bidder.

I couldn't control my emotions any longer; I just started laughing at the police for believing Antonina. I invited the two policewomen into my house and showed them the photos of what Antonina had done to my head. I also showed them my fresh scar.

Thankfully, the two shocked policewomen believed my story and arrested Antonina and put her in jail. At least I finally had something genuine to laugh about. What a relief that was.

It was a Saturday, and Antonina was detained along with all the hookers from Colombia and Venezuela who had overstayed, until she was deported that Wednesday. But not before writing and registering an official statement that I had brought her all the way to the island to murder her. Fortunately, I wasn't the one who had sponsored her return!

That was the last I ever heard of the crazed Kazakh woman.

After she left, I really started to believe that my nightmare was finally over. Stupid me! I still had Haitian and her boyfriend to contend with.

I couldn't face leaving my house until a week later, but I finally decided to take a taxi to the tapas bar next to the hotel I had originally stayed in three years earlier. I sat at the bar talking to a bank manager friend of mine while enjoying my favourite brand of Cuban cigar when a local woman entered the bar with a man I assumed was her boyfriend.

Because I was sitting near the corner of the bar, she made eye contact while rearranging her bra in a very obvious manner with her blouse half open for the entire world to see. That should have been my cue to go somewhere else. She had agreed to go for a drink with the Spanish guy just so she could have free drinks while she looked for a bigger catch.

My first thought was that she looked like a hooker. Unbeknown to me, she was a professional hooker who also worked as a salesperson for a very expensive Italian men's clothing shop on the corner of the Renaissance Mall.

She picked up on my conversation with my friend regarding the best place to buy good quality trousers, and she confidently butted into our conversation. She sat right next to me and explained where the shop where she worked was.

I could see which direction it was going because the guy she had walked in with was now being blatantly ignored. I was fresh meat.

Nevertheless, I had already been at the tapas bar for at least four hours, and I wasn't fit to stay for another four. Thus, I made my excuses and left.

Three days later, I received a missed call from a number that wasn't associated with any name in my phone. I broke my cardinal rule and called the number back. I don't know what possessed me to do that – if I called every missed call I'd received on the island, I would have been bankrupt.

Anyway, a woman answered my call, and I asked who she was. She replied, "It's me, Inez. Don't you remember me?"

I was being completely honest when I told her I didn't know anyone called Inez. She explained that she'd spoken to me in the tapas bar on the previous Saturday.

Okay, I thought, and I began to remember talking to some woman – but I still didn't remember any Inez. I wish I'd never returned that call because another nightmare was about to begin.

She persuaded me to visit the Italian men's clothing shop where she was a sales assistant to show me the quality of the trousers they stocked. She added that they had a tailoring service to turn them up for short-legged men like myself. That last point piqued my interest because I didn't know where to go on the island to get trousers turned up. So off I went … like an idiot.

I found the clothing shop just where I had pictured it from her description, on the corner of the Renaissance Mall. It was located right where taxis dropped people off. The shop was nicely laid out, and a shop assistant quickly approached me.

"Now do you remember me?" the assistant asked. "No," I answered. I really didn't remember her face at all. "I'm Inez. I was talking to you on Saturday night," she said.

I had to be honest and admit that all I remembered from the bar was seeing a woman struggling with her pathetic little silicon bags in her bra.

She seemed to react very well to that, and she took me by my hand as part of her personal treatment to score a new customer. She walked me deeper into the shop.

Actually, she looked totally ridiculous in her free-issue, company-supplied uniform. It was ridiculously tight – at least two sizes too small. Plus, she was wearing four or five-inch heels, which made it look like she was wearing stilts under her trousers as you could see the outline of her heels a few inches up her trouser legs.

She began by showing me the trousers they had in stock. After some sales talk, she persuaded me to buy a couple of pairs before leaving half an hour later.

I needed to return two days later to collect my new trousers. I was horrified to find that, contrary to what she'd told me to secure the sale, they were dry clean only, just like so many I already had, *tailor made in South Korea*. Therefore, I hadn't actually gained a damn thing.

Not to miss an opportunity, she started flirting with me and asked which hotel I was staying in. It seemed like a well-practised speech. She was quite taken aback when she learnt that I had been living on the island for the past three years.

After further interrogation, she uncovered the fact that I was a manager in the oil and gas business and was off the island more than on it. *The thought of housesitting is clearly on her mind,* I thought.

She persuaded me to take her out to dinner, which I did – but on my own terms. She wanted seafood, and I wanted a sixteen-ounce rib-eye steak, so steak it was going to be whether she turned up or not. I really didn't care.

I met her in a cigar bar just across the road from the restaurant that owned it. Amazingly enough, she arrived at exactly six o'clock in the evening, as planned. I was impressed. But that only lasted for about two seconds.

After she had said hello to the barman, bar manager, and waitress, she finally came over to me. Meanwhile, I was just sitting there patiently, waiting to be the last to be greeted.

She sat at the bar next to me and her very first words were, "*Look at me. I'm totally naked from my waist down.*" I didn't react at all because it was perfectly clear from the moment she entered that she wasn't wearing anything, or at the most, something as skimpy as a G-string. Her dress was so short, she looked like a perfect hooker, and I was already starting to feel uncomfortable having her sitting next to me. I really didn't want people seeing me with this new floozy.

I'd only seen such short dresses on the street girls who came over from Colombia and Venezuela to make as much money as possible from visiting tourists. Inez was no different.

The barman, whom I had known for a long time, had known her a lot longer, and he had seen this forty year old hooker with hundreds of tourists for years. He wasn't such a *good friend* because he didn't tell me to drop her as soon as possible. He was Colombian, so he probably assumed I wanted to have my wicked way with her before leaving her as hundreds had done before me.

We finished our drinks and crossed the road to the steak house. All the steaks were always of the finest quality and came from Argentina. The steaks were all grain fed Angus beef. It was my favourite venue when I wanted a steak. The staff knew me very well because I went there two to three times per week sometimes for lunch when I knew it would be quiet.

It was no surprise that the staff had all seen Inez before, but with a different man each time. I noticed the manageress's expression when she saw that Inez was with me this time, and she probably wondered what the hell I was doing with her or where I had been to have met her.

The waiter came to take our order, and after he had patiently waited for Inez to finally decide what she wanted, he turned to me. I simply told him I'd have my usual order – including the wine. He nodded and went away to get the wine. Inez said, "Oh my God, he knows exactly what you want! You've been here before?" I replied, "Just a few times."

Moments later, he returned with a large bottle of chilled sparkling water and a bottle of Saint Émilion Grand Cru. Once Inez tasted the wine, she commented on how nice it was and asked where it came from. I told her it came from Bordeaux, and she asked, "Where's that?" I thought, *I'd be better off ordering sangria for this forty-year-old floozy.*

My American friend, whom I hadn't seen for three years – was on the island making use of his timeshare with his wife. He had arranged to meet me that very same night in the tourist area on the beach pier. I explained to Inez that once we'd finished, I'd drop her off wherever she wanted to go because I had to meet a friend on the pier. She told me she wanted to go with me. That certainly wasn't quite what I had in mind because I wanted to catch up on things with my American friend and didn't want anyone seeing her with me.

After finishing my conch and sixteen-ounce rib-eye, we took a taxi to the beach pier to meet my friend.

Inez explained that she had a Colombian mother and an island father who had jumped ship when her mother became pregnant. Such events were quite normal on the island. Sadly, her mother passed away when she was only seven years old, and her uncle had brought her up.

We arrived at the beach pier, and sure enough, my friend was waiting for me at the bar. It was really great to see him again, and we sat at the bar catching up on all that had happened since we'd last met. Inez kept herself amused by dancing alone in a style better suited for the red light district. It was becoming increasingly embarrassing to be associated with her that night with her dress barely covering her back-side. Looking like a street hooker was certainly the distinct impression she wanted to give every man around her.

We couldn't believe the free show she was putting on while she danced alone, so we both deliberately faced the bar. That way, whenever she looked in our direction, she wouldn't have the audience or interest she was working so hard to get.

We called for the bill and made our way to the main road to drink and chat in another bar. The bar was situated halfway down a street full of bars and restaurants about a ten minute walk away.

Seconds later, I heard a shout. Inez was busy trying to catch up with us, struggling with her ridiculous red plastic high heels in the sand. "Where're we going next?" she questioned. But she should have asked, "*Why are you leaving me behind?*"

Clearly, Inez was not the type to give up easily, and she tagged along even though she was being ignored.

We sat at the bar and ordered a couple of beers. Inez ordered a glass of whisky for herself before I had the chance to ask what she wanted.

My friend and I continued to chat about each other's lives, and he was shocked to hear about all the problems Antonina, Haitian, and Ronnie had caused me in my own house and that under Dutch law, I couldn't kick them out. He also couldn't believe my miraculous escape from Kazakhstan.

I didn't see him again for several months. Instead, I met other frequent visitors to the island who also couldn't sell their timeshares either; so continued visiting the island just to make the best use of them.

I didn't see Inez until the following weekend. Word had got around to her that I was having a barbecue at the house.

She hadn't been invited, but that didn't make any difference to her.

Because so many people she knew had been invited, she didn't want to miss out. She was actually the first to arrive, and she was dressed in a skimpy white bikini and very little else. She asked where my pool was. I didn't have a pool at that time, even though I was getting quotes from various contractors.

Fortunately, soon after her arrival, other guests started arriving, so that took the pressure off me. Only half the number of guests arrived, which was normal on the island. Consequently, there was far too much meat, but nothing went to waste as the Venezuelan's stole as much of it as they could.

Nobody thought to tell me they were making frequent trips to their cars carrying cases of beer and meat packed in take-away boxes they'd found in my kitchen cupboards. Once I knew Venezuelan's had shown up, I couldn't go out of my house as I needed to guard my few remaining ornaments which I'd collected from all over the world.

I'd asked my Venezuelan cleaner to the barbecue along with her three daughters, as I knew she started work in the Hoi Sing bar at four o'clock so couldn't stay long. I hadn't planned on them bringing their boyfriends with them, which I knew would mean trouble.

The islanders never wasted a text message or a quick phone call out of common courtesy to inform they couldn't make it, so I could gauge the number of people coming – that wasn't their problem. Instead I wasted a lot of money preparing enough for everyone just in case they did arrive. I later asked myself, why I bothered?

After quite a pleasant afternoon and evening, the last stragglers left. There was still no sign of Inez making plans to go home. After Inez passed on her last chance to get a free lift home, I began to wonder if I'd be nobbled yet again for the cost of a taxi.

It was soon apparent that going home couldn't have been further from her mind. Inez automatically assumed she could stay the night, even though I hadn't made any suggestions in that direction.

Inez was in full party mode, but with nobody left to entertain, she suggested that we go down the road to the fisherman's bar, built half over the ocean.

We arrived just in time to catch last orders at the bar. We walked down the small wooden pier and sat down at a table on the very end of it. It was a quiet and with a very beautiful atmosphere sitting in the moon light over the Caribbean, only listening to the waves gently lapping against the shore rocks.

We chatted for a while, and most of the conversation was about places to go on the island and what I did for a living. At that point, she told me she had an eighteen-year-old son who had been brought up by his father.

Inez was certainly not the motherly type, and having a son would have really cramped her style. Because the bar had closed, we ended up returning to my place. Inez continued to drink, but she only had me to entertain.

We were in my bedroom watching a pop concert on TV, which provided a little privacy from Haitian and Ronnie who were guaranteed to break up any private little meeting. For all I knew, they were probable eating just outside my bedroom door to listen in, in any case as they had done so many times before to check if I was alone of not.

Inez automatically stripped down to her skimpy white bikini and proceeded to dance provocatively in front of the TV. She was topless, but I just sat on the edge of my bed wondering whether she'd ever suggest calling for a taxi. The suggestion never came. Her intentions were quite obvious: she wasn't planning on going anywhere else that night.

Once the concert finally ended, it was sleep time, which is exactly what I did. Inez stripped naked and cuddled up to me with the hope that something would become of it, but it wasn't going to happen, and nor was I interested or awake enough to last any longer.

To my dismay, she stayed for the rest of the weekend – until the Monday lunchtime, as she wasn't due to work until one o'clock in the afternoon. I really didn't enjoy this floozy's company, as she was so opinionated and confident. I can only admit that as I was lonely, I felt something was better than nothing, I allowed her to stay. I felt that is was clear; that nobody in their right mind wanted her in any case.

On the Sunday, we took a friend's taxi down to the local village to have lunch in a bar. The steak and steamed shrimp were well known in the area.

Before leaving, Inez produced a pair of shorts, which probably would have been too small for a Barbie doll. She somehow managed to squeeze into them, though. With her shorts and red plastic high heels on, she looked like the perfect hooker.

After we ate, we waited outside the bar for my friendly taxi driver to take us back home. Due to her obvious appearance, three cars pulled over to ask how much she charged per hour. But rather than being insulted, she found the questions hilarious. She even said to me, "look at me, I look like a hooker.

Unbeknown to me at the time, Inez regularly walked the streets of the red light district working as a street hooker for additional income. She had spent nights in every single hotel on the island – each time with a different client.

The following week, she told me the most outrageous stories about her time in the brothels. She had stripped naked on stage in front of a full male audience and pole danced naked alongside the other hookers.

To keep in with the various brothel managers, she made her customers pay the bar the usual one-hundred-dollar bar fine, because she was taking customers away from the hookers working the bar.

When Inez became a regular visitor to my house – probably because no one else wanted her – Haitian got involved again. Despite explaining some of the things Haitian had done before, Inez seemed to play into Haitian's hands … as if she enjoyed it.

Inez also had her sick, exhibitionist eyes on Haitian's obese boyfriend. She would rush into the kitchen in the morning, the moment she heard Ronnie, wearing only a short T-shirt and nothing else. She caught Ronnie's attention by knocking something on the floor and bent at the waist to pick it up. I caught her several times, which infuriated her while she was busy giving a free exhibitionist show.

By the time I joined them in the kitchen, Ronnie's face was the colour of a bright red tomato. Also, as I entered the kitchen Inez protested angrily at my presents because she could no longer perform. I reminded her it was my house and my kitchen, but as always, the islanders ignored respect learnt in the civilised world.

Thus, Haitian had an additional motive to cause trouble, as she had done so many times before. At every opportunity, Haitian interrupted conversations I was having with Inez by butting in and speaking in Papiamento to Inez. She knew I didn't understand a word of it.

Naturally, I protested and instructed that only English should be spoken under my roof, but I was always ignored. Several weeks went by, and just like before, the situation worsened until someone had to go.

I had been out of work for four long months, but I still didn't have any privacy in my house. One day, an agency from the United Kingdom called me. It was regarding another contract in Nigeria, which I was interested in because there hadn't been many other enquiries up until then.

The only worry was what Inez would inevitably get up to whilst I was away, as if I cared. The contract rotation was twentyeight days on and twentyeight days off, so there was a lot of flying to do.

I told Inez she could continue living in my house, which she refused because it would have cramped her style with Haitian and Ronnie there. Instead, she chose to return to living in her Colombian friend's house on the north part of the island. There, she could continue to pick up tourists for her own financial gain, just as she always had, before meeting me in the Tapas restaurant a few months before.

So it was back to Nigeria in July of 2011. I was a little apprehensive after previous exploits in the country, but I felt that the island wasn't exactly being kind to me.

CHAPTER 24

Return to Nigeria

Nigeria is a country full of surprises, and I'm not just referring to the wonderful choice of characters living there. Even though I already had so many experiences there, I still loved the people, and still do to this day.

With the usual donations for the immigration and customs staff, I got through with all my possessions intact. My armed escort was waiting outside of the airport in Port Harcourt. It took an hour and a half for the stragglers to be accounted for before we set off to the different places prebooked to accommodate us on our arrival night.

The next morning, I met some others who were assigned to the swamp I was to be based and off we went. It rained most of the night, so the roads were in a terrible condition. It took us over three hours to arrive at the camp where people of many nationalities were busy expanding the upstream oil facilities.

Our accommodation was a typical set-up consisting of rows of narrow containers kept off the ground by concrete footings and all linked up with electrical and tele-phone cables.

Due to the high malaria and dengue fever risk, doors were always kept closed, and the small rooms were sprayed on a daily basis.

Power cuts were a regular occurrence, and the lack of air conditioning was the main discomfort. If any insect was found inside the trailer, it had to be destroyed before sleep was possible. In swamps, almost everything flying or crawling bites – and some bites could be fatal. Even inside the camp perimeter Black Mamba snakes were found on a regular basis. They weren't actually black in colour, but instead a light brown colour. They got their name due to the inside of their mouths being totally black.

We averaged fifteen men per month going to hospital with malaria or dengue fever or both! One South African colleague contracted malaria and went downhill very fast. In the Nigerian hospital, they identified seven different types of malaria parasites in his body at the same time. He lost over twenty kilos in two weeks and was lucky to make it through. It amazed me that so many people walked around in short-sleeved shirts, shorts and flip-flops given the amount of bloodsucking and biting insects around.

I never bothered to take malaria tablets because there were many side effects. Instead, I preferred to soak myself in insect repellent containing a minimum of 50% Deet in the hope that I would evade being bitten in the first place.

On a previous project, one South African colleague was unlucky enough to get cerebral malaria and died in just ten days in a hospital in London. Cerebral malaria has to be treated the moment you contract it. After just a few days it is already too late to cure as he had waited too long to seek help.

While working my twentyeight days on and off rotation, I returned to the Island at the end of every four-week visit. Four weeks doesn't sound like long before a four-week holiday, but four weeks in a swamp goes very slowly.

Due to flights not lining up, each trip required a night in Amsterdam. Amsterdam was one of the most convenient stopovers and gave me the opportunity to buy things unavailable on the island – or cheaper than the goods on the island.

During my first trip to Nigeria, I told Haitian, that she and her pathetic boyfriend had to get out of my house because I was sick and tired of all her voodoo and trouble-making. I gave her until the end of August to find somewhere else so she would be gone before I returned home.

Of course, even though both Haitian and Ronnie had stayed in my house for over one and a half years rent-free, neither of them managed to save a single dollar. Instead of using the opportunity to build up some savings, they ate more and used up every spare cent.

Respecting the Dutch law, I offered to pay the deposit and first two months' rent for them to move out and rent a new place.

Haitian explained that she could never leave the house because she needed to rent a really big house in order to have space for all her personal possessions. She continued until I agreed to send her three thousand dollars, which she claimed she needed for a new place.

I sent the money and found my house empty for the first time since I'd bought it. It was certainly empty! Haitian and Ronnie had robbed me of so many things when they'd left, including clothing, the new laptop I had bought in Amsterdam airport with Antonina, my camera's tripod, some rather expensive jackets, all my kitchens saucepan lids, knives, forks, soup bowls, side plates, and dinner plates. I wasn't left with a full set of anything once they had gone.

That's the thanks I got for helping people out. It was eight months later that I learned Haitian didn't really rent a place at all. She'd lied to me about needing the three thousand dollars. Instead, she moved into Ronnie's mother's house just two streets behind mine.

There was still a bad atmosphere lingering in the house even though I finally had it to myself. The stale and musty stench in the large back bedroom, where Haitian and Ronnie had slept, was unbearable.

I tried to leave the bedroom door open to allow some fresh air inside, but that permeated the air throughout the rest of the house. If I was expecting visitors, I'd have to close the door and spay air freshener all around the living room. I had to completely redecorate the room because Haitian had spat an orange liquid at the walls during her voodoo ceremonies. I wouldn't allow her to perform voodoo any more in the house, but I knew she would continue in the privacy of her and Ronnie's bedroom. They stuck cheap plastic hooks on the back of the varnished bedroom door, completely defacing it, and also on the walls.

I had to put the mattress outside to let fresh air work its way through it. Even without the mattress, the room still had a stale, musty smell, which remained for several months.

While I was on the island, I wanted to get into my storage room, which also doubled as my workshop, at the back of my house. I went to where I always kept the keys, but they were gone.

I looked everywhere, but to no avail. Out of desperation, I called Haitian who admitted to taking the keys so no one – including myself – could open the door. Apparently, her personal belongings were still being stored there.

I demanded she return my keys immediately because I needed to get into my workshop to do some things. She refused until I told her I'd cut my lock off because I needed to get in. She arrived in a remarkably short time with the keys, but she stressed that I must keep my store locked and not allow anyone in.

"What a bloody cheek!" I told her. She was not a friend and not renting the space. Plus, what the hell was the three thousand dollars for if she didn't use it to rent a place? As always, she ignored the question and told me not to touch her things or there would be trouble. *I knew what that meant.*

I opened my workshop, but I couldn't even get through the door because the entire room was packed full of junk, which was no good to anyone. There was a broken, old-fashioned TV, an old plastic typewriter, dozens of empty washing machine soap bottles, old furred up aluminium saucepans, and broken bar stools.

I called her and told her she had to collect it all or I would arrange for it to be taken to the island dump. She freaked and threatened me with voodoo if I touched any of it.

With no voodoo and the absence of the smell of garlic and onions being fried five times per day, Inez moved back in. I just wanted to have some company, but I could have chosen better!

On evening I was standing in my living room talking to Inez who was in the bedroom at the time. Without any warning and for no apparent reason, I found myself lying on the floor where I was just standing in terrible pain. My right knee was badly dislocated and already very swollen. I couldn't understand what could have happened, and neither could Inez. I couldn't make it to the car so Inez called an ambulance to come and collect me.

Almost half an hour had passed before the ambulance arrived. By that time my knee was like a football. The two paramedics secured me onto a stretcher and put me in the ambulance and proceeded to drive off to the central hospital where I'd be treated.

Once in the hospital I was given morphine for the very obvious pain and left to wait until a doctor was available. Soon after being examined, I was sent for an x-ray. The x-ray clearly showed my dislocated knee had half an inch gap between my bones. I waited a little longer, before two doctors returned, and together put my knee back into place. Next I had to have a cast wrapped around my knee. Actually, the cast began at my ankle and continued up the entire length of my leg to my hip.

With my new purple cast I couldn't drive any more. Inez could therefore have full use of my car until my cast could be removed. I was told the cast needed to stay on for at least a month, but as I was soon to fly back to Nigeria, the cast had to be removed after just ten days.

I was determined the cast wasn't going to impair my holiday and managed to keep mobile with the use of crutches and taxi's. Getting up and down steps was the most difficult manoeuvre, not to mention getting on a deep sea fishing boat! I had previously charted the boat and invited a good friend who was also a bar owner to accompany me deep sea fishing. Such trips were certainly not cheap in the Caribbean so I didn't want to lose my deposit, nor let down the boat owner who I had fished with so many times in the past.

I arrived at the quayside where my thirty seven foot charter was moored at six o' clock in the morning on a terrible day. With torrential rain and gale-force winds I worried whether the trip would be cancelled, and also if my friend would even turn up? At 6.15 the captain arrived together with his son who was also his deckhand and five minutes later my friend beeped his car horn as he drove past us to look for a place to leave his car.

With help from the captain and my six foot friend from the Dominican Republic, I was helped to board the vessel and onto a soaking wet chair so I wouldn't risk falling on the very bouncy ride out of the marina. The storm was one of those freak Caribbean types which soon passed by. Unfortunately, the rough seas had caused the fish to swim into deeper water so we knew we wouldn't have too much luck until later in the day. The going was very quiet which was sad for my friend's first fishing experience. Luckily, the boredom wasn't to last.

The storm had loosened a large amount of seaweed from somewhere which was floating all over the ocean. This became a real nuisance as it fouled our fishing lines which we constantly had to reel in to clear them. Sometimes, a large piece of seaweed would foul a line causing the ratchet on the reel to slip making us all jump, *thinking we had a fish on*.

The floating seaweed did have some very good advantages though. Some species of fish liked to shelter beneath it and feed on it at the same time. This was especially the case with Dorado which some people like to call dolphin fish for some unknown reason. They don't have any resemblance to dolphins.

In the Caribbean, they were mostly referred to as mahi mahi. With mahi mahi you could distinguish the males from the females as the females had smaller, more rounded heads than the male's larger, squarer heads. Mahi mahi like to jump out of the water once they are hooked as if they are dancing and usually gave a good performance. They are as tasty, as they are beautiful with their turquoise appearance.

In the afternoon, my captain noticed a large area of seaweed in the distance and headed in its direction to pass as close as he could alongside it without risking our lines getting fouled again. As we began to pass the weed the action started.

Suddenly bang, one of the two rods on the port side was hit and the reel immediately started to spin, a second later, bang again and the second rod on the port side was hooked up too, then again from the rod on the starboard side which was almost bent double. The captain instantly pushed both the turbo diesel engine throttles hard down for a few seconds which hurled the boat forward at a rate of knots to ensure we all had tight lines and firm hook ups.

With the very loud roar from both engines, and a large plume of smoke from both their exhausts, 'game on I thought' as I was handed the starboard rod by the deckhand. My friend was handed the second from the port side and the deckhand took the third.

I couldn't assume the normal fighting position which required both legs to be in a bent position on the foot board sticking out from the base of the revolving chair. Much of the fighting power was gained through the legs and lumber region to get the necessary leverage to '*pump*' the fish to retrieve the lost line from the fishes initial few runs.

It wasn't possible to simply reel in a fish of sizable proportions, especially all the while the boat was moving forward to keep the lines tight. Instead I had my damaged right legs foot on the deck and my left foot on the foot rest making it rather uncomfortable and difficult to play my fish. My fish was particularly frisky and crossed the deckhand's line. The deckhand noticed what was going on and crouched down and got under my line and stood up again, the other side of it. A minute later he had to repeat the procedure as my fish retuned back to my side again. *My fish was trying everything, not to end up on a plate.*

Fish have the ability to spit out a hook the moment you allow the line to slacken. It is as if they are waiting for the opportunity; much to the frustration of many game fishermen. I particularly liked my choice of fishing boat, as the captain always flattened the barb on all his hooks to allow the fish to discard them easily if ever the line snapped. That was another reason, never to allow the line to go slack.

The boat only used 50lb breaking strain line which meant the fishermen couldn't tighten the drag setting on their reels too much, to make the fish get tired sooner. I always set the drag setting on my own reels to 25lb. That meant the fish was pulling away from no more than a 25lb load.

It also meant that the fisherman was also pulling against a 25lb load, even if a fish weighed over 100lbs. If a fish pulled more than 25lbs, the clutch inside the reel would slip, enabling the line on the reel to be stripped until the fish grew tired. For the bigger fish, I used a '*fighting*' belt. My fighting belt was about 5" wide, which spread the load around my lumber region.

It had two narrow belts hanging from its front which were there to clip onto the two lugs on large game fishing reels. It was a great help when I had a big fish hooked. When it was time for a fish to make another run, I could simply release my rod leaving my belt to hold it, which gave my arms the chance to rest, while I waited for my reel to stop getting stripped and, again start pumping back the fish to regain my line. The technique was simple, but very effective.

You needed to smoothly pull the rod back towards you as far as it was comfortable, and then wind the line back onto the reel as you allowed the rod to smoothly fall forwards again. Also, with the boats continuing forward motion, it was impossible to simply reel the line in normally in any case.

Considering we had had a very poor start to the day, catching nothing by 2.30 in the afternoon, we returned back to the marina at 4pm with seven mahi mahi, one barracuda and two tuna fish.

Once back at the marina, the deckhand would skilfully clean the fish and cut them into fillets for me to take what I wanted. I'd always drop some fish off to the seventynine year old lady living to the left of my house, and also some for the family living the other side of my house.

I liked to cook mahi mahi by seasoning some flour to cover a piece of fillet and deep fry it for fifteen minutes. If I ever returned with some lunar tailed grouper, I always kept them and would never give them away. For me, they are the very best eating fish in the sea. They taste as though you have cooked them in honey as they were so sweet. You could identify them by the yellow crescent on the edge of their fins and would only be a couple of pounds in weight.

While I was enjoying what I could of my time back on the Island, it was becoming more and more clear that Inez had very obvious plans for putting the house to good personal use during my four-week trips to Nigeria. She began to receive a constant flow of text messages to her phone, all written in Papiamento so I knew they were from another Islander. She used to show me the messages saying they were from the Colombian woman she rented a room from at the north end of the Island who I knew, didn't speak Papiamento. From the delight on her face, they were obviously from another man or men.

I knew exactly what she'd get up to the minute I left. What I could never have imagined was that she'd made arrangements for a local man to move in the very same day I flew off the island. When I was flying to Amsterdam, I suddenly had a strong gut wrenching feeling that someone was with her in my house. As it turned out, my instinct was right.

She also demanded that I keep my rental car on-hire while I was off the island. It was a pleasant little luxury for her because she could drive down to the red light district just ten minutes from my house, to pick up additional customers when the local guy wasn't staying the night.

Before flying off the Island, I had bought a listening device from a local island conman. All it needed was a mobile telephone SIM card slotted into it and a power supply. I hid it behind the TV in my bedroom thinking she would never find it, but after just a few days, it was unplugged, and after a few more days, its battery had depleted.

It did last long enough to listen to what Inez was doing with several different men in my bedroom. All I had to do was call the SIM's number and listen in. That experience was terribly painful while staying in a trailer in the middle of an African swamp.

I called Inez just to interrupt her, but she always turned her phone's ringer off when she was busy. When I did manage to call her, she was always very aggressive and didn't want to speak. After that, she would hang up on me.

Like a perfect fool, I informed her of my arrival date. In hindsight, it would have been much better if I had given her a date a week later so I could catch her busy. *I could have put it in all the local newspapers.*

After flying from Nigeria to France, France to the Netherlands, and Netherlands to the island, I needed to wait over an hour at the island's Airport for Inez to finally arrive in my rental car to pick me up.

When she finally arrived, she didn't say, "*Hi, darling,*" or, "*How are you?*" No kiss, no nothing. Inez was angry I had returned because she couldn't use my house as a whorehouse for another four weeks.

She drove to the Italian clothing shop where she worked and left me to drive myself home. The fuel gauge was lower than empty. I opened the cubbyhole where I always kept some spare money for parking and petrol, but that had also been emptied.

I got to my place and it was quite a sight. My garden hadn't been touched *even though I'd left money for it to be done.* I had electricity, water, and cable TV bills that hadn't been paid, *which I'd also left money for,* and my air conditioners had all been left on.

She had left plenty of evidence that there had been some wild nights while I was away. Under my sofa, I found the remains of a broken ashtray which I had bought in Amsterdam and the base of a wine glass. Under my coffee table, I found the remains of another glass.

All my beer, whisky, and every other type of spirit was gone, and there was not a single thing left to eat. Inez had certainly been busy milking my house. Like Haitian and Ronnie, the marine and his young Colombian wife, the two young bar girls, and everyone else on the island who had entered my house, Inez had helped herself, together with her clients, to much more than she should have.

Why did I think anyone on that damn island would be different? In the middle bedroom of my house, Inez had stored her fifty-seven pairs of shoes. They were all very high heeled, bright, and multi-coloured − just like the ones all the other hookers wore whilst walking the streets looking for business.

When she returned back that evening, she had a very aggressive attitude towards me. Just like in the past, I was not welcome in my own home because it disrupted the life-styles of those who used and abused it for their own gain.

She demanded I thank her for keeping my place so clean. I couldn't believe it. I asked her what all the broken glasses were doing under my sofa and coffee table? And then I asked her about the broken ashtray and disgusting sheets in the washing machine, which I had already carried out and trashed.

Of course, she knew nothing about any of it and denied everything. I told her to get the hell out of my house and my life and go back to the brothels she loved so much. She ignored me because she didn't want to lose her free, private brothel and free rental car that suited her lifestyle so well.

Instead, she attacked me. She scratched my face and dug her acrylic nails into my chest (adding yet another scar to the ones Antonina had left). Inez wanted me to hit her − it was just like when Antonina threw herself at the kitchen table and chairs in Kazakhstan. *History,* I thought, *is repeating itself.*

I crossed my arms and let her get on with it without returning fire so she wouldn't have any excuses to call the police or anyone else and then went to bed.

The next morning, I did the gentleman bit and made her some coffee, fresh orange juice, and sandwiches. Meanwhile, I started the car and turned on the air conditioning while she was getting ready so she would be comfortable before she began working in the menswear shop.

I did my usual shopping to restock what Inez's sex clients had been encouraged to help themselves to, including my Cuban cigars! I decided that she was going the same night. I picked her up at eight o'clock in the evening from outside the shop where she worked and drove back towards my house.

Inez, as usual, insisted on driving. I moved over and let her take control. When we approached my house, I told her to stop at my favourite Hoi Sing Chinese bar, which she did, *to my amazement.*

She parked the car in true island style – right across two parking slots – and got out. In the bar, Inez was unusually friendly towards me, as she must have known *I was about to kick her out.* She even showed interest in my work instead of quizzing me about my salary to try to find out what I earned.

I wasn't being taken in by her desperate attempt to make things right, though. I just ignored her, looking across the bar whilst sucking on my Cohiba. After a while, I turned to her and coldly said, "We're off."

Of course, Inez asked where we were going next, so I turned, looked her straight in the face, and said, "*to help you pack.*"

She looked dumbstruck at first and asked if we were going somewhere? I replied, "*Me, no; you, yes.*" Startled, she asked, "*Where am I supposed to go?*" I replied, "Anywhere *you want so long as it's the hell out of my life.*"

The three-minute drive home was quiet – very quiet.

As we entered my house, I went straight to the kitchen and took out a roll of black plastic garbage bags that she could use to fill with all her nightlife clothing and 57 pairs of high-heeled shoes.

Inez still couldn't believe she was finally being kicked out, but she only had herself to blame – just like Haitian and Ronnie and every other islander who had abused a good thing.

She didn't start packing anything; instead, she poured herself a whisky and sat next to me on the sofa. She tried to make polite conversation, hoping it would all blow over.

Wrong. After two years of pure unadulterated hell, I was not going to be seduced into changing my mind. I got up and started packing for her, starting with her shoes from the middle bedroom into the black plastic bags.

She figured there was no going back and started to pack her skimpy little clothes from my bedroom drawers into the bags. Unbeknown to me, she took my five-day-old iPad, wedged it against the floor and the wall, and stamped on it. The screen shattered and the frame broke. After that, she put it back where she found it.

After she had finished packing her cloths, she called her Colombian friend to come to collect her, and re-joined me back on the sofa.

Money, gold, and diamonds meant more to Inez than loyalty, love, and security.

After another twenty minutes, she received a missed call from her mobile. Without saying a word, she rushed out the front door, jumped into her friend's car, and left.

Fantastic, I thought. For the first time, I was home alone and feeling so good about the sudden silence that I didn't know what to do.

The next day, I drove into the town to pick up some more Cohiba cigars. I met the same island salesman who sold me the little listening device.

I started talking to him about having security cameras fitted around my house to deter thieves passing by. He claimed to specialise in security cameras and said he'd come over to show me what he had available.

I'd already received a quote from a professional security company, but it was a little high. That hesitation gave the salesman an excuse to sell me his cameras, which later didn't work. He also sold me a computer and said it was necessary for the cameras to record to. Of course, there were no guarantees or refunds on the island, so I lost again.

The time came when I really needed to use the workshop. It was still full of Haitian's junk, so I began to call her from Nigeria several times a week demanding that she remove it. Every time I called, she promised to have it collected, but I knew she had no intention of losing her free storage space. Several more weeks passed before I told her that if it had not been removed by the Friday, I would have it all taken to the dump.

The Chinese bar owner, *who had evicted Haitian* from her bar just down the road said she'd be happy to help me because she knew all I had been through with Haitian. She had experienced so many problems with her, too.

Early that Friday morning, she arrived with her father and one of his Chinese friends who brought his lorry. In no time at all, they had emptied my workshop of everything and even swept the floor clean.

When the bar owner saw the bar stools, she said that they were hers – Haitian had stolen them from her bar when she had been evicted. They left very pleased to have had their stools back.

That day was bright and sunny, like most days on the island with a gentle breeze that took the edge off the thirty-four degree heat. I packed some ice in my cooler bottle and drove down to a nearby beach, which was just twenty minutes away.

Content that I had finally trashed all Haitian's junk and could finally start making use of my workshop, I lay on the beach for the first time in months. I rented a beach bed and it was so nice to just soak up the sunshine and drink a couple of cold drinks.

This is why I bought a house so far from Europe, I thought. I wondered whether a little bit of sunshine had been worth all the pain, stress and murder attempts.

I drew the conclusion that nothing could be worth all I'd gone through, and I started thinking about what to do with the place. After I'd taken in enough sunlight for the day, I made my way back to a peaceful, quiet house to try to begin enjoying it. That was what I hoped would be the case, anyway. Sadly, I was wrong yet again.

I had just finished watching a movie and gone to bed when I heard a police siren very close by. It only sounded for a second or two, and then it stopped. A couple of minutes later, it sounded again.

I got out of bed and peered through a gap in my front window blinds. I saw the flashing lights from a police car parked right outside my house.

Opening the front door to see what was going on, I heard the sound of Haitian's voice screaming, "There he is, there he is! He's the one who gave all my things away!" *What the hell is this all about,* I thought and went to unlock my drive gates to meet the police.

Haitian was screaming for the entire street to hear "This is the man who gave all my things away! Arrest him now! He's got to pay for what he's done!" She continued on and on that I needed to compensate her six thousand dollars.

The police asked me why I'd removed all the woman's things from my store, to which I replied, "Because, after months and months of ordering her to take it – and after telling her that if she didn't remove her junk from my property I would do it for her – I finally did just that."

The police told me I had no right to remove her things. I replied, "My house, my land, my store. I have every right to remove what doesn't belong there, especially considering the space isn't even rented."

To that, she started screaming yet again. Even Ronnie came forward and pointed his finger at me. He said, "You're in big trouble now, Andy. Real big trouble." I asked him to explain exactly what "big trouble" I was in.

I knew what he wanted to say, but he couldn't in front of the police officers. I said it for him: "Voodoo? Is that what you're threatening me with?"

The police looked at them at that point, but she said, "What voodoo? I don't know anything about voodoo." I just started laughing in her face and turned to the police officers and said, "It is because of voodoo and interfering in my life that I kicked his and her ass out of my house and out of my life!"

Haitian freaked again and denied knowing anything about voodoo, so I asked Haitian if she wanted me to show the police officers the photos of her performing a voodoo ceremony for Antonina in my living room."

She looked horrified and said she didn't know what I was talking about. I repeated to the police that I had called her every day since arriving back on the island, including the day before I removed her things, but she still chose to do nothing about it.

Again, she started screaming that I was a liar and had never called her. She was holding her mobile phone in her hand, so I asked her in front of everyone if it was her mobile phone. She admitted that it was, so I asked her how long she had owned the phone. She answered, "You know I've had it since last year. Why do you want to know?

That was what I was waiting for. I snatched her phone out of her hand, opened her call register, opened *received calls,* and showed the police.

My name was recorded every day for the previous two weeks, and then two to three times per week from Nigeria. "Now do you believe me?" I asked the police? I asked again whether they'd like to see some photos of her performing voodoo in my house (dressed in her white gown and wearing a red sash over her shoulders).

The older of the two police officers said that he didn't believe a crime had been committed, that it was more of a civil problem. He turned to Haitian and advised her to get a lawyer to deal with her things because it wasn't really a police matter.

When the police left, I was again in need of relaxation. After all that commotion, however, I was awake almost the entire night.

No longer thinking I'd ever have any peace on the damn island I began thinking positively about cutting my loses and selling the house and moving on.

The next morning, I was outside washing down my paved drive to freshen it up and remove all the dust that always got blown in, when Haitian had the nerve to pull up outside my entrance. She shouted, "I'm walking on your name. I was up all night burning candles in your ass. Soon, you'll be sorry, soon you'll regret trashing my junk, soon you'll be in so much pain you'll want to die. No doctor will ever be able to help you. I'm going to make sure you die!" She drove off after that.

I arrived at the house one afternoon a couple of days later and noticed that someone had drawn a strange kind of sign on the white wall adjacent to my entrance. I walked back from my car and noticed someone had also cut three little chunks out of the rendering on the corner of the opposite wall.

I went to open my front door and noticed three deep hammer marks just under my lock. Someone must have hit my door very hard because my doors were new and made of very hard wood. I grabbed a bowl of warm, soapy water to wash the sign off my wall.

After removing the drawing (which had been created using a stick of charcoal), I inspected the rest of my front wall. I found a small piece of folded paper that someone had taken the trouble to wedge in between the top of my wall and my white aluminium railings.

Later that day, I decided to remove some of the weeds outside my front window because I hadn't done any gardening for a few weeks. Hidden amongst the weeds, I found half an eggshell that contained a piece of folded paper inside with my name written three times.

There was no doubting who had done everything. It was clear that Haitian was continuing with her vindictive, sick ways because she was not being allowed to live for free any more.

I called my Colombian handyman and asked him to do a really thorough cleaning around my house. I also asked his wife to clean the inside.

They spent the entire next day cleaning, and they found several more items outside my house that were well hidden. Haitian had also gone to the trouble of planting several items inside before she'd left.

I knew I would never be left alone to live a peaceful life, and I called a real estate agent to put my house on the market. On Monday, the sign was erected and photos were taken, but the real estate agent was hardly professional. He never bothered to upload the photos to his website.

Two months later, the sign was collected without warning or explanation – not an email or anything. I called another real estate agent who also erected his sign. He prepared a contract and uploaded the photos onto his website.

Okay, I thought, *I'm finally making a move in the right direction.* I felt quietly confident that there was at least a glimmer of hope I'd be rid of the place and never need to return to the damn island again.

I continued rotating back and forth between Nigeria and the Island until an increasing pain in my abdomen finally stopped me in my tracks. It had started soon after arriving in Nigeria in December, but on the 4th March 2012, I contracted chronic pancreatitis. Pancreatitis is known to be the most painful condition a bodily organ can hand out.

The deep, nagging pain I was suffering from since December of 2011 suddenly hit an all-time high, delivering the most incredible agony I could ever imagine.

I can best describe it as having a sword being pushed deep into the pancreas before it is twisted ferociously. At the same time, it felt like a strong hand is squeezing and crushing the pancreas.

I called one of my workers to call the camp doctor because I didn't have his number. In just three minutes, the Nigerian doctor and his nurse arrived at my room. He quickly assessed the amount of pain I was in, and helped me to his clinic where he could take better care of me.

He began by inserting a needle into my vein and connecting a paracetamol drip for my pain. He continued to make several other checks to better make a diagnosis. He said I needed to go to Port Harcourt where they had a better-equipped clinic, so arrangements were made.

The next day, my armed escort – together with a mobile police escort – arrived to safely move me to Port Harcourt. Upon arrival, I was met by a South African doctor and taken directly to a bed where they changed my intravenous needle and connected me to a new paracetamol drip. I never found out why a new Doctor insisted on replacing a perfectly positioned intravenous needle to one of their own?

Nothing by mouth was her first instruction, and that was the way it went for the next three days until I became stable enough to be flown out of Nigeria.

A Nigerian doctor accompanied me all the way to Paris and administered morphine at regular intervals during the flight. Because the electronic flight tickets arrived very late, we only had an hour to make the two-hour drive to the airport in Port Harcourt.

While under the influence of morphine, I called Christopher, a Nigerian airport security friend, to inform him I was on my way because I was dying. He was horrified when he heard the ambulance sirens. He ran around the airport informing all his colleagues that his brother was in trouble, and that they should take out all the stops so I could make the flight.

He did such a thorough job in fact, that they even prevented the Air France check-in desk from closing. Plus, the air traffic control would not allow any flight to leave the country until I'd boarded.

Amazing as it all sounds, my Nigerian security friend did quite a spectacular job holding up a fully loaded aircraft until I was on board. He made me give my passport to my doctor to get my boarding card while he personally escorted me straight through passport control without my passport. We went straight through the body and hand luggage scanners and straight onto the flight, while my boarding pass followed behind.

None of the Nigerian's expected to take a dash from me. They were all too worried about my critical condition and didn't try to ask me for anything! There were absolutely wonderful with their support and understanding.

I can only assume the passengers who had been kept waiting had been informed that the delay was due to a medical emergency. When I entered the aircraft, everyone started clapping. My doctor arrived a short time after me, and the Nigerian air traffic control finally gave the all clear to take off.

Once in the air with the fasten seat belt sign turned off, we started looking for a place to hang my drip. Amie, the Air France flight attendant, rigged up two coat hangers for the job.

Because we were flying business class, the food menu was soon distributed. My wonderful doctor reminded me: "Nil by mouth!" I put my menu back in the slot in the back of the seat in front of me and continued to endure the intense hunger pangs that had been present for four days. The hunger pains were one thing, but the intense pains my pancreas was handing out were really something different.

The flight eventually landed in Paris. My doctor was busy
putting all his equipment back in his bags while I struggled
to put my jacket on with the needle in my arm.

Many people stood in a queue watching me struggle
until a Nigerian lady asked whether she could help. *Wow*, I
thought, *at least there is one person with a heart.*

My accompanying doctor arranged for a wheelchair
to meet us at the door of the plane, which had the added
advantage of being fast tracked to the immigration authorities. Otherwise, it would have been a very long walk – and
another hour spent in a queue.

An ambulance had also been arranged for my arrival,
and it was waiting for me outside. It took me to a hospital in the centre of Paris where they confirmed the

original Nigerian doctor's diagnosis that I was suffering from chronic pancreatitis.

The hospital didn't specialise in pancreas problems, so later that night after having a CT Scan, I was driven by taxi to another hospital in the centre of Paris. That hospital had a surgeon who dealt with pancreas problems.

The next day, they gave me an endoscopy and threaded a stent (tube), into my main pancreas duct, which was blocked. They also gave me another CT scan. Once the results were available, the hospital decided that what I needed was beyond their capabilities, that they couldn't help me.

They kept me for another four nights until I had stabilised more, and then they told me I was free to go because there wasn't anything else they could do.

With a stent fitted, my health insurance flew me back to my point of origin. Thus, I ended up back on the Caribbean Island. The stent must have moved by the time I arrived on the Island though, because I was in the most intense agony once again. The next day, I went back to the airport to book a flight back to Wales because during all this time, my mother had discovered a facility specialising in pancreas problems just forty-minutes from her house which was in Morriston Hospital outside Swansea.

It took seven days to get a seat on a flight out of The Island because it was high season and all flights were fully booked. One morning at 4am I was hit with the most intense agony. I called the Island conman, who lived just up the road, and thankfully he arrived outside my door in just four or five minutes, to take me to the new hospital in the village just down the road. I slowly walked to his girlfriend's car doubled up in agony, bent over and clutching my abdomen.

We arrived at the hospital just ten minutes later. I was crying with the pain. As soon as the Colombian duty doctor was told I had chronic pancreatitis she administered morphine and a paracetamol drip. She told me not to worry as they could carry out an operation right away! I knew that there were very few surgeons in the world who could carry out the Beger procedure, which I needed so I declined her kind offer. Once the morphine and paracetamol had taken effect I returned home with a prescription of oral morphine and tramadol pain killing capsules.

A few days later I succeeded to depart the Island and basically had overdosed on all the medication so I would look fit to fly. I was already flying as I entered the airport, but I knew it was only a temporary relief from what was to come, once it had began to wear off.

I finally arrived in Amsterdam airport and needed to wait another six hours before taking the one-hour flight to Cardiff in Wales. I couldn't show anyone the intense agony I was enduring, as they wouldn't have allowed me to board the flight to Wales. I received some concerned looks due to my grey colour as I passed through the usual scanner before entering the departure gate, but I put on a false smile and was allowed to proceed.

Once in the air, I requested a wheelchair to meet me at Cardiff airport. When I was asked why, I explained that I was no longer capable of walking another step due to having chronic pancreatitis, and I was returning home for an operation. I'd waited long enough before requesting so I knew the flight wouldn't turn around due to a medical emergency.

The only chance I had of surviving was to make it to Morriston Hospital. The flight attendant understood and made the requested arrangements before we landed. By the time I landed in Cardiff, I was *basically on my last legs*, leaning forward and could no longer sit back in my seat.

I was supported while walking down the steps at the aircrafts door as I was in a terrible state once we'd landed and met by a guy with the wheelchair. Time became everything and I was fast tracked through the airport until I finally passed through the little arrivals area. It felt comforting to be back home on my own turf!

CHAPTER 25

Hospitalised

Soon, I left the arrivals area, where my sister was already waiting for me. It was the first time I'd seen her for several years, but it was a comfort to know that family are always around when you most need them.

The airport assistant pushed me all the way to my sister's car, and off we went. Due to the state I was in, my sister drove me directly to Morriston Hospital's casualty wing. My colour was so grey by this time and I could barely talk due to the agony I was enduring.

In the accident and emergency arrivals room, I was taken in by wheelchair (pushed by my sister) and seen immediately. I was asked whether I knew what my problem was, and I was able to squeeze out the word *pancreatitis*. The doctor immediately ordered morphine, which seemed to be routine when treating someone with pancreatitis.

I heard the nurse attending to me tell my sister that I wasn't going anywhere for a few days. Not long after, arrangements were made to admit me to the Ward G, where I remained for the following two weeks.

I was administered a daily regimen of painkillers and a fat-free, light diet that was designed to be pancreas friendly. Basically I ate baby food. It was in Morriston Hospital where I finally learnt what a complex and important organ the pancreas was. Apart from manufacturing digestive fluids, it also manufactured insulin to prevent diabetes.

After two weeks I was discharged with a large prescription of drugs that would last four weeks (until my much-needed operation). Four weeks later, I returned to Morriston Hospital to get prepared for what is known as the Beger's procedure.

Emotions were running rather high while I lay there alone in a different part of the ward, waiting for the surgery I would undergo in the morning. All I kept thinking about was the 67% survival rate after such a massive operation. I wished I hadn't researched that information on the Internet.

I was sure that, with my luck, I would be among the 33% that didn't make it, of the unlucky ones – but I was damned if I was going to loose without a fight!

At half past five the next morning – after no sleep – a nurse came to my bed and told me that I needed to shower and prepare for surgery. That shower felt very different. I felt like I was showering without any feelings or emotions. I felt like I was showering for the very last time. I felt so alone.

I returned back to my bed in a kind of semi-shock, not really aware of my surroundings anymore. Soon after, the anaesthetist booked to take care of my pain and sleep administration visited me to explain the forthcoming procedure and the risks associated with having an epidural needle inserted high up inside my spinal column.

He was extremely detailed in his explanations, which added the fear of God to how I was already feeling. He produced a document that I was directed to sign my authorisation to continue. It cleared him of any responsibility in the event that my body did not perform in the right manner.

In less than an hour, my surgeon came to my bedside to inform me that, because there had been a serious accident, there was not a free bed available for me in the high-dependency unit for post-surgery care.

I was picked up a couple of hours later by my mother for the second time, along with another big prescription of drugs to help with my discomfort and taken back to my sister's house. A couple of days later, I received a second surgery date for a month later. I repeated the very same procedure a month later, but everything felt different. After all the same activities as the previous month, my surgeon greeted me (instead of the anaesthetist).

He informed me that there had been another big accident, that my overdue operation had been cancelled yet again! I told him I was not leaving, as I knew inside I was not able to fight for life much longer, and off he went to see what he could do to change things.

After a half hour, a nurse came to my bed – accompanied by a porter – to take me down to the operating theatre. I owe my life to that surgeon in Morriston Hospital, Swansea and will never forget that he put his neck out to save my life. This is the reason why I was able to write Andy's Story, and no other.

Before entering the theatre, I was pushed into a room where I met the very same anaesthetist who had visited me before. He was already in surgical green, and prepared for the surgery. He started by numbing my spine where he was about to nsert the epidural needle.

Next came a shock: I felt an extremely sharp pain as the epidural touched a nerve that was not yet numbed. The anaesthetist gave me another numbing injection and repeated the process several more times until the epidural had been inserted all the way. He then taped it firmly in place and made me lie back on the bed. While he was carefully positioning the needle, a male nurse pushed gently against my shoulders to stop me pushing forward when I felt each stabbing pain. *This gave a new meaning of being stabbed in the back I thought.* He was also professionally and genuinely sympathetic regarding what I was going through and very comforting and reassuring.

The anaesthetist then placed a mask over my mouth and nose and encouraged me to breathe in the oxygen (*as he put it*), which had a slightly sweet smell about it. I pulled it away from my face and laughingly said it's not just oxygen, smiled and placed it back in position on my face and took a deep sniff. The next thing I knew, I was waking up in the evening in the high-dependency unit with tubes coming out all over my body.

I had four tubes coming out of my neck, two coming out of my left arm, one coming out of my right arm, a catheter, two drains coming out of my lower abdomen, and a tube that had been inserted into my nose and down into my stomach.

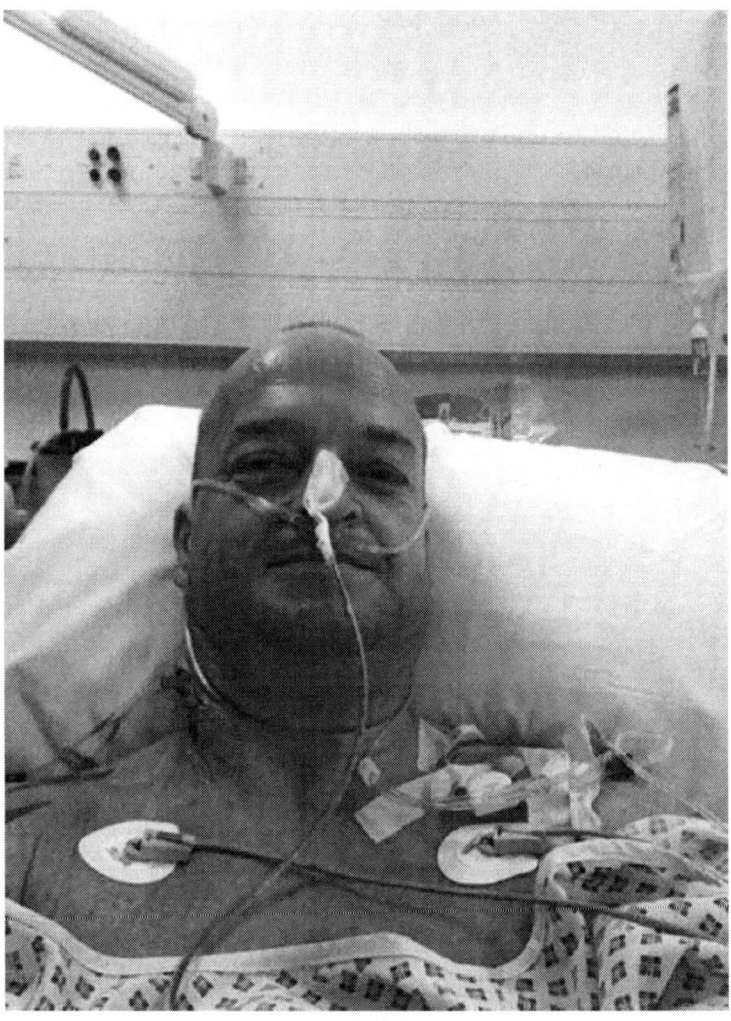

I was assigned a dedicated nurse to watch over me (as well as a doctor). Soon after waking up, my mother arrived to see how I was doing after the ten-hour operation. With all the medication being pumped into me, I was feeling somewhat comfortable considering I just had my stomach, pancreas, gall bladder, and several feet of small intestine worked on.

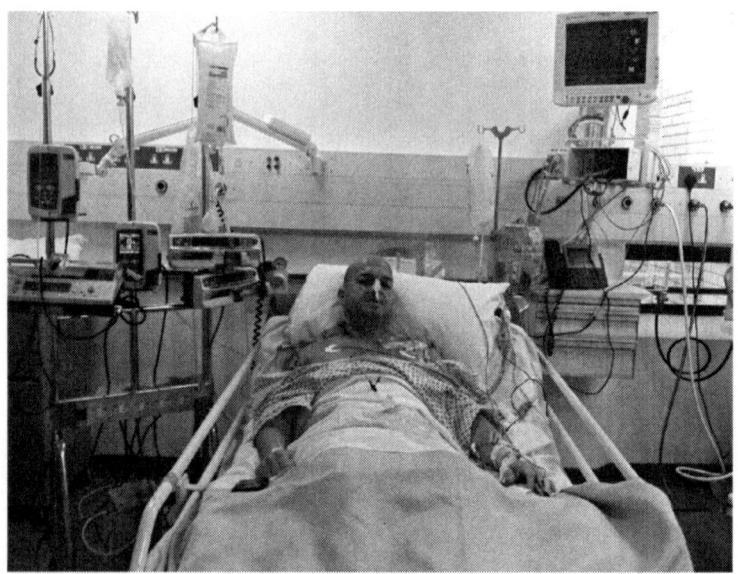

Life seemed to have a totally new meaning. A woman in the next cubicle was not so lucky. After a team spent over an hour and a half trying to resuscitate her after a similar operation, she passed away. It made me feel so guilty to be alive. I was thinking, she must have a husband and children and I hadn't, so why her and not me? I would have taken her place without thinking if only it were possible.

After what I'd seen, I persuaded the high-dependency unit to let them have my bed for someone else more in need than I was. After three nights, they transferred me back to Ward G. I was in a different part of the ward though, close to its reception so they could keep a close eye on me.

The nursing staff were amazing there, and they did everything they could to make me feel comfortable.

Soon after arriving in the ward, they came to remove my catheter and asked whether a young student nurse could remove it – it would be her first time – which I agreed to. Expecting a little discomfort, I waited for the pain. Fortunately, it did not come. Instead, it was all over in just a couple of seconds.

Because I still hadn't been reconnected to the morphine machine, I decided to go for a walk, get some fresh outside air, and smoke a cigarette. I was rather light headed, and it took me about ten minutes to walk down the long corridor before taking the elevator to the ground floor, buy a newspaper from the shop at the hospital entrance and finally get outside.

I continually kept holding my stomach area throughout the walk. After a couple of puffs on the cigarette, I became really faint and giddy. Luckily, I had a wall to fall against. After that, I made my way back to Ward G.

Very soon, an incredible pain beset me where they had done the amazing operation. It grew worse and worse, which caused me to take little tiny steps as I slowly returned the way I'd come. After almost half an hour, I made it back to my bed. Seconds later, one of the nurses appeared and helped me back onto my bed just in time before I passed out with the pain. She wondered where the hell I had been.

She asked where I had got the newspaper from which was under my arm, and I replied, "The shop at the hospital entrance." I received my first reprimanding and was told in no uncertain terms that walking around could result in my insides becoming outsides as I was only clipped together.

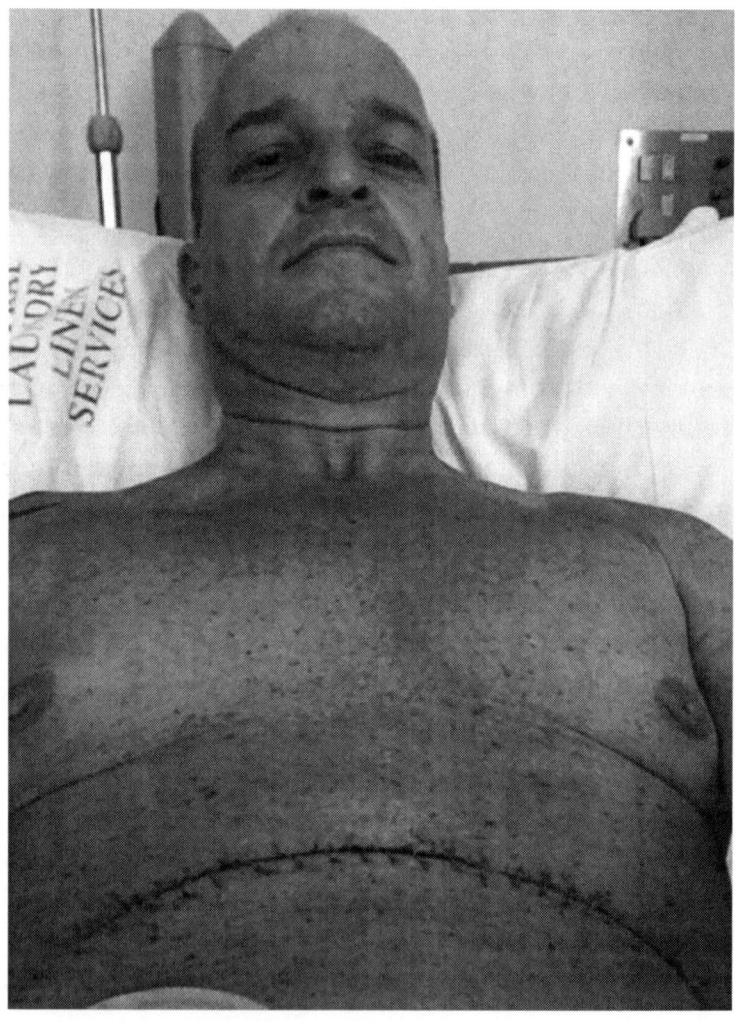

When I was hooked back up to the morphine machine and tinkering with my iPad out, things began to feel more like normal again. My mother visited me every afternoon, and my sister came by every evening. I was well taken care of. The nursing staff in Ward G continued to do all they could for all the patients to help raise moral, and they were simply amazing.

One unfortunate old man was admitted to my ward after having a severe heart attack at the age of ninety-six. He lay on his bed all day, completely still and unable to talk. I often wondered whether he was aware of his surroundings and whether he could hear people talking around him. His tongue was hanging out of the side of his mouth, and it was a very deep purple colour.

Five days after my surgery, I became increasingly aware of my pain level rising. It became stronger by the minute until I could not move or speak. I couldn't even turn and reach for the attention buzzer to call for help. I managed to get the attention of an eighty-six-year-old man in the next bed, and he used his buzzer to call for help.

Every time a nurse came to see what was wrong, the ninety-six-year-old heart attack victim saw the nurse and started making all kinds of noises. He stole the show every time – leaving me completely ignored.

My pain soon became unbearable, and I wanted to die. A few times, I got lucky and a nurse came to my bed and checked my equipment. She said it appeared to be working fine, but something was certainly not fine because I could no longer take any more pain – a fact I made clear for everyone in my ward. Finally, a young anaesthetist came to see what was wrong.

I had a button attached to the morphine machine that I could press for extra doses of morphine in between the pre-set dosages.

It didn't matter how many times the button was pressed, the machine was set to not give any doses more frequently than five minutes. The young anaesthetist noticed that I had pressed the button over four thousand times, so he realised that there was something seriously wrong.

He asked me whether I could lean forward so he could check my epidural needle, but all the pain had made me too weak to move. Two nurses helped me bend forward causing more agony so he could lift up my T-shirt and check my needle.

As soon as he could see my back, he immediately gave the instruction to bring a portable dose administrator because my epidural needle had moved out of position and was not able to block my pain at all.

The ward sister came quickly to my bed to apologise for all my intense pain, and she offered to have another epidural needle fitted. After remembering what it felt like when it was originally fitted, I declined her kind offer and chose to go with the portable unit to see whether it could do the same job.

Actually, the portable unit was not anything like as effective as the epidural block, but I was so well used to being in agony by that time, I basically didn't care anymore and at least I could see the needle in my arm rather than having a needle up inside my spine. The added advantage was that the new unit had wheels, which meant *I could be mobile again*! As a child, I could never keep still for long, much to my mother's dismay!

An hour later, equipped with my new portable machine, I headed down the corridor to buy a newspaper and pop outside for a quick smoke. The nurses began to give me a break because they knew it was better for my circulation to be mobile a few times per day.

On my seventh day in the ward, two physiotherapists visited me.

Much to their surprise, I asked whether we were going for a walk outside. They explained that that wouldn't be possible until a few more days of practise, and that they would just take me as far as the main corridor.

When I explained that I went down to the end of it a few times per day, took the elevator down to the ground floor, and went outside the main entrance, they just looked at each other in total disbelief.

So off we went with my morphine machine by my side in the direction of the shop to buy another newspaper. Halfway to the shop, the two ladies said that I'd gone far enough for one day and that it was time to return to my bed.

Okay, I thought, *I won't be a problem patient.* I did what I was told and returned to my bed and remained there for a few minutes until after they had gone *and the coast was clear.* Shortly thereafter, I went for a newspaper for the eighty six year old gentleman in the next bed and a quick smoke for myself.

My surgeon visited me most days to check on my progress. He was always accompanied by his entourage. He was pleased to see me progressing in the right direction – better and better every day.

Due to a shortage of hospital beds, I volunteered to give up my bed just nine days after surgery and continue my recovery at my sister's home. I guess we all make mistakes, but that was a big one. I nearly undid all my surgeon's handiwork … and nearly succeeded in killing myself.

I did not know which foods I should avoid or which I should never eat again – nor had I been prescribed an amazing medicine called Creon. Creon is a pancreas enzyme that I need to take every time I eat food. Anyway, I chose to have smoked salmon with Philadelphia cream cheese and brown bread and butter.

Because it was so soon after being stitched back together, my pancreas was not able to cope with all the fat and grease, and I became very sick that night. I was awake most of the night with stomach pains that became progressively worse. I had terrible indigestion, and the pain became impossible to deal with.

My sister had already left for work in the morning as she owned the Mumbles Beauty Clinic, so I was alone to cope as best as I could. The best I could do, however, was not enough. All I managed to do was get down the stairs and find a phone to call my mother.

When she picked up the phone, I couldn't speak. She couldn't hear anything coming from my end until I forced one word out of my mouth: "Help". She immediately feared the worst, dropped everything, and drove over to my sister's house. She found me curled up into a ball on the floor of the living room in terrible agony clutching my stomach.

She helped me half to my feet so I could make it to her car, but I was still curled up. I was able to walk a little, and I slowly made my way to her car. A few minutes later, after avoiding most of the holes and bumps in the road we arrived at my mother's house where she could take care of me. Every bump in the road which we couldn't avoid was like being shot.

My condition deteriorated rapidly. Soon, I was in the bathroom vomiting bright yellow bile. I was in intense agony every time my newly stitched stomach muscles went into spasms.

Eventually, after the yellow bile was depleted a dark green fluid was thrown out. At that point, there was absolutely nothing left in my stomach to bring up. But that was only the beginning of my pain.

I continued to deteriorate until I ended up kneeling on the living room carpet with my arms on the sofa. The pain was similar to the pain I experienced when my epidural needle had shifted out of place.

My mother called the hospital, and the reception at Ward G told her to dial 999 and ask for an ambulance because I was in a very dangerous condition. I remember thinking that it was the second time in my life that my mother had called an ambulance for me.

The ambulance was called, but it had to leave from Morriston Hospital, which was quite a long drive away.

The ambulance controllers – true professionals in South Wales – also alerted the quick response vehicle, which arrived in just ten minutes. The paramedic entered my mother's house and found me in the same position I was in when the ambulance was alerted. He couldn't move me in the condition I was in until he had reduced my pain.

He began to give me gas, which was a safe option with no side effects for anyone, but it did not help. He tried to push an intravenous needle into my arm, but it took several attempts because my veins had learnt to hide from needles after my time in hospital.

Eventually, the ambulance arrived with two more paramedics to take me out to their ambulance. I was helped to my feet, but I was still curled up and not feeling any better. The paramedics surrounded me in case I fell as we made our way to the ambulance.

Those guys were fantastic. They were also very understanding and sympathetic to the discomfort I was enduring. They were fully familiar with what the pancreas can hand out. In the ambulance, the quick response paramedic was able to get an intravenous needle into my arm and hook me up to a liquid paracetamol drip. After that, they securely strapped me in for the ride back to the hospital, which I had left only twentyfour hours before.

My mother called my sister, and she immediately cancelled all her afternoon appointments at her beauty salon so she was able to drive back to the hospital to see me.

When my ambulance arrived back at Morriston Hospital and the paramedics were busy wheeling my body into the accident and emergency room, both my mother and sister were right there.

Naturally, they were terribly concerned that I was suffering almost uncontrollably, and they were asked to move aside so I could be wheeled back into the hospital. I was wheeled into a cubicle that was freezing cold, and a Filipino nurse soon attended to me.

The first thing she did was hook up a bag of liquid paracetamol to help ease my pain. After that, she covered me with a blanket because I was shivering so much. Six hours later, I was admitted to Ward G for two more nights so I could stabilise. After I was discharged, I went back one week later because my surgeon wanted to check on my progress. After that, I returned to the Caribbean at the end of the week.

The Island customs stopped me at the baggage scanner and asked me why I had so much medicine in my bag. I wasn't feeling up to giving a long, drawn-out explanation, so I just lifted up my T-shirt to reveal my new scar. He motioned for me to pass through the gate without any further ado.

I arrived at my house twenty minutes later, which looked fine from the outside. When I entered it, I was shocked to see mosquito curtains had be pinned around the entrance to my bedroom.

The conman who was watching over my house for me had turned it into a showroom where he could sell his imported mosquito curtains from China. The plan was for the two of us to share the profits 50/50 – but that was a joke.

He bought them for three dollars each, and he told me he was selling them for just ten dollars each. After paying the import duty, we were left with five and a half dollars to split between us … or so I was told.

I pulled the trashy net off my bedroom doorframe because it was always in the way when I went through it. It left holes (from the pins) all around my new doorframe. I told him I did not want my house used as a showroom for the general public to enter, and I warned him not to do it again. After checking my personal items left in my bedroom drawers, I discovered many things had been stolen.

The salesman encouraged the general public to pass through the net fixed around my bedroom door so they could see how it closed automatically behind them due to its magnetic strips. There was no way of telling who had taken all the gold and money I kept in my room, but that wasn't of any concern to the conman as long as he secured new sales. For all I knew, he might have taken my things?

The next day, I was disturbed by a loud knock on my door. An Islander was returning to buy another mosquito curtain. I told him the salesman wasn't around, but I would look for a curtain. I found one in the back bedroom – along with hundreds more like it.

I asked him how much he paid before because I wasn't sure what to charge, and he held out forty dollars. That was a surprise since my *so-called* partner had told me 50% of each curtain was not quite three dollars.

After checking my emails, I discovered I had been accepted for a six-month contract in Delft, Holland and needed to fly there in just two weeks. I immediately started making arrangements to ship all my personal possessions back to the United Kingdom, and sold off as much of it as I could, including all my beloved fishing gear!

Nobody on that island ever seemed to have money, so I had no choice other than to let people take things with the promise that they would pay me as soon as they had enough money. Of course, the outcome was obvious and I never received a cent.

Five months later, I was paid back just two thousand dollars, but it was given to a Venezuelan friend who had big plans for both her son and I. To be brief, instead of sending me the money, she spent it all on another wreck of a car. She promised to pay my electricity bills every month as a way to pay it back to me. Needless to say, none of my utility bills were paid, and I never saw a single cent of that debt either.

So six weeks after my operation I was off to work again, just a few months earlier than advised.

CHAPTER 26

The Netherlands

I arrived in Amsterdam on the 27th of July 2012, which was a Friday morning and took my time getting to my usual hotel in the centre of the city (opposite the central railway station where Antonina had joined me before). I'd used the same hotel for many years whenever flight connections forced me too.

They had recently renovated part of the old building, and I was lucky enough to get a new room. I went to sleep early that night, and I spent the next day wandering around looking in shop windows before taking a train south to Delft on the Sunday, which just happened to be my 50th birthday. *A birthday I wasn't expecting to reach.*

Just an hour later, I arrived in Delft. I was grateful that it was a warm and sunny day. The taxi driver recommended places to spend the day, and it was a good start to the new location.

I found a nice bar where I could sit outside to enjoy the sunshine, lit a Cohiba, and sipped a cold Dutch beer. It all felt very relaxing until I heard a voice that was deliberately loud enough for me to hear.

The voice said, "I bet he's English with a pint and a cigar." I reacted by saying, "Welsh, actually." I smiled and continued gazing out across the town square.

The man introduced himself as Jack, a bricklayer from Northampton. He explained that he had been working in Delft and around that area for almost five years. He proceeded to recommend all the popular places to eat and drink.

One of his younger Dutch friends turned up – Gordy – and they started taking me from one place to another, which was not bad for my first day in Delft.

I woke up the next morning feeling a little worse for wear considering I was not to drink alcohol for the rest of my life, and took a taxi to the office where I would spend the next six months working as the project quality manager.

The project was still in its front-end engineering design phase (FEED), so there was plenty to do, including writing procedures for the project staff to follow. I was only working from Monday to Friday, so I had every weekend to enjoy and absorb the ambience of Delft. I noticed numerous tourists visiting the quaint little town.

Due to the rather limited choice in my hotel's restaurant, I chose to eat out every day by walking five minutes to the town square. The first bar I passed was called Café Koepoort, which meant *cow gate*. It was the original entrance to the square, where they drove the cows through on market day hundreds of years before.

The owner was a truly amazing lady called Sonja. Sonja and the other Dutch folks in her bar became like family for me. Considering the pressure of so much work in the office, Sonja's bar was a relaxing retreat.

Not long after I arrived in Delft, my *so-called* Island salesman *friend* offered to help me find a courier to ship my remaining cargo back to the United Kingdom. I knew only too well by then that when an Islander offered to help, it was not going to be free.

He quoted me $1,900 dollars to ship my cargo using a local Island courier. He also sent me the company's salesman's name, email address, and phone number. That way I could check to ensure that the quote was genuine. Not.

He also added that it was the last chance to ship anything back to Europe – the next opportunity would be six months later! As if!

Of course, the deal had already been agreed upon (along with commissions and a few hundred dollars extra), but I wasn't accepting it.

My *so-called* local friend reacted very badly to my refusal after he "*had gone to so much trouble to help me.*" He told me to arrange my own courier. My cases were to stay in the house for several more weeks until a Dutch friend helped me find a professional courier who eventually shipped my things.

That wasn't before the conman went through all my things, helping himself to whatever he wanted. Some of the items he took were quite valuable and impossible to replace – especially all of my instruments I used for piping and welding inspection. He probably sold those to the

Island oil refinery workers because they'd be no good for anything else.

His next email included the utilities bill for the previous month, which also horrified me. I couldn't understand why my electricity bills were always double the normal cost when he was looking after my house than when I lived in it.

A few weeks later, I discovered the reason.

My very good Dutch friend Jan, emailed me to ask whether he could buy two small wooden tables from me. His wife had seen them in my living room when they had collected a stereo system they'd bought.

I told him he could have the tables for free, all he had to do was collect them. I gave him the salesman's mobile number so he could make sure the house was open when he arrived. So off he went.

That evening, he emailed me to confirm he had the tables, but he explained how shocked he was when he arrived at the house. The front door was left wide open, and when he walked inside, he saw that all my air conditioners were on full blast.

Also, the damn Chinese mosquito curtains had been refitted onto my bedroom doorframe … and all the other bedroom doorframes. He even put up a curtain on the back door.

My dining room table was completely covered with hundreds of curtains, and my living room was full of boxes. The salesman had turned my house into a showroom and warehouse where the general public could check out the merchandise before buying it.

It was great for the salesman: a rent-free showroom with free electricity. He boasted to my friend that he and his girlfriend spent their free days at the house. There, they got their washing done using the stock of powder and completed other tasks at my expense.

Because my house was on the market, I called my real estate agent and had him visit my house to have the salesman remove everything. I wanted the conman kicked out, and I wanted the keys taken away from him.

The conman sent me thirtyseven abusive emails that weekend, but I didn't bother answering any of them.

Jan found a courier who would fly my cargo back to the UK for just $535 dollars, proving the conman's quote was totally ridiculous. I don't know what I would have done if it weren't for my Dutch friend. He did so much to help me. If only I had met him a few years earlier!

After working a few weeks and trying to achieve as much as possible to bring the project deliverables up to date, I had finally worked myself half to death. I was not supposed to return to work for a few months, so just six weeks after my operation was way too soon.

One Saturday morning, I was wandering around the town square area in Delft watching a brass band playing whilst talking on the phone to my mother. I started to lose the feeling in my left hand, with which I was holding my phone.

After a short time, my entire arm began to go numb. And then my right arm began to feel the same. I was now using both hands to hold my phone because it began to feel heavier by the minute. I started experiencing pins and needles all over my back, and my legs became heavy to move.

I finally made it to a bench seat in the town square, so I took the weight off my feet whilst continuing to talk to my mother. She was getting increasingly worried as I described what was happening to me.

My arms became too heavy to hold my phone to my ear, so I said goodbye to my mother. I told her I would call her back later.

I felt weaker by the minute, and I ended up lying down on the bench. At that point, I began sweating intensely all over my body. I ended up completely soaked. I decided I couldn't stay there indefinitely, so I slowly sat up and gazed across the square. I saw the first bar I went to, where I had met Jack on my birthday.

I slowly stood up, but I felt very giddy. I was walking all over the place like a drunken man. People were looking at me wondering what was wrong with me.

I managed to get to the bar, but I almost fell on top of the outside tables whilst passing them to enter the premises. At the bar, I sat on a stool. The barman came over to me and asked whether I was feeling okay.

I told him I wasn't feeling very well, and he gave me a glass of water. He called the owner who had recently recovered from a cancer operation himself. He tried to call an ambulance, but due to the brass band's performance, all the streets were closed off.

I called a local Dutch friend called Myrthe, but she told me she was out of town coaching hockey and could not get to me. I next called Jack. He was free, and he came straight to the bar to meet me.

In the meantime, Myrthe called Sonja, and she dropped what she was doing to find me. Following the bar owner's directions, she managed to drive reasonably close to the bar. Both Jack and the bar owner walked with me by walking on either side of me in case I fell one way or the other.

Ten minutes later, Sonja arrived and drove me to the Delft hospital. They kept me there until the next morning when I felt fine again and went home.

A strange visitor landed outside my hospital bed window while I lay there alone. It reminded me of the pigeon outside my house back on the Island, the day my mother had visited me. It was a little freaky as even when I walked down the hospital wards corridor to the television room the feathery visitor walked along the outside wall until it could look at me again.

The next day, I went back to Sonja's bar in the afternoon to thank her for helping me the day before, but she wasn't there.

Instead, Myrthe was there along with a carrier bag she had filled with a new razor, toothbrush, toothpaste, other toiletries, and a new pair of pyjamas. She was about to bring it all to me while I was in the hospital as she knew I didn't have anyone else to help me. That was so typical of the thoughtful and wonderful people in Delft.

I moved out of the hotel and into an apartment because the company I was working for said it was cheaper for them. It was a good move because it gave me the opportunity to cook for my local Dutch friends and invite them over from time to time.

The Dutch encouraged me to learn the local customs, and near Christmas, on the 5th of December, they all came over to my apartment with very nice food that they had prepared the night before. They came with little presents, which they'd wrapped up ready to play a *Sinta Claus* (patron saint of children), or *Sinterklaas* game after we had finished eating.

In the Netherlands, *Sinta Claus* came before Santa Claus and added to the build up to Christmas. As usual my wonderful Delft friends helped me clean up before they left. *Sinterklaas* was a very exciting time for children and on the previous weekend, *Sinterklaas* rode a white horse through the streets of Delft. Everyone in Delft was out that day and had lined the streets in readiness to watch *Sinterklaas* riding by. It was so busy that day, and the atmosphere in the beautiful little town was electric.

During December, I'd arranged to spend Christmas back in Thailand. I hadn't been to Thailand for five years and I often wondered how Wi was doing. We had kept in occasional email and telephone contact since I'd left the country and Wi always stressed how worried she was when I told her what was going on in my life so I booked flights and a hotel room in Bangkok and off I went.

Wi was waiting for me at the airport to welcome me back, but where I didn't know? After walking around for an hour I found a kiosk, which was to help tourists. A very nice Thai gentleman had been watching me looking around and offered to help me. As my mobile phone didn't work there he used his phone to call Wi.

Wi answered her phone and explained that she thought she'd seen me walking past her several times, but she remembered me as short and fat, not short and slim so didn't approach me. I told her to go to exit gate number three which I was close to, so she met me a few seconds later. Wi looked exactly the same as I remembered her five years before.

She was amazed how much weight I had lost due to my Pancreas problem and told me that she couldn't call me "Baby Pig" any more. Actually, due to my Pancreas and new diet, I had lost twenty eight kilos so some good came out of it. It also rendered me as a non-smoker much to Wi's delight, but I would still have the occasional beer from time to time, but not too often.

It was also the perfect opportunity to meet up with Neil, or should I say Alan # 3?

We hadn't met for four years so Neil and I had a lot to talk about. It was also a great opportunity to show Neil my favourite restaurant in Bangkok. It was probably the only place Neil hadn't already been to in Bangkok. It was a seafood market as well as a restaurant and located half way down Soi 24, off Sukhumvit road.

To avoid the taxi driver taking advantage of us going there, we had the taxi stop before we entered Soi 24 so we could walk the rest of the way. Actually, I had forgotten how far down the Soi the restaurant actually was and it felt like forever until we could finally see its huge street sign.

You could simply buy your choice of fresh seafood from all around the World and take it home, or have it cooked any way you fancied and eat there. It was the restaurants proud boast, that if is swims, they'd have it! You couldn't possible miss the street sign either.

It was my original plan to fly north to meet her family again as her father wanted to show me how my cows were doing. I had bought five cows back when I worked in Kuala Lumpur, but they had increased since then to over thirty so Wi's father was very proud of all he had done while taking care of them. My time in Bangkok went very quickly so I didn't make it up there. Sad really as I hadn't seen them since my Thai wedding day.

Instead, we spent my short visit in downtown Bangkok and exercising Wi's little dog. She had rescued him from Thai children in the street near her place. They were throwing the newly born puppy up into the air and watching it land on the ground. Wi ran over and rescued the poor little puppy, its eyes still closed, and taken it home to try to bring him up herself.

Wi fed him milk through a syringe and he managed to survive. She took extra special care of him and called him Booboo. Wi also made monthly trips to the local veterinary for Booboo to be checked over and have his injections to protect him from getting heartworm which is prolific in hot countries.

I promised that I'd see her father on my next visit, which would be in July 2013.

My work in Delft was extended until the end of January 2013, which suited me fine because I was busy looking for another contract back overseas. I definitely didn't want a lapse in work after being out of commission for almost five months in 2012 due to my pancreas.

I was happy to leave my job there as it released me so I could return to an overseas location, but deeply saddened with the thought of when I would next see my Dutch friends.

On my last night in Delft, my friends had arranged a farewell party in Sonja's bar. Myrthe had gone to the trouble of cooking very nice Indonesian food for all to eat as part of the get-together. Unbeknown to me at the time, they had secretly got together on the Sunday afternoon prior to my departure to make some team photos which they had framed behind glass and presented to me on the night. They had even attached two pairs of little wooden Dutch '*clogs*' (shoes), to hang down over the front of the frame!

To add to my rather emotional farewell, Sonja's mother and father also joined the party. They were such lovely people and Sonja's father was a famous glass blower, and his products were well known in Holland and extremely valuable. Her father came over to me and began to explain that during his manufacturing career he had only ever made one dolphin.

During his detailed explanation, it was clear that the one and only dolphin he had ever made was a prized possession of his. With no further ado, he carefully un-wrapped the package he was holding and presented me with his dolphin. I felt quite choked to receive such a beautiful keepsake from Delft and it will be something I will always keep on display, but in a very safe place.

After a few weeks I secured a new contract back in the Middle East.

CHAPTER 27
Kurdistan

In April of 2013 I went to Kurdistan, an oil and gas rich region of northern Iraq. My first impression was how nice the people are in Kurdistan, quite comparable to Europeans. Erbil can proudly boast to having the oldest city in the World, the "Citadel" which dates back six thousand years and is currently under restoration to bring it back to its former glory.

On my very first day in the office, I met another Welshman who was also from Swansea. My first thoughts were, what could be the chances of meeting another fellow countryman in Kurdistan and that "*this has the makings of another story just waiting to happen.*"

TO BE CONTINUED....

Lightning Source UK Ltd.
Milton Keynes UK
UKOW04f1047260913

217979UK00001B/33/P